THE UPPER ROOM DISCIPLINES

1992

THE UPPER ROOM

Disciplines
1992

Coordinating Editor
Glenda Webb

Consulting Editors
Mary Ruth Coffman
Lynne M. Deming
Lynn W. Gilliam
Charla H. Honea
Janet R. McNish
John S. Mogabgab
Tom Page
Robin Philpo Pippin
Mary Lou Redding
Mary Lou Santillán Baert

UPPER
ROOM BOOKS
NASHVILLE

The Upper Room Disciplines 1992

© 1991 by The Upper Room. All rights reserved.

ISBN 0-8358-0624-3

The scripture quotations not otherwise identified are from the New Revised Standard Version of the Bible, © 1989 by the Division of Christian Education, National Council of the Churches of Christ in the USA, and are used by permission.

Scripture quotations designated RSV are from the Revised Standard Version of the Bible, copyrighted 1946, 1952, and © 1971 by the Division of Christian Education, National Council of the Churches of Christ in the USA, and are used by permission.

Scripture quotations designated NIV are from the *Holy Bible, New International Version.* Copyright © 1973, 1978, 1984 International Bible Society. Used by permission of Zondervan Bible Publishers.

Scripture quotations designated TEV are from the *Good News Bible,* The Bible in Today's English Version-Old Testament: Copyright © American Bible Society 1976; New Testament: Copyright © American Bible Society 1966, 1971, 1976.

Scripture quotations designated NEB are from *The New English Bible.* © The Delegates of Oxford University Press and The Syndics of the Cambridge University Press 1961, 1970. Reprinted with permission.

Scripture quotations designated JB are taken from the *Jerusalem Bible,* published and copyright © 1966, 1967, and 1968 by Darton, Longman & Todd Ltd and Doubleday & Co. Inc, and are used by permission of the publishers.

Scripture quotations designated NJB are taken from the *New Jerusalem Bible,* published and copyright © 1985 by Darton, Longman & Todd Ltd and Doubleday & Co. Inc, and are used by permission of the publishers.

Scripture quotations designated NASB are taken from the *New American Standard Bible,* © 1960, 1962, 1963, 1968, 1971, 1972, 1973, 1975, 1977 by The Lockman Foundation. Used by permission.

Scripture quotations designated NKJV are from The New King James Version. Copyright © 1979, 1980, 1982, Thomas Nelson Inc., Publishers. Used by permission.

The designation KJV identifies quotations from the King James Version of the Bible.

Any scripture quotation designated AP is the author's paraphrase.

The weeks of May 4-10, July 6-12, and September 14-20 are reprinted from *Disciplines 1986.* The weeks of July 27–August 2 and October 19-25 are reprinted from *Disciplines 1989.* Unless otherwise noted, RSV quotations in these meditations have been updated by the use of scripture from the NRSV.

Cover Design: Jim Bateman
Cover Photo: David Carriere/H. Armstrong Roberts
Typeset by Typecraft Company
Nashville, Tennessee
Printed in the United States of America

Contents

In my travels and contacts as World Editor of The Upper Room, I am reminded again and again both of the growing complexity of life in our time and of the interrelatedness of Christians around the world. This global connectedness among Christians is reflected in *The Upper Room Disciplines*. With the 1992 edition, *Disciplines* enters its second year in a Portuguese edition and its first in a Chinese edition. This year's edition includes writers from a variety of racial and ethnic backgrounds, as well as from several countries, among them Canada, Zimbabwe, and Sweden. The Christian faith has always been lived out in supportive community. *Disciplines* invites us into a broader Christian community than we might otherwise enjoy.

All the writers bring to us a prayerful, studied approach to scripture and share with us their experiences and insights about the incarnational places of scripture—the actual and the potential meeting places between God and persons, and among individuals.

As we read the scriptures and daily hear the writer's response to the word of God, each of us is invited to ponder and pray and then to live the word of God in his or her own daily walk with Christ and with companions on life's way. Through *Disciplines* we are invited to listen first to scripture, then to hear the insights and experiences of another Christian. But we are also invited to dialogue—with the writer and with the scripture passage. We are invited to ask ourselves: Do I agree with what the writer has said about the scripture passage? Have I gained a new personal insight into the scripture, either through the passage or by what the writer has presented? Do I disagree with what the writer of a particular meditation says? Let me converse with the writer's words and thoughts. At what points do I perceive the Christian life and the teachings of scripture differently than this writer does? Why? I am then invited to reread the scripture for the day, perhaps examining it in the larger context of the verses surrounding the assigned lection. In prayer (dialogue with God), I am invited to seek guidance in understanding the scripture message in the context of God's love for me and for the world. I am then invited to show this love of God toward myself and toward those I meet each day—my family, my co-workers, my neighbors. I am invited to be in community and to invite others into community.

Disciplines continues, year after year, to be a vital part of the daily devotional time of thousands of Christians from many different denominations and, increasingly, of Christians from many different cultures and countries.

May we be blessed in our daily walk with God and in turn be a blessing to others as we gratefully accept God's gift of life anew each day.

Janice T. Grana

Janice T. Grana
World Editor
The Upper Room

THE KINGDOM OF LIGHT

January 1-5, 1992   **J. Artley Leatherman†**
Wednesday, January 1   Read Isaiah 60:1-6.

"Arise, shine. . . ." These words announce the dawning of a new day, inaugurating a future glory. Isaiah had a great dream based upon faith in what the Light of God would accomplish.

When John the Baptist sent his disciples to ask Jesus if he were the promised Messiah, Jesus responded in terms of Isaiah's vision. (See Luke 7:18-23; Isaiah 61:1-2; also Luke 4:16-21.) John preached by the Jordan: "Repent, the kingdom is at hand" (Matt. 3:2, AP). Jesus came into Galilee preaching the good news: "The kingdom is at hand" (Mark 1:14, AP). They both reflected Isaiah's dream of a glorious kingdom: "Your light has come!"

Isaiah speaks of "thick darkness" covering the people. A painful parallel occurred in recent history when the army of Iraq left Kuwait with the oil fields burning. More than one observer likened it to what hell might look like: fire, smoke, and sludge polluting the air, scorching the earth and sea, suffocating life. *Darkness* in biblical literature signifies despair, forsakenness, desolation, and fear.

In the new kingdom, God's light and glory are to disperse all that this "darkness" implies. To this kingdom of light, as envisioned by Isaiah, *all nations* shall come bringing gifts—to proclaim the praise of the Lord.

Suggestion for Meditation: *At the beginning of this new year, how might the light of God's presence, love, truth, and compassion shine through my life to give glory to God? Remember, Jesus' words, "You are the light. . . ." (Matt. 5:14-16).*

---

†Minister of Visitation, Trinity United Methodist Church, Elkhart, Indiana.

Thursday, January 2   Read Psalm 72:1-14.

A righteous kingdom

The psalmist applauds the reign of a righteous king and prays that righteousness, justice, and prosperity will be the standard features of a long reign. Today this would be a prayer for a government founded on the basic principles of justice for *all* people; for a government that would defend the cause of the poor, bring deliverance to the needy, and crush the oppressor. This prayer asks for an era of flourishing righteousness and abounding peace, a peace that would last as long as the sun and moon endure. More than just the absence of war, this peace would be alive and dynamic, filled with endless creative possibilities. Hunger and poverty would be eradicated.

In today's reading, kings of other lands come to pay homage to this kingdom of justice, truth, and compassion. Christians have understood that any step toward this kind of rule anywhere on earth is in keeping with the spirit of Christ.

The vision described here in Psalm 72 may not look much like the actual "kingdoms" or governments on earth. But the vision of the ideal kingdom is crucial. Jesus prayed, "Your kingdom come. . . . on earth as it is in heaven." Surely, we must have an idea of what God's reign would be like in order to pray for its coming *on earth*! Dr. E. Stanley Jones appealed to Christians to emphasize "Jesus *and* His kingdom." Jesus always condemned constant worry over material things and earthly treasure. "But strive first for the kingdom of God and his righteousness and all these things will be given to you as well" (Matt. 6:33).

Reflection: *How might our corporate life—family, work, church, community, nation—reflect the glory of God and draw* all *peoples to God's marvelous light? What next step might I take to bring God's kingdom to the world today?*

Friday, January 3   Read Ephesians 3:1-13.

A new vision

The Apostle Paul writes about a direct revelation of the mystery, now revealed through Christ: "The Gentiles have become fellow heirs" of the promise made known in Christ. This marvelous discovery is the realization that the inclusive love of God *is* for *all* people. Bringing all the inhabitants of earth into the embrace of God's grace is part of the eternal purpose.

From the human side of that discovery, anything that fulfills that purpose is in keeping with Christ's mission; anything that separates people is a failure of that purpose and a denial of Christ's sacrifice for all.

Paul speaks of bearing the light *for their sake*. An Alaskan pastor serving two churches separated by a body of water describes a Sunday when the "out-point" church had a special occasion. The pastor and his wife lingered a bit. As they headed home in their small boat, dusk settled and then complete darkness. Panic struck as they realized they were lost. If they made a wrong turn and headed out to sea, it would be a disaster. The pastor's wife suddenly said, "I think I see a light!" Soon the pastor said, "I do too!" Then they spotted other lights and a voice came across the water, "Pastor, is that you?" The members of the home congregation had come out to search for them.

When you know you are lost in the dark, how marvelous to see even a glimmer of light! Paul is saying, "I am bearing this light for you who were once completely outside the fellowship" (AP).Then he adds a P.S.—"Don't worry about my being in prison. I am not bound by the power of Rome—that is nothing. I am a prisoner of Christ—that is everything!" (AP)

Prayer: *Dear God, enable us to be bearers of the light for the sake of others. Amen.*

Saturday, January 4   Read Matthew 2:1-6, 11.

Seeking the light

Around the world, some branches of the church link the visit of the magi with Epiphany on January 6. Since one meaning of *epiphany* is "to show" or "to reveal," the magi's adoration of the Christ-child is a sign that the world-at-large (beyond Judaism) recognized the "manifestation" of the divine in Christ.

We know surprisingly little about these intriguing characters, the magi. Matthew does not say how many; tradition says three. No names are given, though literature outside scripture calls them Caspar, Balthazar, and Melchior. We don't know that they were "kings"; although this would fit the reference in Psalm 72.

Matthew tells us they came "from the East." They must have been learned students of the stars. "We have seen his star at its rising," they said, "and have come to pay him homage." When their best insight led them to new truth, they followed the best light they knew. For Matthew they represent the gentile world acknowledging the coming of the Messiah. The wise men rejoiced when they saw the child; many "religious" people who had waited for centuries for the Messiah missed the great moment of his arrival.

Often, we can recognize God's disclosure or manifestation in unexpected places. In the Persian Gulf War, one of the worst Scud-missile attacks on Israel came during an evening concert by Isaac Stern. As the alarm sounded, performers left the stage and people in the audience put on their gas masks. But Isaac Stern walked to center stage and began playing the victorious music of Johann Sebastian Bach. Somehow, in the darkest hour, the light still shines, and you and I can follow that Star.

Suggestion for meditation: *The wise men gave priority to their search for a new king. Where will you seek the reality of Christ's presence today?*

Sunday, January 5 Read Matthew 2:7-12.

Gifts that enable the light to shine

The wise men were filled with excitement and great joy as the star which had led them on their long journey now lighted their way to the very spot where the Christ Child was staying. They had reason to be profoundly moved. Sometimes the "light dawns" with the realization that our lives, like those of the wise men, are part of a much larger drama.

Filled with joy, the wise men knelt down in an outpouring of devotion and offered their treasures as an act of worship. Gold, frankincense, and myrrh were not mere trinkets to dangle over a child's crib. These were adult gifts, gifts fit for a king.

The scripture says the wise men returned to their own country by a different route. Of course, they were smart enough to defy a jealous King Herod. But we like to think they were also changed men. Could they have gone through this experience of wonder and miracle and remained the same? With all the rushed, sometimes hectic, preparations for Christmas, it seems the season passes so quickly. What is different in your life after Christmas's reminder of the Christ Child's birth?

Prayer: *Lord, make my heart a cradle, where your love can be born anew, and lead me to a total commitment of life and treasure in the service of Christ.*
    As they offered gifts most rare
    At that manger rude and bare,
    So may we with holy joy,
    Pure and free from sin's alloy,
    All our costliest treasures bring
    *Christ, to thee, our heavenly King! Amen.**

---

*From the hymn "As with Gladness Men of Old," words by William C. Dix.

OUR ANOINTMENT AS GOD'S SERVANTS

January 6-12, 1992 **John Clifford†**
Monday, January 6 (Epiphany) Read Psalm 29.

Epiphany. The word means a "revelation of God." To Christians, it means the gift of God's love to the whole world, the Christ Child.

As the psalmist suggests, though, God's people already know a great deal about the Lord. The two attributes that catch our attention in this psalm are glory and strength. Virtually all the scriptural encounters between God and the people suggest that God has to do something quite out-of-the-ordinary to get their attention in the first place. (John 6:30 tells us that crowds followed Jesus because of his miracles.)

The Old Testament, then, has a fairly clear revelation of God under the theme "the fear of the Lord." God's power and glory are overwhelming. We may talk about them; we certainly want to do what we can to be in God's favor, but we only want to *encounter* God secondhand.

In Psalm 29 are those snapshots of power: a voice (remember God's *word* created the worlds!) that breaks the cedars, that flames through the wilderness, that controls the nations and frolics in the floods. We could easily come to rely upon this kind of God. This is the sort of glory and majesty in whose reflected glow we could bask. To be chosen by such a heavenly Being is a special gift indeed!

Epiphany is not a total surprise for us. The surprise, the eye-opening light, is that God's glory is not to destroy us but to love us into eternal life.

Prayer: *Lord, be known to us this day in both your power and love. Amen.*

---

†Pastor, Church of the Good Shepherd United Methodist, Arlington, Texas.

Tuesday, January 7   Read Isaiah 61:1.

To what are we anointed?

This question is likely to get startled looks. After all, we don't install church officers or ordain clergy by anointing anymore.

To what *is* one anointed? The Old Testament, Isaiah in this instance, sees this act as a symbol of call and dedication. Saul and David are anointed kings of Israel. The priests are anointed to their positions. Now Isaiah uses it for his own call—the Lord has chosen him for a special task.

Our Christian belief is that all of us can see our lives as Isaiah did. We speak of the "priesthood of all believers" and imply that every Christian is called for a special task. We try to identify our spiritual gifts to see in what directions God might be particularly leading us. To what are we anointed?

But one thing more: when we begin to find our calling, when we become clear that God has a place for us, then we will find that all of life is filled with times we must give to the Lord. To know we have been anointed for God's service makes all of life different. Every day becomes a holy moment, and we find that not just a part of our life has been anointed for God's service. Rather, God uses all of our life.

The original call expands and fills every bit of our experience. As we follow, we begin to find power of which we were unaware, power to meet the challenges of being God's people, chosen and anointed.

Prayer: *Open our ears, O God, to hear your call. Give us no rest until we know how you would use us for your kingdom, until we know how we are able to be your servants, chosen for our special tasks. Amen.*

Wednesday, January 8   Read Isaiah 61:1*b*-3.

To what are we anointed? The first level of that question has to do with recognizing God's call and commissioning power. The second has to do with the content of the call. After recognizing God's call, Isaiah moved directly to the content of the call: God had sent him to tell good news which will restore the broken, free the unfree, and remind all who hear it that God is still at work in the world.

That's a tall order! Thank God that most of us aren't anointed to such prophetic tasks! Or are we? Jesus echoed this passage to define his ministry (Luke 4:18-19), and we are called to follow Christ.

Of course, each of us is not called to all of this. We are, however, still called to take our part of it. Which part is ours? Encouragement? Healing broken hearts, lives and souls, or even bodies? Helping people escape from prisons of poverty or ignorance or prejudice? Praising, praying and reminding the world that God is still working out the holy purposes of salvation?

There is quite a lot to be done for the kingdom! Indeed, it sometimes seems as though more. comes undone than gets accomplished. It takes all God's people doing our part to get anywhere at all in this mission. We have more than enough possibilities to keep us busy without trying to do it all.

So, since we are called and anointed, where are we going to get to work? Are we going to be people who live up to our commission? Just what is it that God wants from each one of us? What is the content, what is the direction of our anointing? What part of God's kingdom work is ours?

Prayer: *Lord, we really don't want to do any big jobs for you, and so we often reject the small ones too. Help us willingly to find our special place of service and then willingly to serve. Amen.*

Thursday, January 9 Read Isaiah 61:3-4.

We are anointed. We have been given a message by the Lord for the lands in which we live. Now what?

Isaiah suggests that those who speak for the Lord are builders and rebuilders. They take what is ruined and make it into a place where God can be found.

Certainly that seems like a need for our day. We are beginning to understand the devastations around us: both cities and countryside terrorized and bombed into ruins and people and nations who have lost the vision of what it means to live as a people of God. There is a growing sense of hopelessness in the world. Just when we thought world peace might be a real possibility, a hope given life as we watched the Berlin Wall come down, war broke out in the Middle East. And we wonder if our efforts to save our environment are too little, too late.

Into this world, we are sent with a message of good news and glad tidings, with power to bind up the wounds and set free the captives. We are sent with God's point of view, with a message that these scenes of destruction are the natural outcome of our turning away from God.

But we remember that God's anointed people carry that light with them, and with the light the rebuilding begins. We are anointed to be part of that process.

A few years ago I was challenged to state a simple credo, a primary value for my life. I came up with "Be on the side of life." This is God's way—the creativity of life, even eternal life. Side with life and building up rather than with death and destruction.

Prayer: *O God, help us become builders of your kingdom in this world that needs you so very much! Amen.*

Friday, January 10   Read Luke 3:15-17.

Who was John, anyway? This has been a burning question for many people. Except to Luke the Evangelist, who knew the story of his exceptional birth, John was a mystery man.

We are all drawn to mysteries. This man John had a certain power about him. What allowed him to talk about the scribes and Pharisees as he does? What about that unusual diet, the strange clothes? Why was he out in the wilderness instead of in Jerusalem? And why does his message still strike so many of us to the core? How does he know us so well?

All the mystery raises the question "Who was this man?"

There were some popular guesses, of course. Was this one of the prophets come back to life? Certainly the message had a prophetic ring to it. The prophets also constantly called for repentance for salvation; they too had their symbols for forgiveness, like baptism. Was John a prophet?

Or better yet, was this the *Christ*—the Greek translation of "Messiah, anointed one"? Certainly John stood in opposition to the ruling powers of Jerusalem, both Roman and Jewish. Almost by definition a conquering savior would have had to oppose them. Just suppose. . . .

John knew the questions and gave an answer, though it is hardly the expected one. He is the one crying in the wilderness that God *had* come with a Messiah. In that sense, John was a prophet. But the Messiah was someone else, John said.

Who was John? Finally, he was one of us—one filled with God's power, but still not the Savior; one doing God's will, knowing greater works were yet to appear; one who knew God is active and one who looked and longed to see God's work.

Prayer: *Whoever we are, O God, make us aware of our voices, that we may prepare our corner of the world for your salvation. Amen.*

Saturday, January 11   Read Luke 3:21-22.

Why did Jesus come to John for baptism? John baptized for repentance and the forgiveness of sins—neither one a pressing need for Jesus, according to our understanding of the Messiah.

Yet Jesus came and, according to Matthew, was quite insistent on receiving the act of baptism. And John gave in, at least partly in obedience to the holy authority of Jesus.

Jesus didn't need baptism—at least not for repentance or forgiveness. But we sometimes overlook another facet. By coming to the water, each person admits a need and desire for God to be at work in his or her life. To complete the life-change called for, we need help. All those baptized seek God's spiritual counsel.

Jesus came to the Jordan and went down into the waters as though saying, "I'm ready. I will begin to let God's power work through me." This was the starting point of Jesus' mission. It was a declaration of readiness to be used by God. He prayed as he emerged from the water.

So it is not surprising that heaven's gates opened. The spirit of God was visibly and audibly present. The affirmation was made, "You are my Son, the Beloved; with you I am well pleased."

And we who have been baptized discover God asking to be at work in the world through us as well. We too, in these latter days, can be given the Holy Spirit to learn holy living—never as perfectly as Jesus, of course, yet well enough for God to say to us, "You also are my child—and I'm proud of you!"

Prayer: *Lord, find whatever it takes to make us channels for your work in our world. We know the hardest part is for us to say yes to you. Help us through Jesus Christ. Amen.*

Sunday, January 12   Read Acts 8:14-17.

The apostles at Jerusalem faced a major decision. The Samaritans, of all people, had received the word of God! What was to be done with them?

Remember the origins of the Samaritans and the disrepute in which they were held. They were the descendants of the Jews left in the Northern Kingdom during the days of the Exile six centuries earlier; they were Jews who had fallen away from the purity of the faith by intermarrying with those foreigners coming into Israel. Despite being left in the promised land, they were perceived as being less able than the exiles to remain pure, faithful to God. What hate is stronger than hate toward one perceived as a traitor?

But the Samaritans had received God's word, and perhaps remembering Jesus' conversation with the woman at the well, Peter and John were dispatched to check this out. "Can God be at work here? How can we tell? Let's pray for them! If the Holy Spirit comes, we will know God is at work *here* too!" they might have said. And the Holy Spirit appeared bringing with it the realization that anyone—anyone at all!—can receive God's grace and power.

Yes, even we who are wandering through the late twentieth century can receive the Holy Spirit, can hear the call, can see the mission God has for us, can receive the commission. We too are people through whom God may work—if we make ourselves available to the Spirit, that is!

Others may find us unlikely servants of God, but God once filled even Samaritans with power and purpose.

Prayer: *Almighty, ever-working God, grant us a place among the servants of your word, that we may become lights to our world and walk daily in your Holy Spirit. As people who love Jesus, we want to be filled with your love for all peoples. Amen.*

NEWNESS OF LIFE IN GOD'S PRESENCE

January 13-19, 1992   **Elaine M.Prevallet, SL**†
Monday, January 13   Read Isaiah 62:1-2*a*.

In the first lines of this chapter of Isaiah, we see something incredible: we see that God is determined that we should be saved. It seems to matter desperately to God that our lives be transformed from shame and guilt into lives that shine with the power of God's love. "I will not keep silent," God says; "I will not rest" until the salvation of Israel is complete. Can we really believe that God is so invested and involved in our destinies? We often feel—and act—as if God has left us to make our way alone, watching and judging us from some distant vantage point. But scripture gives us reason to believe that we do really matter to God, individually and all of us together. God is not sitting by idly and dispassionately; God is at work to save us.

How is it that God's love keeps trying to turn us around? How does Paul find the insight to say, "We know that all things work together for good for those who love God" (Rom. 8:28)? How do we experience this saving presence of God?

Perhaps one way is as a pull in the direction of continual transformation. God's presence is a power that draws us forward, that refuses to let us rest in our grudges, our selfishness, our pettiness, our fears. God's determination is the reason we cannot feel good when we are unable to forgive. God's presence is the reason that we cannot rest until, small step by small step, we move to overcome our fears, choose to risk a kind action, find the courage to say yes even to suffering, even to the love-power that tugs and pulls us to reconciliation.

Prayer: *O God, open my heart to recognize and respond to your presence that always wills me to be transformed. Amen.*

---

†Director of Knobs Haven Retreat Center on the grounds of the Motherhouse of the Sisters of Loretto, Nerinx, Kentucky.

Tuesday, January 14   Read Isaiah 62:1-5.

What's in a name? In the biblical tradition, a person's self was concentrated in his/her name. To be renamed was to stand in a new relationship with God, to have one's destiny transformed by God. So Abram, whose name-change to Abraham signified his destiny as "ancestor of a multitude of nations" (Gen. 17:5); so Jacob, whose name-change to Israel, "the one who strives with God," marked his destiny as the divinely commissioned ancestor of the chosen people (Gen. 32:28); so Simon, whose name-change to Peter marked him and his testimony of faith as the rock on which Christ's church was built (Matt. 16:18). When God names us, that name becomes our destiny. And God has named us and has placed our true name deep within our hearts. Our task is to live into its meaning.

Today's reading brings a message of hope. God is able to transform us even when we seem to ourselves most hopeless. The images of reversal here are profound: from being named "Forsaken," Jerusalem will be renamed "My Delight Is in Her"; the name "Desolate" will be changed to "Married."

It would be difficult to imagine more tenderly loving ways of naming the relationship God desires to have with us. In our pain and struggle, at times when we feel we have alienated ourselves from God, or when we feel that God has abandoned us, we need to remember that the very pain itself witnesses to the destiny God has written into our being. God's name for us calls out within us as a deep longing to be known, to be loved, to be cherished in a way that only God can fulfill. The promise Isaiah gives us is that God's faithful love is transforming us into a people in whom God's heart delights and rejoices.

Prayer: *O God, let me trust your love for me. Little by little, call me by the name that can transform my being into the person you call and destine me to be. Amen.*

Wednesday, January 15   Read Psalm 36:5-6.

In these lines, the psalmist catches us up in a hymn of praise, exulting in God's *hesed* (faithful, covenanting love). With a cosmic sweep, the psalmist pictures this love reaching up to the skies and down to inscrutable deeps, strong and stable as the mountains, embracing in its scope both human and non-human creatures. What an appropriate motif for our times, when we are becoming painfully aware that in our arrogance, we humans have assumed a posture of superiority over and even of disdain toward the rest of creation. We now recognize with increasing urgency that the amazing diversity of species is a sacred trust that we cannot violate without violating our own fidelity to God's covenant.

For instance, in the tropical forest of Costa Rica, as many as 10,000 different species may inhabit a single tree. That tree stands surrounded by many other trees, each a home to many *other* species as well. Scientists are unable to unravel the complex ways that the nourishment of each single species—and of the tree—depends upon all the others. We catch a glimpse of the fact that our human lives are only one fragile and dependent part of an immensely intricate love. There is an awesome and mysterious economy involved in this covenant our God has made with us, both grander and more subtly particular than we could ever have imagined. We learn to reverence these "least" of God's creatures, the 10,000 species in a single tree, because we recognize that they too have an irreplaceable role to play in God's covenant with us. And we bow in awe of God, who has placed all creation together to nourish and sustain each other.

Prayer: *O God, open my eyes and my heart today so that I may recognize your presence in all things, both great and small. I praise your wisdom and your love manifested in all you create. Amen.*

Thursday, January 16   Read Psalm 36:7-8.

These short lines of the psalm present us with two rich images of our life in God's covenanting love.

"All people may take refuge in the shadow of your wings." These words image God as a safe place. Chicks are gathered under their mother's wings in times of danger. So God is the One to whom we can turn in times of trouble or anxiety, sweeping all our concerns gently into the space where they can be released in remembering God's covenant to be with us and care for us with an all-encompassing love.

"They feast on the abundance of your house." While for the psalmist "God's house" probably meant the Temple at Jerusalem, we can expand the image to think of the whole earth as God's house, for truly God is always present to this marvelous creation, indwelling it, sustaining it. And in a very real sense, the beauties of earth do give us a feast in abundance, without which we literally could not live. We know, for instance, that people deprived of sensory stimuli cannot remain sane. We also know that humans develop relationally as they are loved into being by other humans—and often with the help of a pet. Even the paper upon which these meditations appear for spiritual nourishment is the gift of a tree. These are only minute instances of how utterly dependent we are upon creation. The rich image of creation as God's house, within which we feast with abundance, can help to nurture in us a sense of reverence and appreciation for the whole of creation.

Suggestion for meditation: *Let us today imagine ourselves as God's houseguests, and be careful not to act in a greedy and thoughtless way. Let us regard all that is as a gift to be gratefully received.*

Friday, January 17   Read Psalm 36:9;
                                          John 4:14; 9:4-5.

The images of fountain (water) and light run deep in biblical tradition. However, we now experience water and light more as fact than as image; we have lost their essential connection to life. We have to recreate the images for ourselves in order to recover their power.

The psalmist speaks of a fountain of life; water, of course, is the connecting image. Water—that precious resource without which we cannot live: most of us take it so for granted, having the luxury of simply turning on a faucet. In our image of a fountain, we may think only of human-made constructs recycling water, designed for aesthetics. The psalmist would have imagined a real source of life—a stream of fresh water bubbling steadily from a spring.

Jesus promises that his gift is a spring of water gushing up to eternal life. A spring is a wonderful image of the life of the Spirit within us: a place where we can find refreshment, a never-failing source of renewal. Once we have discovered this source within us, we can turn there with a quick mental glance many times during the day and draw from the fountain the life-giving water of the Spirit.

Light is a power that enables us to see shadow—the dark places in ourselves that we try to hide; the dark places of our world where justice and love have not found a home. Jesus spoke of himself as the Light of the world, a Light in which truth is manifest. The truth is that the world is bathed in the light of God's love; it is the eyes of our hearts that must be opened in order to see.

Prayer: *Gracious God, source of life and light, give me courage to confront with the power of your love those situations where death and darkness seem to reign. Amen.*

Saturday, January 18   Read 1 Corinthians 12:1-11.

A marvelous freedom is offered to us in this passage: the freedom to be just who we are and to do just what we can do. Paradoxically, it is upon this affirmation of the individual that genuine Christian community is founded.

To be ourselves sounds very easy, but in fact it takes a great deal of faith and confidence—in God and in ourselves. We seem to have a built-in tendency to compare ourselves and our gifts with others, and to rate ourselves either inferior or superior. We do this in the smallest ways: someone has longer eyelashes, or better-shaped eyes, or a better voice—there is no end to the comparisons we make. Often it is ourselves we rate poorly. But, more secretly, we may also find ourselves thinking *I could do it better* and refusing to give credit to the contribution of another. Comparisons of this kind are basically destructive of community, for they prevent us from genuinely appreciating ourselves or other persons and evoking their gifts.

Comparison is really symptomatic of a lack of faith. We find it difficult to believe that we are good enough, or that our gifts are valuable enough to deserve God's love—or anyone else's. It is a real breakthrough when we realize that we don't have to be good enough according to anyone else's measure, and especially not our own. We only have to believe deep down that we are God's creation, endowed with the gift of God's spirit, and that the most important contribution we can make is to be ourselves. My contribution to the Body of Christ is who I am, and no one else can do or be that in my place. Here there is no room for comparison, no better or worse. Here lies enormous freedom: the truth of my own being is God's purpose for me.

Prayer: *Help me today, O God, to cherish my own being and the being of every other person. Amen.*

Sunday, January 19   Read John 2:1-11.

The wedding feast at Cana is the first of a series of seven "signs" reported in the Gospel of John as performed by Jesus at the beginning of his ministry. Here is a kind of grand opening, a scene extraordinarily rich in symbolic content.

The stone water jars of the Jewish purification ritual are the vehicle within which a powerful sign of transformation is effected: a new order is being introduced, the old rituals superseded. Ordinary water is transformed into fine wine. The event takes place on the third day—the day of Resurrection—and at a wedding, another symbol of transformation. The whole scene fairly shouts: SOMETHING NEW IS HAPPENING! God's desire to be united with humankind is about to be realized: Jesus, the Christ, is here.

The very fact of Jesus, God's Word enfleshed, himself the union of human and divine, symbolizes God's desire to be united with us. Isaiah has already prepared us for the astonishing news of God's determination to save us. In Jesus, the hour for transformation, the possibility of new creation, has arrived. In Jesus, God has spoken the word that unites us to the very heart of God.

Prayer: *O God, I celebrate your willingness to be with us, among us, in us. Put a new and steadfast spirit within me, the Spirit of Jesus, and let me experience the quickening of your life within me. Transform me, that I may become, ever more fully, a dwelling place for your love. Amen.*

LAW AND PROPHECY: GOD'S GIFTS

January 20-26, 1992   **Fritz Mutti†**
Monday, January 20   Read Nehemiah 8:1-10.

The gift of the law

The law is God's gift to humankind. Is that hard to believe? For most of us this may be a truth slowly learned. We frequently view the law as a burden, something imposed to crimp our freedom, a bondage against which we must rebel.

For those exiles who had returned from Babylon to the land of promise, however, the law was a source of power. It refocused their worship, deepened their understanding of covenantal purpose, and nurtured them to strength. They saw the law in this way, said Nehemiah, because they believed the law had been given by God. What the people heard was no ordinary word. This was the word of the Lord!

With a little imagination we can picture the scene in our minds and feel the difference. When Ezra climbed to the platform and opened the book, the people, moved by a sense of awe, stood out of reverence, raised their arms in adoration, and bowed their heads in worship. During the reading of the scriptures, interpreters moved among the people, helping them to remember the covenantal story and understand its meaning for their lives. But, like us, the people felt the law as judgment, and they began to weep in sorrow. Then Nehemiah and Ezra announced that this was not a day for weeping but a day for rejoicing. The people should be glad, they said; for through the gift of the law, God establishes a covenant that offers the fulfillment of life.

Prayer: *O God, may we receive the gift of law so completely that our lives are filled to overflowing. Amen.*

---

†District Superintendent, Kansas City North District, Missouri West Conference.

Tuesday, January 21   Read Psalm 19:7-10.

The excellence of the law

Try reading these verses aloud in order to catch the grace and power of their meaning. If we speak these lines, key words stand out: *law, decrees, precepts, commandments, fear, ordinances*. These are paralleled by another list: *perfect, sure, right, clear, pure, true*. Now combine these parallel lists: Perfect law. Sure decree. Right precepts. Clear commandments. Pure respect for God. True ordinances. Indeed, God's law is excellent!

This contrasts starkly with the realities of life as human beings try to live it. King David, to whom tradition attributes the authorship of this psalm, certainly had difficulty in keeping the law. His rivalry with Saul, his conspiracy against Uriah, and his adultery with Bathsheba, all point to the frailty of human flesh before the excellence of God's law.

In today's world, we experience those failures no less. In the international community, tyrants defy concepts of law, wheeling out armies and weapons of war to pursue their own ambitions regardless of the threat to safety for vast throngs. Lawless citizens of great cities stalk the streets, sometimes spraying innocent pedestrians with gunfire for no apparent reason. Family members contend against each other so that rules are stretched and distorted. Even in the confines of an individual's personal order, dishonesty and rationalization push aside integrity and truth.

The Spirit calls us back to the law that is excellent in every way. Through the psalmist we are reminded that God is still God. In spite of corruption and sin, God continually offers a way of living that brings fulfillment through righteousness.

Prayer: *Divine Lawgiver, help us to celebrate the excellence of your law and to lift up its precepts in such a way that all people may live together in harmony. Amen.*

Wednesday, January 22   Read Psalm 19:10-11.

The benefits of the law

Before television came into every home, children got some of their morality lessons from radio heroes like Superman, the Lone Ranger, the Green Hornet, Straight Arrow, and Sergeant Preston. Episode after episode taught that crime does not pay and wrongdoing will be punished, while goodness reaps benefits and obedience to law begets blessings.

Perhaps that message is too simplistic for many adults who are aware of the complexities of decision making in an imperfect world, but Psalm 19 insists that there are benefits of God's law more valuable than gold and sweeter than honey.

A generation ago, the modern prophet Martin Luther King, Jr., proclaimed that one of those benefits is equality. While the defenders of segregation and racism railed against him by calling for "law and order," Dr. King held up the possibility that, in a just society of law, "The wolf shall live with the lamb, the leopard shall lie down with the kid, the calf and the lion and the fatling together" (Isa. 11:6). He envisioned a time when all black children could receive a decent education, black youths could expect to find a job, and black men and women could be free to speak their minds and live where they chose.

The struggle for equal justice under the law continues in every country around the globe, and the Spirit prods the church to be in the vanguard. When we accept the challenge of this psalm, we claim a gift more precious than the finest gold.

Prayer: *Transform stubborn resisters of justice, O God, and lead us together into a community of law. Give the benefits of your law to those who are denied equality and justice. We pray through the Savior, Jesus Christ. Amen.*

Thursday, January 23   Read Luke 4:14-15.

The gift of prophecy

As long as Jesus only quoted prophetic scriptures, the people affirmed him and marvelled at his gracious words. When Jesus *became* a prophet, however, they quickly changed from doting neighbors into an angry mob.

The gift of prophecy, sought so vigorously by many, is a risky endowment. Before we ask for the gift we should be aware of the cost. In South Africa, Steve Biko paid the price when he was imprisoned and beaten to death by his jailers. In El Salvador, Archbishop Oscar Romero paid the price when he was gunned down by representatives of his own government while he offered Mass at the cathedral altar. Dozens of other prophets, whose names we do not know, also have given their lives so that the people might hear that prophetic truth.

Few—perhaps none of us—who read these devotional pages daily may expect to be thrust into such demanding prophetic roles. We are not the prophets but those who hear the prophecy. We are the ones who must wrestle with the word the prophets speak. We must decide whether we will work for the changes the prophecy demands.

Prophecy comes to us as a gift that challenges, judges, stretches, pushes, pulls. It confronts us through Old Testament voices, through Jesus of Nazareth, and through the Apostles. It rises up from the midst of common life today, and it beckons from the uncertainties of an ever-pressing tomorrow. If we accept the gift we will be changed. Dare we take the risk?

Prayer: *As Jesus was filled with the power of the Spirit, O God, so may we receive the gift of prophecy to energize every muscle, brain cell, and emotion. May we witness in the communities we call home in such a way that people begin to wonder about the source of the message we bring. Amen.*

Friday, January 24   Read Luke 4:16-21.

The fulfillment of prophecy

After quoting Isaiah 61:1-2, Jesus announced to the people in the synagogue in Nazareth that this ancient word of hope had been fulfilled as he spoke it. Many in that place believed his declaration. They agreed that the Spirit had set him aside to offer good news to the poor, liberty to those in prison, sight to those who cannot see, freedom to those who are oppressed.

A modern example of the freedom Jesus offers lies in the story of "Trouble-Over-Me." Oh, his African name is Matambudziko, but it means "Trouble-Over-Me." Arthur Kanonuhwa, the station chairman at Nyadiri Mission in Zimbabwe, introduced this young man to a group of us who were visiting mission projects in southern Africa.

Matambudziko became a resident at Nyadiri after his parents abandoned him at the age of ten. Believing that the child was possessed by an evil spirit, they had cast him out for fear that the demon would afflict others in their household.

Matambudziko lives with cerebral palsy. His twisted arms and legs are so weak he must remain in bed most of the time. His faltering speech severely limits his ability to communicate. Still, he lives with hope because the church, living out Jesus' proclamation in today's reading, offered him the liberating love of Jesus Christ. He received the gift and is able to have a life of quality in spite of his illness.

When Jesus fulfills the prophet's word, the principalities and the powers are met and defeated, the abandoned find a home, and the broken are restored to wholeness.

Devotional Activity: *Read again the scripture lesson for today, then note on a piece of paper several instances which you believe mark the fulfillment of this passage. Create a prayer of thanksgiving for the fulfillment of prophecy and offer your prayer to God.*

Saturday, January 25　　　　Read 1 Corinthians 12:12-13.

The gift of unity in Christ

If law and prophecy are gifts of the Spirit, so is oneness in Christ. Sadly, however, the church shows the face of shattered unity. Because of doctrinal conflict, political intrigue, class divisions, petty quarrels, or dozens of other reasons, the one Body of Christ splits into detached parts and shuts out the prompting of the Spirit.

In small towns, congregations of two, six, or even a dozen denominations gather separately on Sunday mornings and pretend that they are not divided from other Christians. And in crowded cities, similar congregations baptize persons into competing institutions, each trying to claim a share of the "market." In isolated pulpits and in the forums of mass communication, mission evangelists from multiple traditions tell their version of the gospel, and curious hearers puzzle over the mentality of exclusiveness.

Yet it is God's intention that the Body of Christ be one and that through the Spirit the baptized be incorporated into a single covenant community of faith. Since January 18 in many places, groups of Christians have gathered each day to try to give expression to the unity which the Spirit offers. They have come together in chapels, offices, and homes to share moments of worship and fellowship. As participants in the Week of Prayer for Christian Unity, they have sung, read scripture, and prayed together. In a small way they have witnessed to the gift of unity which the Spirit gives. And in many places the broken Body of Christ has become the unified people of God.

Prayer Suggestion: *Today let us examine our attitudes and behavior regarding unity in light of scripture. Let us repent of any arrogance or judgment in our lives which alienates us from other disciples of Jesus. Let us pray for the gift of unity.*

Sunday, January 26   Read 1 Corinthians 12:14-31.

The diversity of oneness

More than thirty years ago my wife and I exchanged marriage vows and entered a covenant relationship in which the two of us "became one." To our union three sons were added. During that time we have been one family, whether there were two, three, four, or five of us. Of course, this circle of kinship also includes dozens of other persons as well.

Just because we affirm this unity, however, we do not go on to say that we are all alike. Superficial appearances show that. Two of us have brown hair and dark complexions; two are sandy-haired and fair-skinned; one has red hair and wonderful freckles. We do not look alike and we do not act alike. Some are talkers, others are quiet; some are artists, others are athletes; some love intellectual pursuit, others prefer matters of the heart.

So it is in the one Body of Christ. Though we are united in the Spirit, we are many members with diverse gifts. None is better than another or unneeded by the whole. All need each other in order to fulfill God's purpose.

The rich diversity of many natures, cultures, gifts, skills, talents, and visions melds together into a beautiful whole. Apart from each other we are lonely and unfulfilled. Bound together in a covenant of faithful trust, we reflect God's intention that all shall be united in one Body of Christ through the Spirit. Thank God for the diversity of unity.

Prayer: *Make us drink of one Spirit, almighty God, that we may be united with Christ. Use our diversity to bless that unity with creativity and power. May the gifts of law and prophecy be coupled with the gift of unity, that your vision for creation may come to full fruition. Amen.*

ENCOUNTERING GOD

January 27–February 1, 1992   **Temba Mafico†**
Monday, January 27   Read Jeremiah 1:4-5, 9.

An analysis of Jeremiah's call unfolds a profound message concerning our worth before God. Jeremiah believed that before God had formed him into a human being, the Lord already knew who he was. The Hebrew word *yādac* ("know") also refers to a very intimate relationship between people. The same meaning of "know" is found in Hosea 13:4-5. What Jeremiah implies here is that God knew him in a profound and intimate way even before God created his physical body. In other words, Jeremiah believed his spiritual nature pre-existed his human body.

The scripture tells us that Jeremiah was not born by accident. Rather, God consecrated him for his prophetic ministry while he was still in his mother's womb. The Hebrew word translated "consecrate" in verse 5 implies that Jeremiah was individually unique and was created for a task God had preordained. To equip Jeremiah for his commission to proclaim God's word, God put the word in his mouth (see also Isaiah 6:5-7).

Like Jeremiah, we are uniquely created by God and called to our respective tasks. Implied in this idea is that we should always seek God's will in whatever we do. We should constantly pray: "Thy will be done, on earth as it is in heaven."

Suggestion for meditation: *What does it mean for each of us that God has uniquely created us and has called us to our respective tasks?*

---

†Visiting Professor from the University of Zimbabwe serving as Professor of Old Testament and Biblical Hebrew, Interdenominational Theological Center, Atlanta, Georgia; advisory committee member of the Africa University.

Tuesday, January 28   Read Jeremiah 1:6-7, 10.

Many of us despair when we are confronted by the world situation today: pollution of the environment, the high murder rate, greed, poverty, oppression, and other social ills. Naturally, we expect people of some significant social status to do something about it. That is what Jeremiah thought when he initially objected to God's call: "Ah, Lord GOD! Truly, I do not know how to speak, for I am only a boy" (v. 4). In Israel, as in the rest of the ancient Near East, old age was the sign of wisdom based on tested knowledge. Youths were expected to heed the advice of their elders, as the Book of Proverbs teaches. Thus Jeremiah objected to God's commission on the grounds of his youth and his lack of articulation.

But when God assured Jeremiah, saying, "I am with you," Jeremiah was given the confidence that would enable him to speak God's word. Thus Jeremiah's foes would fight but would not prevail against him because God would deliver him. This assurance did not promise that he would not suffer scars and bruises. The Bible gives several examples of people who were called but suffered to effect a change. It was God's word that Jeremiah was given to speak. This passage teaches us that it is God's word *we* must deliver, not our own.

Suggestion for meditation: *God's call is a command, not a request (v. 7b). Breaking down, destroying, and overthrowing must be accomplished within the context of building and planting a new world order which promotes peace.*

Wednesday, January 29   Read Psalm 71:1-6.

Psalm 71:1-6 is a portion of a lament by an elderly person who is being persecuted by wicked and cruel enemies. The psalmist urgently summons God to listen to him and to rescue him. The psalmist does not base his trust in God because God is the One who created the world, who delivered the Israelites from Egyptian oppression. Rather, he trusts in God because throughout his youth he has enjoyed a personal relationship with God. God has been his refuge, and his hope and his trust from his youth. Like Jeremiah, the psalmist believed that God was responsible for his creation as a unique individual and that it was God who took him from his mother's womb and placed him in this world.

The problem with many people's faith is that it is based on what they have heard and not on a personal encounter with God. Some believe in God because of what the preacher has declared to them about the Lord. In other words, they do not personally know God: they know *about* God. Job confessed that he had heard of God "by the hearing of the ear, but now my eyes see you" (Job 42:5). The psalmist, on the other hand, regards God as a personal deity on whom he has leaned throughout his youth. He found God to be a rock of refuge and a fortress.

Suggestion for meditation: *Do the majority of Christians believe in God only because of what they have heard through sermons? How can we experience a personal relationship with God? To a personal God, we can direct our praise (Psalm 66), our complaints (Psalm 22:1-2), and our frustrations (Jer. 20:7-10).*

Thursday, January 30   Read 1 Corinthians 13:1-10.

This chapter from Paul's letter to the Corinthians is often used in marriage ceremonies. As such, the emphasis is on the invincibility of love in sustaining a marriage that must endure many trials and tribulations. But there is an even more profound message that Paul was communicating to the believers at Corinth, a message that is applicable to believers of modern times.

The early church had become too involved in religious acts, and this preoccupation sometimes tended to de-emphasize divine service to humankind. The early Christians were focusing too much on gifts of the Spirit they had received and too little on acts of service to others. In this passage, Paul is encouraging the Corinthians to realize that while all gifts are good and divinely accorded, love is superior to all of them. Speaking in tongues, knowledge, prophecy, and other spiritual gifts are knowledge intended to be used hand in hand with the gift of love.

There is a big difference between our faith, which moves our own mountains, and our love, which moves the mountains of others. There is a difference between our knowledge of all mysteries and our knowledge which, through love, enables others to know mysteries. There is a big difference between merely observing Christian teachings and practicing love (Matt. 19:16-30).

Suggestion for meditation: *Does 1 Corinthians 13:3 suggest to us that charitable acts not motivated by love, though helpful to the poor, receive no divine blessing? Love makes itself known in a kind act and not a pious gesture (cf. Matt. 6:1-4). What motivates my charitable acts?*

Friday, January 31   Read 1 Corinthians 13:11-13.

Paul's metaphorical phrase "seeing in a mirror dimly, but then face to face" is elucidated only by reading it within its context. In verse 12 Paul makes a clear distinction between what we did as children and what we are expected to do as adults. The way children speak, think, and reason would not be appropriate for adults. Children think like children, speak like children, reason like children. But when they become adults, they are expected to give up childish behaviors. The phrase "give up" indicates that growing up involves a conscious effort on the part of a young person to adopt adulthood and maturity. Paul appears to be alluding to a rite of passage. Among many tribes, particularly in Africa, the rite of passage was a time when adolescents publicly renounced childish behaviors and adopted adulthood with its responsibilities.

Childlike attitudes and behaviors remind Paul of seeing in a mirror dimly. Just as a mirror does not give a perfect image, faith without loving acts is a talent which bears no fruit. Similarly, as knowledge must keep growing to perfection, Christians must realize that faith without works is dead (James 2:17; see also Gal. 5:6). Perfect faith is manifested by sacrificial love that suffers and endures all things, like the love of God revealed in Jesus Christ.

Suggestion for meditation: *What did Paul mean by "If anyone is in Christ, there is a new creation; everything old has passed away; see, everything has become new" (2 Cor. 5:17)? How does 1 Corinthians 13 help us understand what it means to be a "new creation"?*

Saturday, February 1   Read Luke 4:21-24.

Jesus' first visit and rejection at Nazareth is more vivid in Luke's description. Matthew and Mark are sketchy on the visit but are more detailed on the people's reaction to the gracious words Jesus spoke there.

While Luke records that the people marveled at the words that proceeded from Jesus' mouth, Matthew and Mark report that the people marveled at Jesus' wisdom and at the mighty works he performed. In various ways the other two Gospels make it clear that Jesus, prior to the commencement of his ministry, was a commoner who suddenly became prominent. In spite of the miraculous nature of his birth, Jesus remained as ordinary to his kinspeople as were his parents, brothers, and sisters. His fame was due neither to his unusual birth nor to his great learning, for according to Matthew 13:57 and Mark 6:2 (cf. John 7:15), the Jews remarked: "How is it that this man has learning, when he has never studied?" While Jesus was not formally schooled, he nonetheless possessed wisdom (cf. Luke 2:52), God's natural gift to all people who ask for it (1 Kings 3:5-12).

Jesus' visit to Nazareth is therefore a great lesson to all people. Wisdom is God's natural gift to all people and it surpasses theoretical knowledge learned in classrooms.

Prayer: *God, give me wisdom to distinguish between right and wrong. Amen.*

Sunday, February 2   Read Luke 4:25-30.

I have always wondered why this group of Jews reacted so strongly when Jesus told them about Elijah's miracles. After all, they should have been familiar with this story from the Hebrew Scriptures. On closer examination of the text, however, I realize that they were hurt because Jesus told them the truth they did not want to hear. They had been too accustomed to thinking of themselves as God's chosen people. Even though their religious lives were in conflict with God's covenant, they still expected God to show them special favors.

One characteristic of Luke is his firm belief that the idea of election (being chosen by God) did not exclude God's salvation to other nations. Luke repeatedly underscores this point by showing many foreigners (non-Israelites) as having greater faith than most Israelites and thereby being more worthy of the kingdom of God. For example, Luke tells the story of ten lepers who were healed, but only the Samaritan returned to give his praises unto the Lord (Luke 17:11-19). The familiar parable of the Good Samaritan was intended to underscore how despised people such as Samaritans were actually demonstrating God's love more than those who believed in God but did not practice their faith. Luke shows that there is a big difference between upholding doctrines or liturgies and spontaneous love to a needy human being.

Suggestion for meditation: *"Not all those who say to me, 'Lord, Lord,' shall enter the kingdom of heaven, but those who do the will of [God]." What do these words mean for you?*

February 3-9, 1992   **John O. Gooch**†
Monday, February 3   Read Isaiah 6:1-4.

When God appears, we see God's glory! Isaiah's vision suggests he was in the Temple, stationed where he could see both the altar and the sanctuary. Right in the middle of ordinary worship, he "saw the Lord" and around the Lord the great hosts of seraphs, crying aloud God's holiness and glory.

Whatever else one might say about what happened in the Temple that day, one point is crystal clear—Isaiah became aware of the Reality behind the liturgy. He saw that worship was focused on a living God, a God of holiness and glory. Today is Monday. Were we aware of a living God behind the liturgy yesterday? Or was it business as usual?

Most commentators on this text are in a hurry to get past the vision of God to the "important stuff "—the confession of sin. True heirs of the Augustinian tradition, we know how to handle sin and guilt and confession. We're less comfortable with the vision of the glory of God.

Today, linger in the glory. Just stop and be aware of God. Drink in all of the beauty and power and majesty and wonder and glory of God that you can. Let the glory of God roll over you like the waves of the ocean and fill your being with joy and wonder. Then, when you are ready for confession, you will know to whom you pour out your sense of sin and failure.

Prayer: *Glory be to the Father, and to the Son, and to the Holy Ghost. As it was in the beginning, is now, and ever shall be, world without end. Amen, and amen.*

---

†Clergy member of the Missouri East Conference; editor, Youth Division Staff, The United Methodist Publishing House, Nashville, Tennessee.

Tuesday, February 4   Read 1 Corinthians 15:1-11.

When God appears, we see God's glory! Think what it must have been like to see the risen Christ and catch a glimpse of the glory and wonder of the world to come. To know that this rabbi is Lord of heaven and earth must have been heartbreakingly beautiful. And then think what it must have meant that this Lord of heaven and earth had appeared to you, that even in the glory of God's perfect kingdom, you were known and loved by name!

So the Lord appeared to Cephas, then to the twelve, then to over 500 at once. Interesting—Paul makes no mention of an appearance to Mary Magdalene. Yet one of the most certain points of Christian history is that the risen Christ appeared to Mary (making this appearance all the more valid, because being a woman at that time meant that Mary had no legal standing as a witness). Then he appeared to James. What a special moment of glory that must have been for this younger brother of Jesus! Early traditions suggest that the appearance to James involved a meal, like the appearance to the disciples on the road to Emmaus or the disciples on the shore of Galilee.

The risen Christ was known "in the breaking of the bread" (Luke 24:35). For us, that statement suggests that one place we see the glory of God and of the risen Christ is in the Eucharist. When we celebrate Holy Communion, when we remember, when we eat and drink, we see God's glory.

We will never see the glory of the risen Christ with our own eyes, at least not in this life. But one of the great comforts of the Christian faith is the awareness that when we share together in the Eucharist, we know Christ "in the breaking of the bread."

Prayer: *Lord, help me see your glory in the bread and wine, and in the ordinary events of this day. Help me to live in the hope your glory brings. Amen.*

47

Wednesday, February 5   Read Isaiah 6:1-7.

When God appears, we become aware of our own sin and of God's forgiveness. As Isaiah's exultation pierced his consciousness, he became aware he was in big trouble. "Woe is me . . . for my eyes have seen . . . the Lord." No living human can see God and live. Only Moses, in all the long period from the twelfth century B.C. to the eighth century B.C., had seen God and lived. More: "Woe!" is the proper response for humans when we become aware we are in the presence of the Holy. We recognize the gulf between Creator and creature, between holiness and all the ways in which we fall short of holiness.

So it was with Isaiah. He recognized—in the presence of God, the Holy One—that he was unclean. Part of being unclean had to do with sin; part had to do with the reality that he was ritually unclean, not consecrated as a priest of YHWH. So he deserved to die.

But no sooner does Isaiah cry out his fear and anguish than God acts to redeem. The seraph carries a coal from the altar and touches Isaiah's lips. In terms of ritual cleanliness, the coal carries the holiness of the altar and, because of that holiness, purifies Isaiah's unclean lips. In that touch of holiness, Isaiah is cleansed—his guilt is taken away and his sin forgiven.

Those of us who live our lives consciously as servants of God need to learn from Isaiah. How can God forgive and purify anyone who feels no touch of impurity, no need of forgiveness? And who among us is not unclean before the holy God?

Look again—the story is as much about death/life as it is about sin/forgiveness. No one can see God and live. But God bridges the gap through the seraph, who enters into relationship with Isaiah and makes him holy. Truly we are justified by grace.

Prayer: *God of grace, I too am a person of unclean lips. Cleanse me, purify me, renew me, so that I too might live in your presence. Amen.*

Thursday, February 6   Read Luke 5:1-10.

When God appears, we become aware of our own sin and of God's forgiveness. I am struck by how much this account sounds like John 21. Many scholars think both are accounts of the same resurrection appearance. Luke has moved the account to this setting to explain how Jesus called Simon in the first place.

The great catch of fish prepares Simon for something even greater to come. But before the something greater, there is Simon's reaction to the miracle. Like Isaiah (in Isa. 6) he knows he is in God's presence. Like Isaiah, he knows he is in big trouble. And, like Isaiah, he falls on his knees and cries, "Go away from me, Lord, for I am a sinful man!" (v. 8)

I wonder what Peter meant. Did he mean that, like Isaiah, he was unclean and could not stand in the presence of holiness? Was he begging Jesus to go away because he, Peter, did not want to be reminded of his failures? Was he doing a short form of the Prayer of Confession and saying he had sinned? In any case, it is clear Simon knows he is unworthy to associate with Jesus.

Jesus' response was, "Do not be afraid." That is a common Lukan phrase. We find it in the words of the angel to Zechariah (1:13), to Mary (1:30), to the shepherds (2:10). It is a common phrase in Luke because it is the way God reassures us when we behold God's glory. When we become aware of the divine, we also become aware of how far from God we really are and how dangerous it is for us to be in the presence of the Holy. More even than the forgiveness of our sins, we need the assurance that God is disposed toward us in kindness and mercy. "Don't be afraid" means that God does not come to us to do us harm, but good, and to call us to God's service.

Prayer: *Lord, don't go away from me, even though I am sinful. I need the assurance that you love me and want me to be with you. Amen.*

Friday, February 7   Read Psalm 138.

When God appears, God's people are strengthened and renewed. Like Isaiah, the psalmist is in the temple. His mind is full
of the knowledge that God has appeared in this place. So he gives
thanks for the love and faithfulness of God (v. 2). Those are
covenant terms, so it seems clear that a part of the strength the
psalmist feels comes from being in a faith heritage that celebrates God's mercy and faithfulness even when God's people are
unfaithful.

The psalmist finds strength and renewal in remembering that
his prayers have been answered (v. 3). He remembers that God
has helped him in time of trouble (v. 7). So the psalmist knows
grace, steadfast love, assurance, and the power of his heritage as
a part of the people of God.

Verses 4-6 are a little hymn of praise that says God's appear-
ing is important for the whole world. Even great kings will sing
songs of praise when they see the greatness of the glory of God.
More: this great God, whose glory humbles even the mighty of
the earth, has a special care for the lowly and dispossessed.

Then, in a flash of glory as blinding as Isaiah's vision, the
psalmist becomes aware that this great God has saved him
personally (v. 7). His own salvation is a part of the salvation of
the world, a part of the revelation of God's glory.

Because the Lord's love endures forever, the psalmist says, he
is sure that God will "fulfil his purpose for me." He knows he is
safe in God's love and is content to leave the future there.

Strengthened and renewed, the psalmist leaves the temple to
live another day.

Prayer: *O God, help me know the assurance of your love and to go
forth to live my day strengthened and renewed because I have been in
your presence. Amen.*

Saturday, February 8   Read Isaiah 6:8-13;
                                            Luke 5:10*b*-11.

When God appears, we are called to spread God's message. A funny thing happened to Isaiah. He wasn't struck dead when he saw God, even though he was unclean and deserved death. Instead, a seraph came with the live coal, touched his lips, and sanctified him. Then Isaiah learned that he could hear God's word and had the power to obey it. "Here am I! Send me." Chances are that Isaiah had not anticipated his day would end with a commission to go and speak God's word to his people. And what a word! Isaiah was called to go and preach "bad news" to a people who did not want to hear about justice and judgment.

A funny thing happened to Simon. He started out that morning just a tired fisherman, frustrated because he hadn't caught anything all night. Then Jesus got into his boat, and his life changed forever. He cried out for Jesus to leave him—and found himself sanctified. Before the morning was over, he had heard the words, "From now on you will be catching people."

"Sanctified," in both stories, means made clean, complete, consecrated. Not a Wesleyan meaning of sanctification, perhaps. We would more likely call it justification, or perhaps being called to preach. But for both Isaiah and Simon—and for us— being sanctified means we can hear God's word. The noise of the world that keeps blocking our ears and distracting us is cleared away, and we *can* hear God's call. More: we have the power to obey. Go, speak to the people. Tell them about the realities of life, of justice and judgment. Stir them from their comfortable lives, from their world of fantasy in which they get lost so easily. Go, bring them to God, where they will find life.

Prayer: *God, sanctify me so I can hear you clearly. Clear away the noise that keeps blocking my ears and help me hear you. Help me be open to you and obey you. Amen.*

Sunday, February 9   Read 1 Corinthians 15:1-5.

When God appears, we are called to spread God's message. Paul reminds the Corinthians how they received the good news—he preached it to them. But Paul himself had received it from someone else. The traditions he handed on were handed to him. Did he hear them from Ananias in Damascus? From some unknown Christian in Arabia? From Peter and James the Just during those fifteen days he spent in Jerusalem?

In any case, Paul did not treat the received tradition lightly. He handed it on as a matter of "first importance." He told the Corinthians how Jesus died and rose again "in accordance with the scriptures." The scriptures means the Hebrew scriptures (the Old Testament), of course, and this statement tells us that, as early as Paul, there was already a tradition of searching the scriptures for signs that pointed to Jesus. The key to the meaning of the statement, however, is found in Paul's faithfulness in passing on the message he had received.

We, too, have received a message and a call to pass on the message. We have a call to pass on the tradition as a matter of first importance. Unfortunately, it is all too often clear that we have not treated passing on the tradition as a matter of first importance. Sermon preparation is often relegated to moments snatched after other tasks and not treated as of first importance. Teaching the faith to children and youth is too often seen as a task that calls for as little time and effort, instead of as a matter of the first importance.

We are called to spread God's message—and we can learn a lot from Paul's model of treating that as a number-one priority.

Prayer: *Lord God, help me take more seriously the importance of preaching and teaching your word, of handing on the tradition that I have received. Help me be faithful in this task. Amen.*

GOD'S WAY OF LIFE

February 10-16   **Keith Beasley-Topliffe†**
Monday, February 10   Read Psalm 1.

Every day, in everything we do, we make choices. From the first thing in the morning (Do I get up or pull the covers over my head for just a little while longer?) until the last thing at night (Shall I go to bed or try to watch one more television show?) we are faced with alternatives. We must choose. We can't avoid it— even refusing to choose is a choice.

Of course, a lot of the time we aren't really aware of the choices we are making. We are simply repeating choices made long ago and don't even think about them. We don't usually agonize over whether or not to brush our teeth, whether to go to work, or what our job will be when we get there. We can travel through much of the day on a sort of auto-pilot, doing the same things we've been doing without even considering alternatives. The choices are there, though. Every time we repeat them, the deeper the ruts become, the harder it is to break the pattern. Choices become habits, and habits become a way of life.

The lessons this week remind us that the choices we make— our goals, our conduct, where we place our trust, even our theology—are signs of a more basic choice between two fundamental ways, or, better, between God's way and the many ways which are not God's. Not every way of life is a way of life. Traveling some ways will lead us only to destruction. "The LORD watches over the way of the righteous, but the way of the wicked will perish" (Psalm 1:6).

Prayer: *Keep my steps steady according to your promise, and never let iniquity have dominion over me. Amen. (Psalm 119:133, AP)*

---

†Pastor of the Saltillo United Methodist Parish in South-Central Pennsylvania.

Tuesday, February 11   Read Psalm 1.

What does it mean to walk in God's way? It means that in all of our choices, we seek to choose as God would have us choose. We seek to know and do God's will. For many choices, that could mean spending time in prayer, asking for guidance and carefully listening for God's answer. But for the ordinary choices of everyday life we need some general guidelines.

God has already given us such a basic guide to living. It is called *Torah* in Hebrew, which means "Instruction" but is usually translated "Law." It is the law which we contrast to gospel, the law that is a terrible burden from which Christ has freed us. We have taken Jesus' critiques of pettifogging legalism and Paul's overscrupulous conscience and created a caricature of Torah (Law).

The picture in the Old Testament is quite different. Torah is God's gracious gift. In Psalm 19 we learn that God's instructions are more desirable than gold and "sweeter also than honey, and drippings of the honeycomb" (v. 10). Psalm 119, from which the prayers for this week are taken, is the longest chapter in the Bible: 176 verses about how wonderful the Torah is!

Who are the people who walk in the way of righteousness, the way of life? According to today's lesson, they are those whose "delight is in the law of the LORD, and on his law they meditate day and night." We are doubly blessed, for we have not only Torah, God's will for us in words, but also Jesus, God's will for us in action. As we meditate on both, we learn what it means to walk in God's way.

Prayer: *Teach me, O LORD, the way of your statutes, and I will observe it to the end. Give me understanding, that I may keep your law and observe it with my whole heart. Amen. (Psalm 119:33-34)*

Wednesday, February 12   Read Jeremiah 17:5-6.

I do well in a structured environment. Something like a retreat setting where meals, worship, prayer time, and recreation time are all scheduled takes a great load off my shoulders. I don't have to make decisions about when to do things. I can relax and enjoy the day. But when I have to create my own schedule, I never seem able to stick to it.

Sometimes I think, *If only someone would come along who could make all our decisions for us!* Of course, it would have to be someone very wise, so we could be sure those decisions would be good ones. We would want to be very careful about choosing such a leader. Once that choice was made, though, we could sit back, relax, and let the leader lead.

No wonder, then, that we demand perfection in those who would be our leaders. After all, if they can go astray, they might lead us astray. We don't tolerate bad behavior in political candidates. But once we have invested our trust in leaders, it's a different story. We don't want to believe they can do any wrong. That would call our choice into question. We deny incompetence and misconduct as long as we can—as long as the press will let us. When we are forced to face their failure, we become angry. How could they have betrayed our trust?

Jeremiah reminds us that such betrayal is inevitable. No human is able to bear the weight of making our decisions for us. No one should have to try. When we expect so much of our leaders, we set them up for failure. When we ask our leaders to make all the choices for us, we guarantee that we will be misled. We might as well plant a bush in the desert and expect it to thrive as to place complete trust in a human being and expect all to be well. It just won't work.

Prayer: *I have gone astray like a lost sheep; seek out your servant, for I do not forget your commandments. Amen. (Psalm 119:176)*

Thursday, February 13   Read Luke 6:20-26.

It's no wonder Christians are often confused about how wealth and poverty are related to the two ways of Life and Death. Different biblical passages seem contradictory. Some texts promise that the righteous will prosper and the wicked will perish here and now. Other passages acknowledge that real life often isn't so tidy. The wicked profit from their evil while many good people live in poverty and suffering.

And then there are sections like today's lesson. Jesus says God's blessings are exclusively for the poor and down-trodden. He warns the rich to enjoy life now. There's no good news about their future. His word for them is, "Woe!"

We really wish Jesus wouldn't say such things. We know he's talking about most of us. We try to get out of it. We think of someone who has much more than we do, so we feel comparatively poor. We turn to Matthew, where Jesus declares blessings for those who are poor in spirit, and go on about detachment and right use of wealth and other rationalizations about how wealth isn't really so bad.

Deep down, though, we know we are struggling to justify our desire to hang on to our posessions. Wealth is addictive. Whatever we have whets our appetite to get more. I keep telling myself I really need the latest best seller, a CD player, a new car. St. Francis warned his friars that even if all they wanted now was to own a Bible, soon they would want a shelf to put it on, then more books to fill the shelf, and so on. The way of grasping, coveting, and pursuing posessions is not the way of life God offers. What is truly important is loving and serving God.

Prayer: *Let my cry come before you, O LORD; give me understanding according to your word. Let my supplication come before you; deliver me according to your promise. Amen. (Psalm 119:169-170)*

Friday, February 14   Read Jeremiah 17:7-10.

One way of talking about God's way of life is to speak of being focused on doing God's will, as revealed in Torah and in the life and teaching of Jesus Christ. The emphasis here is on our action, our response to God's call by girding our loins, gritting our teeth, and living the way God's people live. Jesus leads the way and we set out to follow.

In today's scripture reading, Jeremiah offers an alternative image. Following God's way is like being rooted in God. We can draw upon God as the source of all we do. It is like being a tree planted in an oasis, with an unending supply of water. Now the emphasis is on God's action, on how we would wither and die if cut off from our Source. Whatever we do begins in God and prospers only through God's grace.

We need to keep both these aspects of our journey in mind. God is both source and goal, Alpha and Omega, beginning and end of our faith. Our life in Christ is our co-creation with God. God calls and we respond. God instructs and we act. We grow weary and God gives us strength. As we go, stronger and more sure-footed in the way, God calls us to even greater challenges, fills us even more with God's love. In all we do, we work together with God as we travel in God's way.

John Wesley called this mutual effort "going on to perfection." The process is not over until we are all God intends us to be, until we do indeed love God with all our being (heart, soul, strength), until we love our neighbors as ourselves (see Luke 10:27). Few Christians reach that point in this life. Wesley never claimed he had done so. Instead, he expected to continue to grow in this life and in the life to come.

Prayer: *I implore your favor with all my heart; be gracious to me according to your promise. Amen. (Psalm 119:58)*

Saturday, February 15   Read 1 Corinthians 15:12-20.

Although there seem to be many ways which are alternatives to God's way of life, they all have one thing in common. They are all near-sighted. That is, they all seek something less than God, something more concrete, easier to see. It is quite possible that whatever we seek is good in itself: food, security, freedom, self-confidence. It just isn't God. And so our quest turns into gluttony, avarice, wrath, pride.

We may ask God for power to help us achieve our own ends, or at least to be gracious enough not to hinder us. We often seem concerned only with what God can do for us today.

One of the splinter groups in Corinth seems to have argued that this life is all there is. When you die, you're dead. They didn't look for any resurrection, any return of Jesus, any judgment. Yet still they were Christians. Why? They looked for power through Christ, for the spiritual gifts which seemed to flow so freely in their church. They reveled in the message of freedom and equality which Paul had proclaimed. They took what they wanted and ignored the rest. In that, they weren't very different from many of us.

Paul is astonished by their position. If there is no resurrection, then how can Christ be raised? If Christ isn't raised, then how can they speak of life? How can Christ send them power or the gifts of the Spirit? If there is no resurrection, then what is the point of the stonings, imprisonments, and other sufferings Paul has endured in his ministry? Christianity without resurrection is pitiful. But Christ has been raised! And our hope extends beyond this life and into eternity.

Prayer: *Uphold me according to your promise, that I may live, and let me not be put to shame in my hope. Amen. (Psalm 119:116)*

Sunday, February 16   Read Luke 6:17-19.

In the patches of grass around the National Gallery of Art in Washington, D.C., there are small signs. They don't say KEEP OFF THE GRASS. They say Please use the sidewalks. Instead of forbidding, they offer a positive alternative.

The way of life is more than just God's negative way of self-denial which we follow in hope of abundant life in the future. Jesus does not intend us to be so intent on avoiding evil that our lives are dried up, sterile, empty. His way is life now, a way which makes us alive, renews us.

In C. S. Lewis's *The Lion, the Witch, and the Wardrobe*, the land of Narnia is under a curse. It is always winter, but never Christmas! What could be worse? Then one day things begin to change. The snow begins to thaw. Bare ground appears. The grass grows, flowers bloom, and birds begin to sing again. Is it that spring has come? Not exactly. Aslan, the great lion, the rightful King of the land, has returned to Narnia. Where Aslan is, winter cannot endure. Life blossoms in his presence. At his breath, even those who have been turned to stone come back to life.

So it was when Jesus walked the earth. Healing flowed from him, even from the hem of his robe. The lame walked, the blind saw, lepers were cleansed, and the dead rose. Life abounded.

This is this life which Jesus offers to those who follow his way. It is God's own eternal life, breaking into our world. It is the breath of the Holy Spirit blowing through us to set us free. It drives us to share love with our neighbors as well as to avoid evil. It fills us with joy in the midst of sorrow, hope in the face of despair, love in a world of apathy.

Prayer: *Let your steadfast love become my comfort according to your promise to your servant. Let your mercy come to me, that I may live. Amen. (Psalm 119:76-77a)*

JOSEPH, OUR BROTHER

February 17-23, 1992   **William H. Willimon†**
Monday, February 17   Read Genesis 45:3-5.

By the time this week's reading from Genesis takes up the story of Joseph and his brothers, much has happened. In Genesis 37, little brother Joseph had a dream which infuriated his brothers because it foretold that he would rule them. So the brothers conspired to put away their upstart little brother.

If you have never read or have forgotten the story of Joseph, read it in Genesis 37–45.

Whatever we say about the story of Joseph, let us first say that it is *a story about a family*.

Genesis 45 is the narrative's climax, that point where Joseph reveals to his brothers that the one whom they sold into Egyptian slavery is none other than the royal official to whom they beg for bread.

He says in a regal tone, "I am Joseph" (v. 3). Then, his voice cracks, tears cannot be restrained, and he falls upon them saying, "I am *your brother*, Joseph" (v. 4, italics added). Official speech gives way to intimate talk of family.

We have here a story about envy, cruelty, jealousy, love, tenderness and all the other sometimes painful, often blessed experiences of human families. And the story says, *this is where God meets us*. God uses even the messy brokenness of our families for divine purposes. "God sent me before you," says Joseph, "to preserve life" (v. 5).

Prayer: *Loving God, help us to see your hand moving among us, using us and our families for divine purposes. Amen.*

---

†Dean of the Chapel and Professor of Christian Ministry, Duke University, Durham, North Carolina.

Tuesday, February 18   Read Genesis 45:6-8;
                                                      Psalm 37:1-8.

Most law enforcement officers would rather try to stop a bank robbery than a family dispute. Most murders occur among family members. Domestic violence has reached horrifying proportions in our society. A psychiatrist friend claims that "most of the real damage occurs in the family."

Such thinking collides with our romanticized notions of family. On television, the family is idealized—"Ozzie and Harriet," "The Cosby Show." These are happy families.

But this family story of Joseph and his brothers is in the Bible, not on television. Far more truthful than we, the Bible depicts family life as deeply problematic, full of opportunity for envy and hurt. There has been much heartache in Jacob's family. Jacob favored his son Joseph and for that, Joseph's brothers hated him and sold him into slavery.

Despite the reality of the hurt in this very real family, today's scripture reveals that God used this family. The story is not about "important" people like Pharaoh. It is a family story about how God works among little people (like us) in ordinary, ambiguous places (like our families). If Joseph or his brothers thought that theirs was too ordinary a story to have significance beyond their family, they now learn that behind their daily cares and conflicts, God was working to bless all people. Joseph says, "It was not you who sent me here, but God" (v. 8).

It is not just our children, parents, brothers, and sisters who love us, make demands, challenge us in our families, but also God.

Prayer: *Dear God, help us to seek your will for us and our families. Amen.*

Wednesday, February 19　　　　　　Read Genesis 45:1-4;
　　　　　　　　　　　　　　　　　　　　　Luke 6:27-38.

We are taught, you and I, to keep our distance. A little child, unself-conscious, trusting and open, willingly reveals feelings, openly talks to most anyone. As we grow older, we hold back true feelings and keep our distance.

We learn to detach ourselves from others after we have suffered great hurt. Having given ourselves to others, only to be rejected, we are slow to give ourselves again. We value our "right to privacy." We learn to be suspicious of those who too quickly become intimate with us, fearing they might ask of us that which we are unwilling to give.

With time comes distance.

Joseph has been separated from his brothers for many years. Though he stands before them, they don't recognize him. Little brother Joseph has been transformed into a big man in the Pharaoh's court. He has adopted royal ways, succeeded in a sophisticated culture a long way from his family's nomadic roots. Can such distance be overcome?

Watch. There is an unseen hand nudging Joseph toward his brothers. He can't hold back. Joseph weeps so loudly that he is heard throughout the palace (v. 2).

"Come near to me," Joseph begs (v. 4).

Is not that our prayer also in a society which tends to make strangers of us all, a culture of competing rights and feuding factions? *Come near to me.*

Our God is a God who brings us together, overcomes barriers, reaches out across the distance and prods us to do the same.

Prayer: *Great God of togetherness, nudge us near to one another, break down our boundaries, and encourage us toward embrace. Amen.*

Thursday, February 20   Read Genesis 45.

You will notice something about this story of Joseph which you see in other Bible stories. *It is all very specific.*

Fairy tales begin with, "Once upon a time, in a land far away, there was a king . . ." Bible stories begin with, "There was a father named Jacob who had some sons, one of whom was named Joseph." Fairy tales can happen to anybody, at anyplace or anytime. Bible stories happen in specific, real places like Canaan or Egypt.

Something in us wishes it all were not so specific and concrete. We prefer to drink religion in the form of clear, distilled nectar from which the gross particularities of history or geography have been removed. We thrill to the enunciation of universal, timeless truth. We rally around high-sounding generalities like "humanity," "justice," "compassion." We are put off by the squabbles, trials, and tribulations of Jacob's famished family who went down to Egypt looking for food only to meet there their brother whom they once hated—a brother who was now their only hope of survival.

The good news amid this story's particularity and specificity is that the Bible says this is how God chooses to deal with us. Not on cloud nine or in some generalized idea but here, now, among real people caught in real life dilemmas in real places like Durham, North Carolina. *Here*.

And that is good news, because we do not live in fairy-tale kingdoms. We live here, now. And this is where God wants to touch our lives and use us to accomplish God's plans for the world. *Here*.

Prayer: *Help us to look for you, gracious God, not somewhere else but* here. *Amen.*

Friday, February 21   Read 1 Corinthians 15:42-50;
Genesis 45:7-8.

Back in Genesis 37, Joseph had a dream. The dream foretold a dramatic future for him and his family. And yet, Joseph, his father Jacob, and all his brothers have had to wait for nearly nine long chapters in Genesis before anyone has a clue about how things will turn out. Everyone in this story has had to keep moving, to continue living, not knowing for sure how it will end.

As in the Joseph story, so it is in life, *Our lives are formed by hands other than our own*. If we are parents, one of the greatest challenges we face is in being patient, waiting for the purposes of God to be worked out in our childrens' lives. Who will they be as adults? I wish I knew, now.

We do not know. The future is not totally of our devising. We choose, deliberate, plan, prepare, but none of us knows how it will end.

I believe in providence—the notion that God works in and through our lives for God's good ends. Not that I know how God is working in my life at this moment. Few of us know that. All we know about is that eventually, in the end, our lives end in God. "Just as we have borne the image of the man of dust, we will also bear the image of the man of heaven" (1 Cor. 15:50).

As Joseph's family was united at last, so shall we be at last with God. We shall look back in wonderment at how our ordinary, everyday lives were somehow woven into the purposes of God. We will be able to say, with Joseph our brother, that it was God who chose, planned, prepared when all along we thought it had all been up to us.

Prayer: *We thank you, good Lord, for not leaving our lives solely up to us. Work in us for your good. Amen.*

Saturday, February 22   Read Genesis 45:3-11,15.

A couple I know in their early forties have just received the joyful news that in this later stage of their marriage they are going to have their first child.

"We had given up hope that we would ever be parents," he said to me.

The family of Jacob, estranged by a violent and tragic break many years ago, is brought back together in a stunning reversal of fate. By chapter forty-five of this story, we had about given up hope that this family would be preserved.

Such newness and reversal of the expected path of history invariably surprises us. "There is nothing new under the sun," we say. "Accept the facts." We have many ways of encouraging ourselves to accept the inevitability and intractability of discouragement.

Caught off guard by newness, we don't know what to make of it. Joseph, stunned by an outcome so completely new, so utterly unexpected, has but one explanation for his tearful reunion with his brothers—this is the work of God (vv. 5,7,8). Beyond the will and work of people, God was busy creating life where there was death, creating newness out of "caughtness."

In Genesis 1, the Spirit of God breathed over dark waters and brought forth new life where before there had been none. In Ezekiel, the creative breath of God made life out of a valley of dry bones (see Ezekiel 37). In Acts, the holy breath made the church out of strangers (see Acts 2).

God still does.

Prayer: *Breathe on our lives, holy breath of God. Bless our tired old lives with new life and fresh possibility. Amen.*

Sunday, February 23   Read Genesis 45:3-11, 15.

"Holy, Holy, Holy, Lord God Almighty!" we sang as our opening hymn this Sunday. For many of us, Sunday worship is a primary way for us to experience the holy sovereignty of God.

The story of Joseph and his reunion with his family, despite being an account of ordinary people, is a story about the majestic sovereignty of God.

We modern people cut all things, even God, down to our scale. God is the kind but not too powerful friend. History is a matter of human-initiated acts. What happens to us is accredited to either our human choice on the one hand or bad or good luck on the other. We waver between thinking of ourselves as incredibly powerful beings who are the captains of our fate and the masters of our souls or else as sadly impotent creatures who are at the mercy of impersonal forces of fate.

The story of Joseph refutes both the proud notion that human beings autonomously shape their own destinies and the pitiful despair that we are victims of nothing but luck.

By the end of the story, God is sovereign. God works through even the terrible things that we do to little brothers like Joseph in order to create newness.

Read your Sunday newspaper—its sad accounts of wars, pestilence, violence, injustice—and you're apt to wonder, "Who's in charge here?"

Listen to the end of the saga of Joseph. You will hear a confident affirmation that God yet reigns, that God's sovereign purposes will not be defeated.

Prayer: *O God, who is both loving and powerful, grant us the faith to see you at work in our world. Amen.*

Our Veiled View of God

February 24–March 1, 1992   **Robert L. Reddig†**
Monday, February 24   Read Exodus 34:29-35.

Moses had a direct encounter with God, the force of which neither he nor the people of Israel fully understood at the time. God had descended in fire and smoke, lightning and thunder, to the peak of Mount Sinai. Moses was called to the mountaintop not simply to pray but to be directly confronted by God.

We can only imagine the moment in which briefly and powerfully the barriers between heaven and earth, between God and God's servant Moses were lifted. We can only imagine the exhilarating transformation Moses experienced in the encounter, since we are all too aware of our own veiled and faulty vision, the barriers of our own making between ourselves and God. And we can only imagine the adjustments Moses had to make in departing the presence of God after forty days and nights.

We do know that Moses returned to his people with two remarkable testimonies: one, of God's law written on stone, and the other, of God's presence shining on his face. Moses carried the stones, but he was unaware of the radiance about him. The people looked upon him with fear and fascination. Yet, as a true servant of God he was unaware of his own glorification or of the barriers he had crossed. Though he could bring to his people the word of God, he could not bring to them the transformation he had experienced. Their vision and spiritual formation remained incomplete.

Prayer: *God, we both seek and fear a direct vision of your majesty and power, just as we seek and fear a transformation of our lives. Remove the barrier of fear that lies within us. Amen.*

---

†Branch Director, Williamson County Counseling Center, Franklin, Tennessee; ordained elder, Hillsboro Presbyterian Church.

Tuesday, February 25   Read Exodus 34:32-35.

As Moses spoke to his people and conveyed to them in commandment all that God had revealed to him, his audience was more immediately taken with the medium than the message. The face of Moses shone, and that was a problem. His very appearance became a phenomenon. But Moses brought to his people the new covenant, not his own glory. He chose to wear a veil and in doing so concealed his face and revealed God's word.

In an age of mass media and spectacular forms of communication, we have come to expect "good visuals." Often the messenger is more significant than the message. We see in our news anchors, sports figures, and other celebrities a polish and glitter which our lives often lack. We are vicariously engaged, powerfully entertained, but rarely transformed. We enjoy looking, and could do so with the sound turned down. As we focus on the power of the messenger, we can too easily overlook the message. We become enthralled rather than inspired.

Spiritual visions, spiritual truths are meant to transform us and draw us closer to the source of life itself. As such they call for a response, for sacred human activity. Moses was doing much more than bringing the people of Israel the news of his own encounter with God. He was calling them into active covenant and leading them in a new spiritual direction. He pointed to a new vision even as he hid his own visage.

Prayer: *God, when we look upon others who have inspired faces and inspired lives, help us to see beyond our admiration of them. Help us to see you. Amen.*

Wednesday, February 26   Read 2 Corinthians 3:12-13.

The Apostle Paul proclaims a boldness and a hope that was not known by Moses. He suggests that when Moses wore a veil after speaking with God and his people, it was to conceal the inevitable fading of his countenance, the fading of the brightness of the encounter. The veil was, by Paul's interpretation, an essential illusion to sustain the hope of a people with tenuous faith. Dependent upon the dramatic and recurring interventions of God, the people of Israel no doubt hungered for permanence, hungered for certainty. If the fading face of Moses led inevitably to a fading of his people's faith, then the veil had a certain practical utility.

In our personal and spiritual lives we, too, find ways to veil our fading vitality. We smile at the expression, "It's more important to look good than to feel good," but we've all practiced some gentle deceptions. Makeup and artful clothing can conceal our fading youthfulness. When the stress of daily work and career advancement depletes our energy, the process can be veiled with vigorous denial and determination to work even harder. When the fragile bonds of marriage and family are frayed and torn, we can veil the pain with casual new relationships. And in our spiritual lives, when the passion of our immediate contact with God dissolves into pleasant memory, we can easily veil our losses with religious routine. When we despair of recovery, we go to the veil.

It is God's promise that when we wait upon God we "shall renew [our] strength and mount up with wings like eagles" (Isa. 40:31). We are given a promise that endures forever; we are invited to a faith that need not be veiled.

Prayer: *God, when we are tempted to veil our failures and shortcomings, draw us unto you. Amen.*

Thursday, February 27   Read 2 Corinthians 3:14-18.

Paul is reluctant to let go of a good metaphor. After referring to the veiling of Moses' splendor, he points to the veiling or clouding of the Israelites' hearts and minds as they read scripture. Truths that ought to be seen and known are obscured. Paul speaks historically and theologically when he says that only through Christ is the veil taken away, only through Christ is the full and final covenant revealed.

Most of us claim our veils. When we wish to be less than open and honest with one another, we veil our intentions, we veil our threats or promises. We do so not out of modesty but out of our wish to control the encounter. And often our veils take on a life of their own. We decorate and embellish them, as with a favorite prejudice, bias, or judgment. We wish to see others yet not be seen behind our veils. When we are called to promote peace and justice, we often veil our reluctance to change our hearts and call only for law and order. When we are called to forgive, we often veil our reluctance and become merely tolerant. And when we are called to love the seemingly unlovable, we often veil our reluctance to deepen our personal involvement by offering only money or pity.

The new covenant through Christ unveils the true worth of others, the true nature of our own hearts. The veils we choose to wear darken our visions, darken our minds. Through the living example of his sacrificial love, Christ casts light upon every obscure corner of our lives. Christ invites us to relinquish our veils.

Prayer: *God, when we seek to disguise and obscure parts of our lives, dissolve the veils we wear. Give us a clear vision of your love. Amen.*

Friday, February 28   Read 2 Corinthians 4:1-2.

Paul presents a vigorous defense of his ministry and makes two points. First, that he even exists to be able to minister is a testimony to the mercy of God, and thus Paul's grateful response has no self-promotion about it. Second, the truth he brings is presented not with artful deception or trickery but in plain and straightforward appeal to the conscience of all who hear and in the clear and full view of God.

Very early in life a child learns that he or she is free to do many things, in curiosity, play, or passion, when adults aren't looking. Eventually, however, repeated external constraint forms a core of internal constraint, or what we popularly call a conscience. Like our distant memories of being warmly held and rocked, we have distant memories of acting with reckless abandon, with secret and unwitnessed willfulness. And all too often adult character is formed more by fear of being exposed and shamed than by earnestly and openly desiring the good.

As a small boy I was once told to shell peas on a morning better suited for baseball. Unwitnessed, I mixed unshelled pods with pod husks, and threw half of my task into the slop pail destined for the hogs. In less time than it took me to join my friends, the plump unshelled pods floated to the top of the pail and betrayed me to my parents. No glorious home run for me, only a guilty walk.

Like Paul, when we can tolerate and welcome the full view of others upon our actions, when we can accept God's full knowledge of our very being, we will have gone beyond the constraints of merely meeting our obligations. We will have become free.

Prayer: *God, we know that much of our goodness is an appearance rather than a reality. May we accept and acknowledge your clearer, deeper view of us and in so doing become free. Amen.*

Saturday, February 29   Read Luke 9:28-31.

The account of the transfiguration of Christ recorded in Luke provides a remarkable panorama of God's continuing covenant with creation. For a brief time, history is compressed, as Moses and Elijah appear in their heavenly splendor with Christ, now radiant and dazzling in full identification with God. Three disciples, initially asleep, are there as well. Peter, John, and James had been invited by Christ to join him in prayer on the mountain. They had seen their master and friend daily, yet there was more about him than met their eyes, more connections to be fully revealed.

In our relations with others we commend ourselves when we see them for what they are. Yet all of us are accumulations of events, past relationships, developing character, and evolving meanings. I, for one, am immensely grateful when my family or my friends forgive me a bad day, a blunder, a shabby appearance. I am grateful that they see more than my immediate presence and that they value history, memory, and the invisible bonds of affection. Each of us is multidimensional, and our worth is not evident at a glance.

The transfiguration of Christ was an illumination of his connections to God the Father, to the patriarch Moses, to the prophet Elijah, and to our representatives—the sleeping disciples.

Prayer: *God, even when we get a clear view, we miss many of the connections between ourselves and others, ourselves and Christ. Help us see and respond more fully to the bonds of your love. Amen.*

Sunday, March 1   Read Luke 9:32-36.

Jesus took his disciples Peter, John, and James with him to the mountain, and once there he began to pray. Once there, the disciples fell asleep. They were roused to see the spectacular vision of Jesus in company with Moses and Elijah. They were roused to hear the voice of God proclaim, "This is my Son, my Chosen; listen to him!" In a fog Peter lurches to do the right thing, proposing to make three tents. He and his fellow disciples were there, but not really with it. This event seems to foretell another which Luke records in chapter 22. Once again these disciples, and others, are called by Jesus to accompany him to the Mount of Olives to pray. Again they fall asleep, their full awareness dulled by fatigue and grief.

It is not surprising that we, like the disciples, fail to see, hear, and feel all that we are invited to experience through Christ. What is surprising is that we continue to be invited. Christ knew the shortcomings of his disciples. He knew their occasional pettiness about rank, their frequent misunderstandings about his ministry, their slowness to grasp the depth and implications of sacrificial love. And he knew their continual underestimation of the costs of discipleship. He knew they had dirty feet, that they sometimes tired easily, and that they often worried about non-sense. But he always took them along, he always loved them. In the end he commissioned their telling the story of themselves and the story of his perfect love.

We too are called not because we are perfect but because we are loved. We are called to be obedient not because we see everything but because we see enough.

Prayer: *God, we are grateful that you continually invite us along, that you overlook our frailty and honor our willingness. Amen.*

In the Face of Temptation

March 2-8, 1992   **Rick Helms†**
Monday, March 2   Read Luke 4:1-2*a*.

We start with a basic question: What does it mean to say that Jesus was tempted? One possibility is that the Gospel writer is saying Jesus was "challenged" by the devil. If that is the meaning, it merely shows that the devil attempted something with Jesus and failed. But if the Gospel writer is suggesting Jesus felt what we feel when we are tempted, then the temptation narrative takes on an entirely different sense.

When we are tempted, we desire to do something that we believe to be wrong. We all know the feeling. Some temptations are as innocent as desiring that extra piece of pie, while others are very serious and cause great pain to ourselves and others.

Because temptation is a part of life, admitting that we know what it means to be tempted is no great confession. However, it is quite another thing to say that Jesus was tempted. Yet that is the startling announcement that begins the reading for today—Jesus was tempted by the devil. We may recoil at the thought. How could Jesus, the sinless one, truly have had the desire to do that which he believed to be wrong?

As we continue our study of the temptation narrative, we will discover that what the text says is true. Yes, the Son of God was tempted in the same way that we are tempted. Jesus shared our nature even to the extent that he could know what it means to be tempted.

Suggestion for meditation: *Am I willing to consider that Jesus truly was tempted? Does it change my idea about his nature?*

---

†Attorney; pastor, Elkton Christian Church (Disciples of Christ), Elkton, Kentucky.

Tuesday, March 3   Read Luke 4:2*b*-4.

Yesterday's reading raised the proposition that Jesus was tempted in the truest sense, that he experienced the internal conflict of desiring to do that which he knew was wrong. But how could one who was sinless desire to do that which was wrong?

The first temptation was that Jesus turn stones into bread. The text states that Jesus had not eaten for forty days, so perhaps this was merely a suggestion that Jesus use supernatural power to meet his own physical needs. But Jesus would not have needed the devil to tell him he was hungry or that he had the capability to satisfy the hunger, so perhaps the real temptation went far beyond that specific situation.

Jesus knew the world was full of starving and needy people, and that must have saddened him. Perhaps the temptation was not only to satisfy his own needs but to reach out to humanity. It was as if the devil had said, "If you are the Son of God, love your brothers and sisters by giving them bread."

It is easy to see why Jesus might have desired, or even longed, to do that which the devil suggested. We then have to wonder, *Why was it wrong?* How was that different from the miraculous feeding of the five thousand? The problem was that Jesus knew it was not God's will for him to use his power only to meet the physical needs of humanity. And so he answered, "One does not live by bread alone."

Perhaps Jesus was sorely tempted because of his love for humanity. Certainly Jesus had great desire to heal the pain of the world, but his focus was on a wholeness of life, not on bare survival. To survive is to have physical needs met, but to live is to come to know God and to accept God's love.

Suggestion for meditation: *Am I willing to ask God for more than meeting my physical needs? Am I able to ask for wholeness of life?*

Wednesday, March 4 (Ash Wednesday)
Read Luke 4:9-12.

In the third temptation of the narrative, Luke describes how the devil tempted Jesus to throw himself down from the pinnacle of the temple. According to the tempter, Jesus would be protected by the miraculous intervention of God. Why would Jesus have been interested in such a demonstration? It would have been an opportunity for Jesus to prove his faith in God. It also would have served to identify who he was and to call attention to why he was there. Surely such an event might lead people to believe, and was that not the very purpose of his coming?

Why, then, would the action be wrong? Was it wrong for Jesus to use miracles as a test of faith? How was that different from Jesus calling Peter to step out onto the water? (See Matthew 14:22-33) Each act required faith, and each actor depended upon the miraculous intervention of God.

This action in the temptation narrative would be wrong because it was against God's will. God had a time and plan for how Jesus would be revealed to humanity. It would not be in the way that Jesus or Satan would choose but in the way that God would choose. Jesus would prove his faith in God and his identity would be revealed, but this was not yet the time.

This lesson teaches us that we do not glorify God by doing great feats or by performing miracles. God is glorified by the simple obedience of those who call themselves believers. No one, not even the Christ, is to force the hand of God. So Jesus answered the challenge by saying, "Do not put the Lord your God to the test."

Suggestion for meditation: *Do I have a secret desire to test God? Are there any subtle ways by which I attempt to call God to demonstrate either power or love?*

Thursday, March 5   Read Luke 4:5-8.

The second of the three temptations was, I believe, the most significant. It was the most significant because it was the one that had the most chance of succeeding. It is also the one that is the most difficult to understand.

In this dialogue, Satan promised to give Jesus the world in exchange for worship. If we are to believe that Jesus was tempted, we must believe that he desired to do that which was suggested. We might wonder how Jesus could possibly have considered such an exchange. What could there have been in the devil's offer that would have made Jesus consider worshiping the enemy of God?

In this temptation, the devil offered the one thing that could have made Jesus consider the proposal—creation itself. Jesus was not tempted by the power or the glory. Jesus was not tempted because he would be able to avoid suffering and death. Jesus was tempted because the devil offered the very thing that Jesus had to accomplish. Jesus was offered success, not for himself but for God.

This was a temptation born of love. In fact, the price called for the greatest act of love imaginable. Jesus knew he was willing to give his life, but could he give his soul? That was the decision he would have to make. He made his decision and answered, "It is written, 'Worship the Lord your God and serve only him.'"

God is never truly served through disobedience. We have no better ways than God has. We can never love better than God. Jesus chose to be obedient by abiding in God's time and God's method. We can do no better.

Suggestion for meditation: *Do I believe that God has a plan? How do I know what part I am to play?*

Friday, March 6   Read Psalm 51:1-12.

In these verses, we can hear the cries of torment as the psalmist struggled to find some relief amidst the agony of overwhelming guilt. In pain the writer called upon the mercy of a loving God. Who is the psalmist, and what sin caused this overwhelming anguish?

The psalmist is David, and he was agonizing over his actions with Bathsheba. David saw Bathsheba and desired to have her as his own. Unfortunately, she was the wife of another. This posed little problem for King David, for he merely arranged for the husband of Bathsheba, his loyal soldier Uriah, to be killed in battle. David had his way, but the pleasure that he anticipated was short-lived because soon he was called to account by the prophet Nathan (see 2 Samuel 11:1–12:15).

In verse 4, David claimed that he had sinned against God alone. Now, it may be that all sins are against God, but is it likely that any action is a sin against God only? What transgression against God is free of human victims?

In this particular case, David had certainly violated the law of God in many respects. He had murdered, committed adultery, and coveted his neighbor's wife. He had every reason to ask the forgiveness of God. But is there not a problem here? What about the others he harmed by his actions?

In order for King David to have that which he desired, two innocent lives were lost—Uriah and the child born of the illicit union. Bathsheba was also a victim because she would have been powerless to refuse the advances of the mighty king. We are right to seek the forgiveness of God, but we must never forget those whom we victimize by our actions.

Suggestion for meditation: *Whose forgiveness is it easier to seek, God's or that of someone I have hurt? Why?*

Saturday, March 7   Read Matthew 6:1-6.

The byword for today's reading is secrecy. Jesus encouraged his listeners to act, to give, and to pray secretly. Of course, history has taught us that secrecy is not always a positive thing. It is often used to gain advantage or to conceal those activities which would fail the test of public scrutiny. However, in this teaching Jesus insisted that secrecy was necessary. Why should this be so?

Jesus issued a warning. Many acts which in and of themselves are commendable can be ruined by the desire that motivates them. The text describes three activities that fall within that category: piety, giving, and prayer. In each instance, improper motivation has made them unacceptable.

Jesus' words should not be taken too literally. Much of piety consists of how we relate to our fellow human beings. So how can pious acts be conducted other than before people? Surely Jesus was not condemning all public giving. (Paul praised the gift to the Jerusalem church; Rom. 15:25-26). Surely, Jesus was not condemning all public prayer, for he himself prayed publicly.

In this text, Jesus was concerned with a specific issue—motivation. Most all our actions spring from motivation, and there are always proper and improper motivations for the same acts. In acts of piety, giving, and prayer, the proper motivation is the desire to please God. The improper motivation is the desire to please people. Jesus knew that judging our own motivation is often difficult for us, and so he suggested a test. Do the act secretly. If we are willing to do what we do without others knowing about it, we can have some assurance that we are not doing it for their approval. It is a good test.

Suggestion for meditation: *What would I be willing to do for others if I knew they would never know?*

Sunday, March 8   Read Deuteronomy 26:1-11.

The Book of Deuteronomy is comprised primarily of the laws of God given by Moses to the people of Israel. Chapter 26 is the concluding section of what is called the Deuteronomic Code, and it is there that Moses described how the people were to respond to the gifts they had received from God.

First, the people were to bring an offering of thanksgiving. The object of their thanksgiving was the recognition that God had given them an inheritance—the promised land.

Second, the people were to confess. When the offering was brought to the priest, the story of God's deliverance was recounted. The telling of the story reminded the people of the need for thanksgiving and preserved the story for future generations.

Third, the people were to obey. As part of the offering, the people recounted their acts of obedience regarding the specific instructions given by God.

Thanksgiving, confession, and obedience were the key concepts in this ancient passage. Are they not key concepts for us today? The Israelites were giving thanks for their inheritance—the promised land. For what should we give God thanks? What is our inheritance?

The Israelites loved to tell the story of God's deliverance because it was their story. What is our story? What story do we tell when we want to confess the deliverance of God? What tradition are we passing on to the next generation?

The Israelites were not always obedient, but they knew the laws for which they would be held accountable. How do we express our obedience to God? In our day, the emphasis seems to be on freedom rather than obedience. Are there any rules which require our obedience to God?

Suggestion for meditation: *Is having a faith story to tell important for each of us? Why? What is my story?*

TRUSTING IN GOD

March 9-15, 1992   **Patricia D. Brown†**
Monday, March 9   Read Genesis 15:1-4.

Abram was in a desperate situation, for he was both childless and homeless. Two times God took the initiative to come to Abram in a word. God promised that Abram would be the father of many children and would possess the land God would give to him.

In this covenant word God assured a unilateral obligation. God promised to shield, protect, and care for Abram. Abram was not asked for anything in exchange. Abram was the recipient of God's grace.

What is God's grace in our lives? My toddler, Stephen, went with my husband, Dale, and me to an arts festival at our local park. As we enjoyed the canvases, Stephen wandered over to a pond where he could view the ducks. Then he saw a stick a few yards away and ran to pick it up. A squirrel caught his eye, so he hurried over to watch it scurry up the tree. As we watched, a look came to Stephen's face which said, "Where are my mom and dad?" As his facial expression scrunched into what would quickly become tears, his father walked up behind him and placed his hand on Stephen's shoulder. As his little body relaxed, I could see in his face the feeling Dale's touch gave him.

> You see, that is God's grace:
> One who answers before we ask.
> One who comes before we call.
> One who touches before we reach.

Prayer: *Gracious One, while we were yet sinners, Christ died for us. Jesus, you found me even before I knew I was lost. Amen.*

†Executive Secretary for Mission Evangelism, General Board of Global Ministries of The United Methodist Church, New York City.

Tuesday, March 10   Read Genesis 15:5-12.

Since Abram had no children or land, God's gracious promises evoked Abram's doubt and opposition. Abram could see his
situation only from his own perspective. He understood only that
he was childless and a nomad. So Abram asked God to show him
some proof that God would fulfill the promises made. God
answered Abram's doubt by showing him the thousands and
thousands of stars, too many to count.

Abram's second response was one of faith. Abram put his
trust in the Lord, in spite of the fact that from his human perspective God's promise seemed nearly impossible. Abram's trust and
faith placed him in the right personal relationship with God.

Do we, in faith, place our trust in God? Consider a woman
hanging from a cliff.

"Help! Help! Lord please save me. If you'll just get me down,
I'll do anything. What's this fluttering? Who are you? An angel
of the Lord? Great! Get me down. . . . You have three questions
for me first?"

"Do I believe in God? Yes, . . . now get me . . . Do I believe in Jesus Christ as my Lord and Savior? Yes! Do I believe
and have faith that Jesus Christ has the power to save me? Yes,
now please get me down. What? You're telling me to let go? H-E-
L-P!!!"

Abram's response to God's coming to him could have easily
been like the woman's response. But God overcame Abram's
skepticism by bringing Abram into relationship, thus enabling
Abram's trust. The miracle is that God does not give up in the
face of rejection. Instead God comes and keeps coming to us
because God is the faithful One who is bound to us in Jesus
Christ.

Prayer: *Steadfast God, help me to trust in you that I may live these
days in your name, in your way. Amen.*

Wednesday, March 11   Read Psalm 127:1-2.

The author of this psalm knows that no building can be erected without the worker's labor. The psalmist is not condemning work in general. Instead, the writer calls into question the selfish *attitude* of control which leads people to believe they can build their lives without God.

Do we work in ways that show evidence of leaving God out? This type of work is in vain because it fosters the delusion that we are able to achieve by our own efforts what is reserved for God. What does not spring from faith stands empty without God. When we begin to believe that we can and must accomplih everything by our own efforts, then we are standing in mistrust of God and standing on our own powers.

For me, growing up in an alcoholic home meant living on the daily "out of controlness" of life. I now find myself trying to do what could not be done in my childhood years. I like to be in control. I compare this to a game we played as children. We would set up dominoes on end, side by side, and continue until one domino would tip over, causing a chain reaction. Then all the dominoes would tumble down.

Like this game of dominoes, I have tried to build my life in an attitude of control. I have carefully made decisions and choices, built from my own labor, but something always happens to make the "dominoes" tumble down so I realize I cannot be in control. Now I ask God daily to help me release my tight grip of control. When I let go and allow God to be in ultimate control, I am released to live in ways which are freeing.

Prayer: *Merciful Lord, forgive my delusions of control and guide me in confident surrender to you. In your sustaining grace I will find blessedness and peace. Amen.*

Thursday, March 12   Read Philippians 3:17-19.

Living the disciplined life means living by the example of the great Christian saints of ages past. Perhaps we have been blessed with contemporary saints who model a faithful and obedient life centered in Christ. Consider this conversation of one new Christian as she struggles with God about her cross.

"Well, here I am, Lord. You said to take up your cross and follow you. It's not easy, you know, this self-denial thing. But I've counted the cost. So let's get on with it. I've come to pick up my cross. I'd kind of like a new one. I'm not fussy, you understand, but a disciple has to be relevant these days.

"Uh-huh . . . Oh, excuse me, God. There doesn't seem to be much of a selection here. Only these rough, coarse, wooden ones. I mean, that could hurt! I was thinking of something a bit more distinctive. I can tell you right now, none of my friends will be impressed with this shoddy workmanship. They'll think I'm a nut or something. And my family would be mortified.

"Now, I was thinking of something smaller, to fit in my side pocket—one shouldn't appear too radical! And perhaps in different colors . . . to attract different kinds of people.

"What's that? These are the ones I choose from? But, Lord, I want to be your disciple. I mean, just being with you is all that counts. But life has a balance, too. In this day who's going to be attracted to that self-denial bit?

"I mean, being a disciple is challenging and exciting, and I want to do it, but I have some rights, you know. Now let's see. No blood. OK? I just can't stand the thought of that. And another thing, Lord. . . ."

Prayer: *Thank you, God, for coming to me in and through other people. Like the great saints, help me to take up your cross and follow. Amen.*

Friday, March 13   Read Philippians 3:20-21.

A missionary story, passed on through oral tradition, was recently shared with me. The story was of a missionary couple who were traveling to the United States from Africa, where they had spent their lives in ministry. On the same boat was President Theodore Roosevelt, who was returning from a hunting trip. On the journey home the missionaries felt forgotten by the ship's staff and passengers. As the ship entered the harbor, musicians and banners welcomed the President home. With no one to welcome or receive them, the missionary couple left the deck quietly.

Once on land, the husband began to grumble loudly, "All that I've done for the Lord! All these years I've served the church, and now not even one person welcomes us home!" After a few days of listening to these laments, his wife asked him, "Why don't you tell the Lord about it?" The husband did just that and spent many hours in his closet praying.

Reappearing, the husband shared how the prayer conversation had gone. "I complained to God. I told God how we had been ignored and unvalued, how after all our service we returned home to find no musicians, no banners, and no welcome."

Again his wife asked him, "And what did God say?"

Her husband replied, "God answered, 'You're not home yet.'"

The Apostle Paul makes clear to us where our citizenship and real homeland is. Our homeland is in heaven. Our outlook goes beyond this world to the hopeful expectation of the Savior who will come from heaven. The Lord Jesus Christ will remake our bodies to resemble his own glorious body.

Prayer: *Living Christ, lead me daily to stand firm in your way. Even as I struggle through the challenges of these days, let me remember that my real homeland is in you. Amen.*

Saturday, March 14   Read Philippians 3:21–4:1.

Transformation is perhaps the word which best describes how God is at work within us. Let me explain what I mean by transformation. My four-year-old son has a toy at home that works like the original Transformer toy. You move the parts of the toy around, and presto! His toy egg changes and transforms into the shape of some sort of creature that is a completely new creation. That is how I envision what Paul meant when he said that our present limited bodies would be transformed into the body of glory which is Christ.

To be transformed and changed into a new creation is not a process which happens overnight; instead, it is a process which takes patience and perseverance. We also must have a willingness to place ourselves in God's presence and power.

The baptismal shell has become a symbol of my own spiritual journey of transformation. The shell represents to me newfound grace. This fresh grace-fullness releases me from my old ways of trying to change my life through a works-righteous mode of living and frees me to live boldly in God's power, confident in a God who names me acceptable. This grace-fullness allows me to live in ways that can be both open and freeing to myself and others. In God's grace and power we can change and be transformed, take the risks, and even make mistakes, confident in a God who loves us and names us acceptable.

Christ invites us to a life of transformation, relinquishing our old plans into an openness to God's new possibilities.

Prayer: *Grace-full God, the good news is that I don't have to depend on my own power alone to face my days. With your power in my life I can overcome that which would keep me from being the person you intend for me to be. Amen.*

Sunday, March 15　　　　　　　　Read Luke 13:31-35.

In a befriending way, the Pharisees came to warn Jesus that his life was in danger. In these verses Jesus depicted Herod as a fox and himself as a hen as if to say, "Tell that fox that the hen will not be intimidated. I still have work to do." Herod's desire to kill Jesus is a clear example of rejecting God. Jesus responded by lamenting over Jerusalem's continuing rejection of God's gracious coming and its opposition to those who come in God's name.

In comparing himself to a mother hen, Jesus voiced God's desire to embrace and protect. The language is reflective of Psalm 36:7, "How precious is your steadfast love, O God! All people may take refuge in the shadow of your wings." Yet Jesus once again points out the rejection poignantly when he states, "And you were not willing!"

Nothing hurts so much as to go to someone and offer love and have that offer spurned. To give one's heart to someone only to have it rejected is one of life's greatest sorrows. That is what happened to Jesus throughout his ministry. The miracle is that Jesus did not give up in the face of repeated rejection, but instead he came and keeps coming because he is the faithful one who has bound himself to his people.

God in Christ invites us to gather under protective wings. It is the picture of the unrelenting grace of God constantly coming to humankind. God's chief desire is to gather all people under God's wings in order to provide safety, protection, and meaning in their lives. Faithful God constantly seeks us to give us blessing and hope. We are to be responsive and glad in our recognition of the one "who comes in the name of the Lord."

Prayer: *God, in the midst of life's hardness I take refuge under the fold of your wings. Open my heart to accept your love. Amen.*

MERCY AND JUDGMENT IN GOD'S REALM

March 16-22, 1992   **K. Cherie Jones†**
Monday, March 16   Read Exodus 3:1-6.

A clergywoman friend spent several years serving a church in the California desert. She once said to me, "You wouldn't believe the things people are trying to escape by moving to the desert!" For them the desert became the only perceived place to escape from problems, and even God. Perhaps they thought their problems could not pursue them through the mountain passes. In the desert, they could make a new start. Or so they hoped.

Moses fled to the desert to escape the retribution of Pharaoh. He fled so deep into the desert that Pharaoh could not find him; and there he built a new life for himself.

But although Moses could evade Pharaoh in the desert, he could not avoid God. Pharaoh did not hate his adopted grandson Moses enough to chase him there, yet God loved the murderer Moses enough to pursue him to the far side of the desert. Moses did not look for God, but God found Moses. In an act of mercy to one who had done nothing to earn it, God pursued and engaged Moses.

In that moment, Moses learned what we too learn time and again: We cannot flee from God. We may perceive the desert as a haven from people or from problems—or even from ourselves. But God always finds us there and comes to us in mercy. And that is good news for those of us who seek to hide in the desert.

Prayer: *Pursuing God, I flee for so many reasons. Often my first response to a problem is to escape. I even try to escape from you. Yet you are merciful to me, and I am never lost to you. Show me again today that I stand on your holy ground. In the name of Christ. Amen.*

---

†International Director of The Walk to Emmaus, program of The Upper Room, Nashville, Tennessee.

Tuesday, March 17   Read Exodus 3:7-15.

My tendency when offered a new job is to stay put. I can think of many reasons why I should continue at my present job, many reasons why I am not the right one for the new job. And so my initial response to a new job offer is, "No thank you." It takes a lot of prayer to discern God's call to a new task. In this text about the call of Moses, I see an image of myself.

God prefaces the call with a description of the sufferings of the Hebrews, God's own people. God has seen and felt their suffering and is ready to act on their behalf. With these introductory comments, God then calls Moses to go to Pharaoh and bring the children of Israel out of Egypt.

Moses is not so sure. "Who am I that I should go?" *After all, I have never really led people. I have never spoken in front of large crowds. I am a shepherd. I know how to handle sheep. But the Hebrew people? And don't forget, I am a murderer. Surely someone will remember and then who will take me seriously?* (Like me, and perhaps like you, Moses is good at coming up with reasons why it should be someone else on whom God should count). Yet even as God pursued Moses to the far side of the desert, so would God go to any extreme to free the Hebrew people. God patiently responded to each of Moses' concerns with the promise to enable and empower him for the task.

The message is clear. Because we have experienced the mercy of God, we are called by God to be agents of holy mercy—in our homes, in our workplaces, in our world. The story of Moses reminds us that God is patient and persuasive and will give us what we need in order to live out the call. Thanks be to God!

Prayer: *Merciful God, I am often reticent to heed your summons. When I am reticent, remind me of this story of Moses and of your desire to be merciful not only to me but to others through me. Amen.*

Wednesday, March 18   Read Psalm 103:1-14.

"My life has been punctuated by moments of blessing and grace." Earl, a member of one of the congregations I pastored, described his experience as a fighter pilot in World War II, his work after the war, his marriage and his life recently. I realized I was hearing a litany of thanksgiving. Earl is acutely aware of God's blessings and grace in his life. It was an honor to hear his litany.

The psalmist describes for us the ways in which *our* lives are punctuated by God's blessing and grace. Notice the descriptions of God's activities in verses 1-6. God is the one who forgives sins, heals diseases, redeems from the Pit, crowns with love and compassion, satisfies with good things, and works righteousness and justice for the oppressed. God's actions for us cover the spectrum of our needs and concerns. We are reminded that every aspect of our lives is embraced in the loving care of our Creator.

In verses 7-14, the psalmist offers more descriptions of the character of God. God's initiative with us is rooted in love; our Creator knows how we are formed and remembers that we are dust. Our response is not always in kind. Notice how God responds to our rebellion and sin. God's basic posture toward us is that of abounding mercy. We would be mistaken to think that our behavior never angers God, as though divine love offers a carte blanche to any and all behaviors. But the psalmist assures us that God does not hold grudges against us. Nor are we punished according to the magnitude of our sin; God retains the right to soften the penalty. And more, God removes our sin from us totally. At each point, God treats us with mercy.

Suggestion for meditation: *"My life has been punctuated by moments of blessing and grace." The psalmist has described the ways in which God punctuates our lives. What is your litany of blessing and grace?*

Thursday, March 19   Read 1 Corinthians 10:1-5.

In this week's passages from Exodus and Psalms, we find mercy. Now we read our New Testament texts for the week expecting to find mercy and are caught off guard by the strong warnings of judgment. But to have judgment without mercy would be cruel. The story of the Hebrew people is, like our own stories, an example of this dynamic tension. In mercy, God set out to free the Hebrew people. In mercy, God summoned Moses to take a leading role in that liberation.

In today's text, Paul summarizes the actions of the people and God's subsequent judgment upon them. God redeemed them. They "all passed through the sea, and all were baptized into Moses." They all received spiritual food and water. Yet God was displeased with most of them, and they did not enter into the promised land. The warning is clear. Passing through the sea and partaking of the supernatural provisions were not guarantees of escape from God's judgment of their self-indulgence and arrogance.

This was a tough warning to the Corinthians, some of whom had decided that their baptism into Christ and their participation in the Eucharist precluded them from judgment. They thought that as long as they participated in the sacraments, they had the license to do whatever they wanted to do. They failed to remember that they would be accountable to God for their actions.

During Lent, we are challenged to question whether we are succumbing to self-indulgences. Lent is a time for us to remember that, while participation in the sacraments is vital, more is required in order to live lives that are pleasing to God.

Prayer: *Merciful God, through this scripture, you warn me of the serious nature of my actions and responses to your grace. Help me be honest with myself and with you. Amen.*

Friday, March 20   Read 1 Corinthians 10:6-13.

As a resident of Southern California for nineteen years, I heard repeated warnings about being prepared for earthquakes. Residents are urged to set aside emergency rations of water and food with extra clothing, flashlights, radios, and other items. The warnings are urgent, given the seismic history and potential of the region. For the entire time I lived there, I heard the dire predictions regarding the potential destruction of "The Big One."

Still, for the most part, like so many other residents, I ignored the warnings. We tend to delude ourselves into thinking that "it" will never happen to us. "The Big One" may hit, but it will not damage my family, my house, or myself. Even the devastating earthquakes in Mexico City, Armenia, and San Francisco only gave me momentary consideration of taking extra precautions. Soon I was back to thinking that it would never happen to me. Such thinking can lead to disastrous results. The truth is that "it" *can* happen to me and I would be wise to listen to the warnings.

Paul's warning in today's reading may sound harsh to us. The stories of the Exodus serve as examples to us of what may happen if we set our hearts on evil things. God's response to the Hebrews' evil was death on a large scale. This is not an easy passage to read or to apply to ourselves. (*Surely Paul is warning others, not me; I would never do such a thing!*)

Yet there is good news: God is faithful! God will provide us with ways to resist the temptations that come to each of us. We will not be tempted beyond our endurance. We can count on God's promise and offer of consolation and hope.

Prayer: *God of warnings and promises, help me consider both the temptations which are alluring to me and your promise of faithfulness to me. I do not want to be one who ignores warnings. Amen.*

Saturday, March 21   Read Luke 13:1-5.

In the prime of his life, Dale was diagnosed as having a rare form of cancer. Several months later his wife, Pam, was asked if they had ever questioned why he had contracted this disease. Her response was that as Christians they both knew they were not exempt from suffering. They did not assume that this disease was a punishment for some sin on Dale's part. And they knew that God loves them. Their faith is empowering them to deal with this illness.

Their attitude stands in stark contrast to the attitudes of so many of us who look for cause-and-effect relationships to explain why bad things happen to people. "Surely," we reason, "she must have done something to deserve this misfortune." "Surely he must have sinned some horrible sin to account for this traumatic occurrence." And so we attempt to find meaning when an infant drowns or a drive-by shooting occurs or a natural disaster strikes. Conversely, it is easy to assume that because our lives are going well and nothing dreadful is happening to us, we must be leading guiltless lives.

But according to Jesus, we cannot assess the quantity of another's sin (and subsequent need for repentance) by the quantity of that one's suffering. And for that matter, we cannot assess the quantity of our own righteousness by our lack of suffering. "No," says Jesus, "unless you repent, you will die too!" The strong warning is to stop looking at others in order to evaluate their need for repentance and, instead, to look first at one's own need to repent.

Prayer: *Just and merciful God, it is not always easy for me to see my need to repent. When my life goes smoothly, I assume I am doing all the right things. When I suffer, I wonder what I did to deserve this. Through your Holy Spirit, reveal to me of what I need to repent—and in your mercy, forgive me. In the name of Christ I pray. Amen.*

Sunday, March 22   Read Luke 13:6-9.

Dr. Butrus Abd-al-Malik, a Coptic Christian from Egypt, was entering his sixtieth year of teaching when I enrolled in his course. His name means "servant of the king," and his form of service was to teach Hebrew to seminarians. He wanted us to have a deeper understanding of the Old Testament, and he painted word pictures to clarify its meaning.

His word picture for repentance was climbing a mountain trail that grows steeper, narrower, and more treacherous with every step. Finally the climber stops to consider this precarious situation. To continue up the path would be at best foolhardy, at worst fatal. To go back down the mountain would be to return to safety. The climber, having come to his or her senses, decides to descend the mountain and seek a safer trail. Thus, the image of repentance is that of choosing life rather than death.

I confess that all too often, the summons to repentance has negative connotations to me. It sounds more like a threat than an invitation to life. I do not always remember that repentance offers the possibility of another chance to choose life.

The New Testament lessons this week have included strong calls to repentance. Paul and Jesus do not pat us on the hand and tell us that we have done nothing wrong, that everything will be okay. Instead, they proclaim that we do experience temptation, we do sin, we are on the edge of that mountain path and we do need to repent.

Yet, like the vineyard owner, God is willing to delay judgment to give humans yet another chance to repent (cf. 2 Peter 3:8-9).

Suggestion for meditation: *Where, in your life, are you on a steep, treacherous mountain path that is perilous? Will you continue on this path? Or will you descend and find a safe path? May God give you courage to make the necessary decisions. Amen.*

A FATHER'S LOVE

March 23-29, 1992   **Jung Young Lee†**
Monday, March 23   Read Luke 15:11-32.

The scripture reading this week is commonly known as the parable of the prodigal son. However, I would like to call it the parable of the loving father. In this passage we find what a father's love ought to be. In our time of social unrest and family crises, we must be aware of the importance of parental responsibility. Jesus, in this parable, helps us understand that the fatherly love is more powerful than the prodigality of the son. Many problems of children in our society might be prevented if they felt loved by their parent(s). We know that persons who have never felt that they are loved have difficulty showing love to others. Parental love, therefore, becomes the foundation of good family relationships and a good society. If you are a father or mother, this week's meditations based on this parable may help you reassess your understanding of love for your children.

In the parable, the father's love has several recognizable characteristics. First, the father's love allows trust in his children, in spite of his own doubt. Secondly, the father's love allows them freedom to act independently. Thirdly, it allows them to suffer as a consequence of their actions. Fourthly, it allows them to repent and return by themselves. Fifthly, it rejoices in reunion. Finally, it reaches out to reconcile conflict and to restore peace. These six characteristics of the father's love in the parable will be explored in this week's meditations.

Prayer: *Thank you, O God, for the love of human parents. May we experience that love more richly through your immeasurable love. In Christ's name. Amen.*

---

†Jung Young Lee, Professor of Systematic Theology, Drew University Theological School, Madison, New Jersey.

Tuesday, March 24   Read Luke 15:11-12.

Trust

Trust is required for the father in this parable to give the prodigal son his portion of the inheritance. If the father had not trusted his son, he would not have agreed to the son's request. The father may have feared that the property would not last; but, in spite of that, the father gave it as an act of love based on trust.

Trust is fundamental to human relationships. It is an essential ingredient of love. Trust is synonymous with faith, which is the basis on which our relationship with God is built. Likewise, the relationship between the father and the son or between parents and children is based on trust. When this trust is not present, our relationship is fragmented and love ceases to exist. Contemporary crises in our families and our society are often due to the lack of trust. When trust is absent, the life of our family and our society is fragmented. In a fragmented society it is no longer love but fear that controls our lives. When we cannot trust each other, the world becomes an unsafe place to live.

One method to control human behavior is to create a climate of mistrust. This method was used in the formative period of communist reign during the time of the Cultural Revolution in China (1966-1969). During this period, children mistrusted their parents, students distrusted their teachers, the youth mistrusted the old, and the uneducated mistrusted the educated. This atmosphere of conflict and fragmentation was used to manipulate the Chinese people.

In the parable the father trusted in his sons because he loved them. It was his love that created the condition of trust and that nurtured them to love. The loving family begins with trust.

Prayer: *Help us, O God, to trust each other, as you have trusted us as a loving parent trusts their child. Let our trust become the foundation of a loving family. Amen.*

Wednesday, March 25   Read Luke 15:13-14.

Freedom

When the son received the portion of the property that came to him, he sold it and left home with the money. In early tribal society property was passed from generation to generation. Especially in biblical culture, which was an Oriental culture, selling inherited property to someone else was regarded as a disgrace. Such an action risked non-care for aging parents and the family as a whole. Moreover, moving far away from the family was generally not an accepted practice. But still, the father gave the son the freedom to choose how he would handle his share of the property. Real love allows freedom while false love fosters dependence.

In our family life we confront very much the same situation. When our children grow up, they should be given freedom to choose, freedom to go away from home.

The father allows his children freedom to be independent because he loves them. Love helps them grow in their own way, creates room for freedom and self-realization. Love does not make us cling for our security, but it helps us go on our own way. Thus love contains risk, adventure, and even sacrifice. The father's love in the parable is precisely this kind of love that takes risk for his son's freedom and autonomy.

Prayer: *God, give us love that is strong enough to risk our lives and allows us freedom to grow and to mature in your grace. In Christ's name we pray. Amen.*

Thursday, March 26   Read Luke 15:15-16.

Suffering the consequences

The parable now turns to the consequence of the son's act. Independence can be costly and dangerous, and freedom is not without responsibility. The son wastes his money in reckless living and faces degradation and suffering. The question we ask then is, "How does a loving father allow his son to suffer?"

From the parable, it is difficult to know whether the father knew the suffering of his son. In a parable from the Buddhist tradition that tells of a prodigal son, the father was aware of his son's suffering and sent his servants to bring him back by force, although they failed to do so.

Let us suppose that the loving father in Jesus' parable was aware of the suffering of his son. Why didn't the father go to save the son? Was it because the father knew that suffering can be redemptive? Did the father then knowingly allow his son to suffer? If so, in this respect, it would be similar to the suffering of Jesus. According to Shusaku Endo, a Japanese writer, Jesus himself was identified with the prodigal son, and the parable was based on the reflection of his own life. Although we may not agree with this interpretation, we can say that the suffering of the prodigal son served to strengthen his character. (A Korean proverb says that the suffering of youth is more precious than gold.) The prodigal son's suffering, albeit a self-imposed consequence of his choices and actions, brought about the realization of the depth of his sin. This realization led to his repentance. Similarly, our suffering is necessary for our consciousness of evil and suffering in the world.

Prayer: *Whenever we suffer, O God, remind us of the redemptive suffering of Christ. Help us to realize the mystery of suffering that gives us meaning in love. In Christ's name. Amen.*

Friday, March 27   Read Luke 15:16-20*a*.

Repentance

Through suffering, the prodigal son came to his senses. He recognized his mistakes and repented. This was then the response of the son to the loving father who was waiting for his return. The son recalled the life he had lived with his father and decided to go back to his father's house. He confessed his sin and submitted himself unconditionally to his father. In the same manner, our response to God's love is expressed in our repentance and submission. The father's response to his children is always expressed in his outpouring love, while the son's response to his father is expressed in obedience.

The act of returning is an expression of love, for love is the power that reunites the separated. The son was separated from the father because of his will to be free and independent from the father. This separation was essential for their reunion. In other words, often love is not realizable unless separation takes place. Separation often awakens the consciousness of love. We experience this in our family life. Our children begin to appreciate our love when they are away from home. Likewise, the more we are separated from loved ones, the more we want to be united. The love of the father in Jesus' parable is like God's magnetizing love for us that calls us to return to God's all-embracing love. In the parable, the son's response to the power of the father's love is to return with repentance and submission.

Prayer: *Loving God, because of our sin we want to run away from you; but, paradoxically, because of your love we also want to come back to you. Help us return to you with repentant hearts. In Jesus' name. Amen.*

Saturday, March 28   Read Luke 15:20*b*-24.

Reunion

In this passage we see the actual reunion of the father with his son. This then is the reality of love. The long suffering of waiting love is transformed into the joy of embracing love. This is the realization of love that reaches its climax in the parable.

It is important in this passage to observe how the son and the father met. The son hesitated, but the father ran out, embraced him, and kissed him. The son asked the forgiveness of his sin, but the father transcended this request. The father was not interested in what the son tried to say. The father loved him in spite of what he said or what he did. The father loved him because he was his son, not because he was good or acceptable. The father's love for his son had been there all along. He said, "This son of mine was dead but now he is alive; he was lost but now he has been found" (TEV). Before the son could finish his request to be allowed even to be one of the hired servants, the father welcomed him as a son. He gave him the robe and ring (symbols of authority) and placed sandals on his feet (signs of being a free man).

If you are a father or mother, perhaps you would behave in the same way that the father of the prodigal son did. Perhaps you would freely and joyously welcome a returning and repentant son or daughter. Parental love at its best is unconditional love. When this occurs such love is comparable to God's love. We begin to realize why Jesus called God the Father.

Prayer: *Loving Father, help us experience the reality of love, the joy and ecstasy of reuniting the separated. Let our unity with you be the basis for our love of humankind. Amen.*

Sunday, March 29   Read Luke 15:25-32.

Reconciliation

The parable ends with the story of the elder son who had stayed with his father. He was known as a faithful and obedient son, yet he was also a jealous and arrogant man. In fact, because he had not been independent from his father, he was unaware of the real meaning of the father's love. The elder son became conscious of autonomy because of his younger brother. He, therefore, reacted against his father. This reaction became his attempt for his autonomy and independence. It created conflict and fragmentation.

The father's love is then expressed in his act of reconciliation. When there is no justice, conflict arises; and when there is no love, fragmentation takes place. The conflict among the family members can be overcome only through justice; the fragmentation of their relationship can be mended only through love. Love and justice are inseparable. Genuine love does not exist without justice, and justice must be maintained if love is to be genuine.

In the parable, justice is restored by the father's love: "My son, you are always here with me, and everything I have is yours" (TEV). When justice is restored, reconciliation takes place. The father has laid the foundation for the process of healing and transformation to begin. The father's love embraces both sons. The conflicting forces can be overcome through the creative power of the father's love.

Prayer: *Grant us, O Lord, the power of love that reconciles our differences and transforms us into new creations in Christ Jesus. Amen.*

OLD EMPIRES AND "NEW THINGS"

March 30–April 5   **Bob Roth†**
Monday, March 30   Read Psalm 126.

When we join the chorus that says God "has done great things for us; we are glad" (RSV), we remember to look forward in hope. God's leadings will flow like a river in the parched Negeb. There's some "juicy news"! Beginning with this psalter lesson, the week's readings affirm that God has used (and will use) prophets, servants, and even prisoners to redeem the times.

If we lapse from remembering our past or envisioning our future, the news of our day can deeply discourage us. Redemptively, the psalmist offers a personal memory that inspires a public faith. With refrains of laughter, the songs of a joyful day are sung. God delivered. God redeemed. God restored.

Is our day any bleaker than when the psalter was first sung through exiles and restorations, under empires both benevolent and evil? Or has the private comfort of our religion diluted a public faith that would prophetically claim God's "new things"?

In human chronicles, memories seem to fade. Then the image of God reviving a temple and a people begins to evoke our deepest trust in the future. Can you hear it? One who "goes forth weeping . . . shall come home with shouts of joy" (RSV).

Suggestion for contemplation: *To con- ("with") template (the temple) is to allow oneself to be in the presence of the holy.*

Look at your hands. Reflect on how God has used them to aid the life of one other person. Remember how God has used many hands together to affect the course of public events. Looking at your hands, pray that God will use them to help those who need you. Together with God, we can write a righteous history!

---

†Writer; associate pastor, Grand Ledge First United Methodist Church, Lansing, Michigan.

Tuesday, March 31   Read Isaiah 43:16-19*a*.

War. Homelessness. Dislocation. Greed. Some days, every headline seems to be but a translation of: "Today—More of the Same." Then along comes the prophet to remind us that empires come and empires go while, even now, our God and Maker is "doing a new thing" (RSV).

Isaiah's wake-up call alerts his people to distinguish between tired cliches about public affairs and the stark realization that those driven into a diaspora really are coming home.

Hear Isaiah well. We cannot live the life of faith independent of our history, God's land and its geography, and the politics that precede us. However, we must see how our faith can *inform* and *transcend* world events.

The second part of the book of Isaiah (sometimes known as Deutero-Isaiah or 2nd Isaiah) is written at a time when the sweep of peoples from Persia through Assyria, Syria, Israel and Judah are all being realigned. Quite a bit like the 1990s! Call them empires or superpowers, political dominions still vie for land, resources, and allegiance.

There is also spiritual news. Revelation begins with noticing the hand of God inspiring those who are powerless. From God come new perceptions. And new visions. Soon, new hopes. The prophet proclaims that superpowers rise and will someday fall, but the God who parted the waters lives forever.

Even benevolent kings, like Cyrus of Persia in Isaiah's day, are understood to be God's unwitting agents. Our own hope is to be found not on the surface of events but in the subtext of a surprising reunion of the scattered.

Suggestion for prayer: *Look at your hands. Now, envision the hands of the rejected and refused. Have your hands held theirs? Looking at your hands, pray for the hands of God's children to come together someday.*

Wednesday, April 1   Read Isaiah 43:19*b*-21.

Fashioning bears and fish and bald eagles and bumblebees, our Creator provided a lush earth and a crawling, flying, swimming, and walking cast of characters. In the final act, God made humanity—maybe the oddest species of all!

One dynamic of ongoing creation is the saga of the human family. Wondrously, every arriving baby is another new creation. The Creator breathes life into each one. Things begin anew. Life goes on.

The natural order astounds us with its beauty and feeds us with its plenty. Our very survival is rooted in creation, but our greed for creation breaks us apart. There are breaks in the family and even breaks in creation itself.

The people of Israel in Babylonian exile symbolize this brokenness found age after age. Nations war regularly over the very natural resources we were sent to steward and share. In ancient times the "Fertile Crescent," which included Israel, was a bounty for which empires battled. Over the span of a few centuries, the region was controlled by the Assyrians, the Neo-Babylonians, and the Persians.

The prophets present new creation and public redemption as threads of the same cloth. Isaiah 40–55, with earthiness and groundedness, preaches through a poetry of nature. God's waters refresh. The people echo the creation's praise of God. They even give language to praise!

The prophet announces that God sees our plight and cares. Now, we have a choice: will we help accomplish the new creation?

Suggestion for prayer: *Fold your hands: pray for wholeness. Open your hands with your palms to the sky: pray for oneness. Fold your hands again: pray for the new creation that is peace.*

Thursday, April 2   Read Philippians 3:8-11.

Paul writes to the Philippians from jail. Like John the Baptist and Jesus the Christ before him, Paul is imprisoned by the empire of his day. Like them, he is later killed by that same empire.

With Philippi on a main communications path of the empire, we might expect the persecuted Paul to write words of despair or simply to offer judgment. Wouldn't he despise those who attack him?

Paul moves beyond judgment because his relationship to history—which is to let go of it for a time and transcend it—is born of his relationship with God in Christ.

On a spiritual pilgrimage, Paul chooses to live for a while in that mystical fullness of time called *kairos*. Living "above" history doesn't mean Paul is unaware of it, only that he needs to be renewed fully in God's spirit.

With Christ, Paul dies so that with Christ, Paul may rise again. Paul believed that God cares about history—even guides salvation history. But there are times (as in persecution) to let go of history and simply trust Christ.

Sometimes history can be almost unbearable. As I am midway through the writing of this reflection, the U.S. and coalition forces have just gone to war with Iraq. How can we transcend history so as not to lose heart? How can we find a spiritual context for news that might otherwise leave us drained and depleted?

Suggestion for contemplation and prayer: *Again, examine your hands. How do they discover, even touch, the holy? Fold your hands, let yourself relax, and pray through silent listenings. Hear the good word God has for you now.*

Friday, April 3   Read Philippians 3:12-14.

Paul "leaves" his time and place in history that he might return again, renewed and centered in Christ. Having transcended history spiritually, he can look again with a clear vision. Most of all, Paul steps beyond the past and above the present to become deeply future-oriented.

Over the long haul, Paul is in no sense an escapist. In fact, with the assurance that "Christ Jesus has made me his own," Paul is "straining forward to what lies ahead." The humility of his limited gains does not bring discouragement but an excitement for the possibilities ahead. Paul's spiritual search has become a holy adventure.

In a personal sense, Paul knew that some very tough times lay ahead. Paul writes as he comes into his first direct contact with Roman power and persecution. His lively assurance is not naive—he knows the worst is yet to come. (Paul was to die around 64 A.D., probably under Nero's persecution of Christians.)

With Christian faith comes a radically new power, before which even the majesty of empires is dwarfed. Paul identifies with the life, death, and resurrection of Jesus. Like Jesus, Paul was arrested in Jerusalem. Through Christ's empowerment, Paul can drain the power from violence and hatred and domination.

Before the power of the Spirit, an empire is a small thing indeed.

Prayer: *O Lord, as we hold the day's paper or the week's newsmagazine, keep us mindful that these are also the hands that pray and that hold your word. Take away our fears and the wounds of the past, and fix us in a grace-filled world view. Empower us in a Christ-centered hope, come what may. Amen.*

Saturday, April 4   Read John 12:1-8.

Human recognition and acceptance of Christ's sacrifice (like Mary's anointing of Jesus) turns history on its head. In worldly loss can come the paradox of ultimate gain.

Sometimes God works in the gaps of a sorrowful day. Sometimes the Spirit revives the human spirit by transcending the day's events. Here, Mary moistens the feet of a weary Savior with expensive ointment and dries them with her own hair. The trickery of Judas and the empire that could so easily buy him off is made transparent.

There are days when it is faithful to step back from history. Jesus stepped forward—in the flesh—to change history forever. He shows, in his affirmation of Mary's profound faith, that changed hearts and lives are the truly "new things" in our midst.

Mary focuses attention on the identity of a Jesus who would soon enter Jerusalem and suffer toward a final victory. The powers and principalities, who would use death as their greatest threat and sanction, would find that death had lost its sting.

What of the poor? Jesus shows his *present* incarnation and Mary's recognition as enabling *future* compassion. What of Lazarus? Christ's healing of him was part of the threat to the institutional religious and state powers. He, too, points to the tragedy and triumph to come.

And what of Judas? Is there not a little of him in each of us? Peace comes when our faith and values can no longer be sold for a bag of gold. With Jesus, we see the "new thing" Mary has done. That sight is power.

Prayer: *O Creator God, you have given me a unique set of fingerprints on these hands. What other "new things" do you have in store for me? As the world tells me I'm weak, show me my power-from-within this day. Amen.*

Sunday, April 5   Read John 12:3,7-8;
                                              Isaiah 43:18-19.

To smell the fragrance and delight. To perceive the new thing and know. These are poignant beginnings for a worldview full of faith. The prophet, the psalmist, and the Lord all invite us to use our memory, our vision, and all of our senses to know when "our" history and salvation history meet. Ordered in creation itself, this meeting amazes and awakens.

Yes, we each have power. Size up the empires and superpowers, then remember what God has done. Expect the unexpected. To do otherwise would be to be satisfied with a God-less view of history.

To witness the majesty of this God of history is to see One greater than anything a nation-state can embody. Prophetic vision always calls into question our might-makes-right triumphalism. It becomes more difficult for nations to say, "God is on our side."

Yet when it comes to the cross and those who bear it in each place, we might envision God somewhere on every side. Who really are the defeated? The good news is that, not despite the cross but through it, our loving God shifts the course of events.

Through this death will come life. Pour the ointment! Prepare for burial! If the empires deal death, the faithful will embody self-sacrifice. As God continues to seek and save the lost, their thankful response will form the new creation that nourishes salvation history.

We end the week where we began it: in remembrance. Here we will find the energy and the hope to look ahead. New things are coming!

Prayer: *O gracious God, forgive these hands when they hurt or reject others. Guide these hands when they work or play. Free these hands to be your hands in this chapter of history. Amen and amen.*

STRENGTH SUFFICIENT FOR THE DEMAND

April 6-12, 1992   **Jim Sargent†**
Monday, April 6   Read Luke 22:14-46.

During the last hours of his life, Jesus watched his disciples erupt into angry dispute, heard one disciple dismiss the possibility of personal weakness, and witnessed men prepared to use violence in order to protect themselves. All that Jesus had attempted to teach his disciples appeared to be for nought. At this late and crucial hour the disciples still did not comprehend the demands of discipleship. What kept Jesus from giving up in disgust and disappointment?

Jesus did not concede defeat; he did not give up. Instead, Jesus continued on his course. How? Luke gives us glimpses of the source of Jesus' faith and courage. During the last meal Jesus gave thanks for the bread. Jesus promised Peter that he would be praying for him. Later, in the garden of Gethsemane, Jesus warned his disciples that they must pray in order to resist temptation. Jesus was a man of prayer. Through prayer Jesus learned how to trust God's power. Prayer accompanied every major decision Jesus made.

When life's demands challenge us, we, too, will be able to find courage and faith sufficient to the demand through prayer. Even when all outward circumstances look dismal, we can trust that God continues working. God still hears prayer. God sustains us through all of life's demands.

Prayer: *Lord Jesus, through the scripture we have seen you give prayers of thanksgiving and utter prayers of need. Grant us the gifts of courage and faith so that we, too, may learn the power of prayer. Amen.*

---

†Preacher and writer; pastor, Bluffton First United Methodist Church, Bluffton, Ohio.

Tuesday, April 7   Read Isaiah 50:4-9.

We have seen that Jesus was a man of prayer. Where did he learn about prayer? Luke portrays Jesus as a student of scripture. One of the most important tasks of any disciple is the study of God's word. Jesus had read the prophet Isaiah. Remember that Jesus read from Isaiah when he visited the synagogue at Nazareth (see Luke 4:16-20). Jesus could also have studied the "servant" images in Isaiah; chapter 50:4-9 is the third of these. In these verses we learn what must be done in order to sustain God's work:

1. The prophet must pray regularly, every day.
2. Through prayer the prophet will be able to speak to others.
3. Through prayer the prophet has learned identity and what is supposed to be done.
4. Through prayer the prophet has sufficient strength in time of need.
5. Through prayer the prophet knows that God's intention will outlast any resistance or persecution.

It is possible that when Jesus said "This is your hour, and the power of darkness!" he was remembering the prophetic words, "Who will declare me guilty? All of them will wear out like a garment." A lifetime of study and prayer helped Jesus interpret even the most arduous and unjust circumstance in the light of God's promises.

When we are faced with tests and trials, we too can draw on what we have gained over the course of a lifetime's discipline of study and prayer.

Prayer: *O Lord, I ask for the will to study and learn so that I will be able to understand God's work for me. I pray especially for insight and courage when darkness seems to overwhelm me. Help me to trust as the prophet and as Jesus did. Amen.*

Wednesday, April 8   Read Luke 22:63-71;
                                          Psalm 31:9-16.

Luke tells us that worship in the synagogue was a regular part of Jesus' life. Doubtless he had heard the psalms as a regular element of worship in the synagogue. How many times might Jesus have heard the psalm we are reading today? We have no way of knowing. However, in the hours of greatest stress and personal peril Jesus may have silently drawn on that psalm.

Surely Jesus' sufferings emulated the sufferings that the psalmist confessed in his prayer. Jesus prayed during every major crisis. Prayers that he had learned while growing up probably helped sustain him in his critical hours.

Similarly, elements of our prayer and worship sustain us, sometimes in ways we are not even aware of. Many years ago a young man blurted out that the church meant nothing to him. The wise preacher allowed the young man's outburst without public censure. However, afterwards, in private, the preacher asked the young man if he had ever prayed the Lord's Prayer, or sung "Amazing Grace," or called upon God during his schooling or illness. The young man responded, "Of course." Then the wise preacher challenged him to think again about the importance of the church. That young man finally realized that the church had been much more important to him than he had appreciated.

We will never be able to fully fathom the importance of regular attendance in worship services. As Christians, however, we can give thanks for the many times when we depended upon the memories of church.

Prayer: *We give you thanks, O God, for the prayers that we have learned, the hymns that return to our memory during trying times. We are grateful for the power of worship. Amen.*

Thursday, April 9   Read Luke 23:13-25.

The crowd's choice for the release of Barabbas should not surprise us. The crowd, after all, knew Barabbas. He was one of them. He had been jailed for something that many in the crowd had wished they could do. Barabbas had been jailed for insurrection against detested Roman rule. All of Judea seethed under the oppression of the occupation forces of Rome. Barabbas's crime would have been considered a virtue by zealous and patriotic men and women in Jerusalem.

Jesus, on the other hand, had never counseled violence against Rome. Jesus' attitude surprised and disappointed many people. The mob remained convinced that violence and hatred are the way of this world, that one has to be ready to fight. The people understood and knew Barabbas. They did not understand Jesus. The crowd chose Barabbas whom they knew and with whom they agreed. For them Jesus remained an unfamiliar man from a distant place whose teaching contradicted what they had always been taught.

During the readings for this week, we have been considering the importance of prayer. Jesus' teaching and call to discipleship will never fully be understood without the insight and courage that prayer makes possible.

Jesus' way will often contradict popular opinion. When majority opinion threatens to shout down the minority voice of truth, we can pray that we will have insight as to what God's will is and sufficient courage to remain loyal to Jesus' call.

Prayer: *We ask for insight, O God. We want to discern your will and follow Christ's way. Be present with us in wisdom and courage. Through Christ we pray. Amen.*

Friday, April 10   Read Luke 23:26-31.

Simon of Cyrene must surely have been one of the most shocked people in all of Jerusalem on that Friday. Luke tells us that Simon was just entering the city when the gruesome procession passed by. Roman soldiers abruptly seized the visitor and laid the execution timber on his shoulders, roughly instructing him to carry the beam to the execution site on Golgotha.

Without any warning or chance for preparation Simon of Cyrene had to shoulder Jesus' cross. We will probably not have to carry an instrument of torture and death. However, we may be required to bear the moral burden of Christ's will. What happened to Simon of Cyrene may well happen to any one of us. Didn't Jesus indicate that disciples must be willing to bear the cross (Luke 9:23; 14:27)?

The opportunity for service and bearing Christ's cross may come at any time. If the demand comes suddenly, without warning, will we be ready? A young man sat practicing the church organ. A handful of people listened to him play. Later, upon learning that the group of people was the church music committee, he wistfully said that he would like to audition sometime for the position of church organist. A wise man then told the young man that in all probability he had already received the audition. This example shows that we must always be ready. Our opportunity to serve Christ may be veiled as chance or accident. How tragic it would be not to be prepared or not to recognize the chance.

Prayer: *Dear Lord, we want to be your disciples; we want to be able to bear the cross. Give us insight into what your cross means. Grant us sufficient strength to do your will. Amen.*

Saturday, April 11   Read Luke 23:32-43.

The scenes are of a travesty of justice and of unmitigated horror. Jesus has been convicted, beaten, and now suffers the humiliation of public execution. His friends have abandoned him, the crowd has turned against him. What sort of person will Jesus prove to be? How will he react in the hour of his greatest trial?

It is often said that in moments of greatest stress our real character is revealed. Therefore, the final words of Jesus are of utmost significance. What will Jesus say?

The importance of prayer in the formation of identity and character can hardly be overstated. All those years of preparation, worship, study, and prayer come to focus in Jesus' final hours. What is the word? *"Father, forgive them . . ."* Under the cruelest of circumstances Jesus prays for forgiveness for his executioners.

Each of us wants to prove sufficient to the trials we face, no matter how difficult the circumstance. We need to be prepared ahead of time because we will not be able to draw on what isn't already a part of us. We can begin preparing ourselves for the great challenges of our lives through the disciplines of study, worship, and prayer.

Prayer: *Heavenly Father, we don't know what we will have to endure or encounter, but we want to be ready. Strengthen and guide us in the disciplines that will prepare us to face the trials that life brings us. In Christ's name. Amen.*

Sunday, April 12 (Palm Sunday)
Read Philippians 2:1-11.

Immediately after the crucifixion men and women began to interpret the meaning of Jesus' life and death. In Luke's Gospel the first words that interpreted Jesus are the centurion's "Certainly this man was innocent!" (Luke 23:47)

The Christian church has always interpreted Jesus. In his letter to the Philippians, Paul reflected on Jesus' life and ministry by quoting from a hymn that was already being used in the church in the first years of the Christian movement. Remember, Paul did not have a library at his disposal. Writing to the Philippians while imprisoned, he had only what he could remember. Very much like his Lord, Paul had to live on the basis of what he had learned and practiced throughout his life.

We should not be surprised, therefore, that the apostle drew on a part of Christian worship. Prayer and worship equipped Paul for the extraordinary demands of apostleship.

First century Christians emulated the humble life of Jesus, strengthened through prayer and worship. Modern Christians are still called to discipleship. We are still summoned to a Lord who emptied himself and took the form of a servant. We too are summoned to lives of service and humility. We will only be able to do this if we continually commit ourselves to Christ.

Luke tells us that the final words that Jesus speaks are, "Father, into your hands I commend my spirit" (Luke 23:46). Paul utters a confession that Jesus is Lord. Today, let us once again commit ourselves to the purposes and manner of God.

Prayer: *Gracious God, we give you thanks for people who live by your calling and who commit themselves to lives of service and humility. Grant us strength to join with them in the life of faith. Through Christ. Amen.*

April 13-19, 1992   **Mary Lou Redding†**
Monday, April 13   Read Isaiah 42:1-9;
                                           Matthew 7:17-21.

Levi

My name is Levi. I am a tax collector, though I have been traveling with Jesus, a prophet from Nazareth, to hear him teach.

I love the Law. I have spent many hours talking with the rabbis. The Lord God has given us the Law, and the rabbis say we, Israel, are called by God to be a sign in the world, to establish justice, to change things. But Jesus makes some incredible claims. For instance, the prophet Isaiah speaks of Israel as a suffering servant. Jesus said in the synagogue that passage applies to him! That's not the way the rabbis have explained it.

But Isaiah also says God's servant will open blind eyes and give food to the hungry. Jesus touches blind people and their eyes are healed; he breaks bread and there is enough for everyone. You can't argue with results. We've been waiting a long time for the Anointed One, the Messiah, and I'm ready to say Jesus is the one. There is real power in him, and I believe it comes from God. But I get uncomfortable and a little nervous when he keeps using Isaiah's words about God doing a "new thing."

Yesterday some were even calling him king. The authorities don't like that kind of talk. The rabbis don't like the way the crowds gather to listen. But I just keep coming back to this: I know Jesus. If Jesus is part of any "new thing" God is doing, I can trust it, because I trust him.

Suggestion for meditation: *Who is Jesus to you? What names for him do you respond to most?*

---

†Managing Editor, *The Upper Room* magazine; writer; workshop and retreat leader; Nashville, Tennessee.

Tuesday, April 14   Read John 12:1-10.

Mary of Bethany

My sister Martha and my brother Lazarus and I have come here from Bethany. I don't think it's a good idea for us to be here. The religious leaders are nervous about Lazarus, and people make such a spectacle of him once they find out who he is. But Lazarus wants to celebrate Passover in Jerusalem. So here we are.

I'm frightened for Lazarus. And I'm frightened for Jesus, too. Several days ago Jesus was in Bethany, and there was a strange air of determination about him. At first I thought it was just weariness; he's always exhausted after the crowds come to him for healing. But after a while I could see it was more like an enormous sadness. The longer I looked at him, the more I knew I had to do something special for him. I wanted him to know how wonderful I think he is.

Then I thought of the spikenard. I am always the one to wash Jesus' feet (Martha gets embarrassed), and after I washed off the road dust, I poured the perfume on his feet. It was extravagant; I know that, but I thought the special attention would help him. My hair was loose, and it got in with the towel as I dried his feet. Martha looked scandalized that I had allowed my hair to come unbound and touch him. She always gets upset when I do something she considers unconventional, and this time she was furious. So was Judas. They just didn't understand.

But then Jesus said something about the perfume being for his burial and about his not always being with us. I am scared. I don't want Jesus to die; I want him to live!

Suggestion for meditation: *Do you consider yourself conventional or unconventional in the way you express your faith in Jesus? What might you gain from the example of those unlike you?*

Wednesday, April 15   Read Psalm 118:14-24;
                                          Hebrews 4:14-16; 5:7-9.

A follower

I have a name, but even if I told you what it is, it wouldn't mean anything to you. I'm not one of the twelve or even one of the seventy.* I haven't been healed of blindness or had demons cast out. I'm just an ordinary person. But I've been listening to Jesus teach, and I have seen some of the healings.

All my life I've wondered about God. But I'm puzzled by some of the stories—fire raining down from heaven, Lot's wife turning to a pillar of salt, awful stories like the prophet calling a bear to eat the children who were taunting him. I want to know God, and at the same time I've always been a little afraid, too.

But God is also called the "gate of righteousness," and one day I heard Jesus call himself "the gate of the sheepfold" and "the door." I decided to ask him about that. And the strangest thing happened. When I got up close and looked into his eyes, I didn't have to ask. He understood, even before I said a word. I don't really know how to express it, but somehow he made me feel—welcomed. I got the feeling that he'd just been waiting for me to approach him. And it's not just me. He welcomes everybody. He even touches lepers.

I've seen God's mighty works now, and I see that God is powerful—but powerful in a way that heals people, not hurts them. That's a different kind of God, one that Jesus has helped me want to know more. There are some who say Jesus is the Messiah. I don't know. I just know this: he changed me.

Suggestion for meditation: *What images for God have you given up? What images for God are most important to you, and how are they linked to Jesus?*

---

*Luke 10:1-17

April 16 (Maundy Thursday)

Read John 13:18-30.

Judas Iscariot

I am Judas bar Simon. I'm from the town Kerioth, in Galilee. One of Jesus' brothers is called Judas, too, so some call me Judas Iscariot. Judas is a common name.

I have been traveling with Jesus for over two years, and I really thought he was the one. Many of us did, and I thought we were going to succeed. A few days ago the people were ready to make him king—but he wouldn't let them. He is throwing over our cause, and we are all going to look like fools.

I don't think he understands. He's an idealist, a dreamer. He believes absolutely in what he's doing. The healings and the teaching are fine as far as they go, but that's the place to begin, not the place to stop. I've tried to tell him you can't change the world just one person at a time. You have to deal with the bigger issues. I really thought God was going to use him to restore the kingdom to Israel. But if he won't take the reins politically, he can't change the system. The time is right for us to act now, but he stands in the way of building any other widespread alliance. As wonderful as he is, he has become a liability, too.

The authorities would like to see Jesus out of the picture, and I think I've figured out a way to use that: I am going to turn Jesus over to them. They're stupid. They don't realize what making him a martyr will do for us. It's a desperate move, but this is a time for desperate measures.

Sometimes there are things that are bigger than one person. I really believe Jesus loves his ideals enough to die for them. Maybe the time has come for that. Maybe.

Suggestion for meditation: *At what places in your life is Jesus not what you want? How do you deal with that?*

April 17 (Good Friday)

Read Luke 22:7-20, 31-34.

Simon Peter

I am a coward! I'm even worse than Judas. At least Judas did something. Me—I was cowed by a servant girl! And what hurts most is knowing that Jesus could see in advance what I'd do.

After the Passover meal, as we talked privately, he said, "Simon, Satan wants to sift you like wheat, but I have prayed for you, that your faith may not fail." Then I said—like always, almost before he even finished talking—"Lord, I'm ready to go with you to prison and even death." What a laugh!

In the courtyard, after they'd taken him in for questioning—and the Lord knows what else; I've heard about their "interrogations"—this servant girl came up to me. She had been inside; she might even have had a message from him for me. But when she asked if I was one of his followers, I was too scared to even look her in the face. I denied I even knew him. Two more times people asked me if I knew him, and two more times I denied it. Some friend I am.

And Jesus is the best friend I've ever had. He doesn't get mad at me when I shoot off my mouth. He just waits until I cool off and then asks me the same question again—and again, until I see what he really means.

I feel like going out somewhere and never coming back. But Jesus said something else last night, something like, "and when you have turned back. . . ." I don't see what there is to turn back to. I don't see how anything good could come from this. But maybe there's something I'm not seeing here. It wouldn't be the first time I didn't understand.

Suggestion for meditation: *In what ways do you nurture your friendship with Jesus? In what ways would you like to be a more faithful friend to him?*

April 18 (Holy Saturday)

Read John 19:25-30.

Mary

My heart is broken! They have killed my son. I stood by as they hurt him, and I could do nothing. He suffered so! He was thirsty and called out for a drink, and one of the soldiers wet a cloth with vinegar and put it to his lips. Why did they have to be so cruel?

They beat him and tortured him, and then they humiliated him. If I could have taken some of the pain, I would have. But I just had to stand there, helpless. John stood beside me, weeping. John, the "Son of Thunder"! John, the one who wanted to call down fire on the village in Samaria that would not welcome them. John, the ambitious one. And from the cross, even in that pain, Jesus thought of me. He said to me, "Here is your son," and then he said to John, "Here is your mother."

I don't want to be John's mother. My son is dead, and no one could ever replace him. I knew Jesus was born for something different. Joseph knew it. Years ago, when we brought him to the Temple for circumcision, Simeon knew it, too. He said to me, "A sword will pierce your spirit." Now I know what he meant. This world will never be the same for me.

I prayed that it would not come to this. Jesus had his own way of listening and his own way of being faithful. But I don't understand why it had to end this way.

I hear John calling. He is brokenhearted, too. I guess I should answer him.

Suggestion for meditation: *At what points in your life has your relationship with Christ led you into new relationships? How has God used these people in your life?*

---

*Luke 9:54.

121

Sunday, April 19 (Easter)

Read Luke 24:1-12.

Mary Magdalene

I really don't blame them for not believing us. Joanna and Mary and I went with some others to the tomb. We had gathered spices and were going to tend to Jesus' body. It was early—none of us slept much last night—but we needed to be doing something. The least we could do was prepare his body for a proper burial. Yesterday they only wrapped him and put him in a tomb.

Chuza, Joanna's husband, wasn't sure we ought to do this. Chuza said Joseph of Arimathea had put the body in his own tomb, and we'd have to find him to go with us. But Jesus' mother seemed a little comforted when we told her what we had in mind, so we went on to the garden.

At first I thought we must be in the wrong place, because there was no stone at the entrance to the tomb. I went inside, and there was no body. As we were trying to figure out what to do next, two men *appeared*. None of us saw them walk up; all of a sudden, they were just there. And one of them said, "Why do you seek the living among the dead? He is not here. Don't you remember what he said to you?" And in a flash, I did remember. He said he would be raised from the dead! We stood there, stunned.

He was telling the truth! And if he was telling the truth about this, then I knew he was telling the truth about all the rest, too. He was telling the truth about the demons being gone for good.* I don't have to be afraid. They won't come back. The change in my life—in me—is permanent. I really know that now.

Suggestion for meditation: *What things has Jesus banished from your life? How has knowing him changed you?*

---

*Luke 8:2.

WITNESSES OF EASTER

April 20-26, 1992   **Donald D Wachenschwanz†**
Monday, April 20   Read John 20:19-23.

This passage is unusual for the Gospel of John. First, although John shows a recurring interest in signs as a means of arriving at belief, Luke (24:36-43) actually develops better the two signs of this Resurrection appearance—Jesus showing his disciples his hands and feet and Jesus asking for something to eat. John skims over the first and omits the second.

Secondly, John rarely shows interest in matters related to institutional religion. Yet this passage seems to contain a commissioning service. After Jesus appears and shows his disciples the marks on his body, they believe. Then Jesus commissions them, empowering them to forgive (or not forgive) sins.

Imagine a commissioning service in which the celebrant says to the candidates, "Peace be with you. As I was commissioned, so I commission you." Then he breathes on them and says, "Receive the Holy Spirit."

As we reflect on the scripture readings for this Easter week, we remember that Easter is the central fact of the Christian faith. Every aspect of our theology is informed by Easter—even the creativity and providence of God are understood in its light. The world is remade at Easter. We are given life. This life is given to us for a reason: We, like the disciples, are commissioned to be witnesses to the Resurrection and its power in our lives.

Prayer: *O fill me with thy fullness, Lord, until my very heart o'erflow in kindling thought and glowing word, thy love to tell, thy praise to show.* * *Amen.*

---

*From "Lord, Speak to Me That I May Speak" by Frances R. Havergal.
†United Church of Canada minister, Hawkesbury and Cassburn congregations, Ontario, Canada.

Tuesday, April 21   Read John 20:24-29.

In Mark (16:11) none of the disciples really believed the Resurrection. Here, only Thomas needed signs. In Mark (16:14) Jesus scolded the disciples for their unbelief. Here, only the doubter gets special attention. Again, the doors are locked, and yet Jesus appears in the room. Jesus lets Thomas actually touch his wounds.

Jesus' actions in John's Gospel suggest that Jesus understood why Thomas doubted. However, Jesus called "blessed" those who believe without seeing proof. Thomas needed answers; he was searching. He was open to solutions—indeed, to new solutions. Thomas did not want to rush into belief simply because he wanted to believe—and he wanted very much to believe. Jesus did not condemn that in Thomas but said simply, "Do not doubt, but believe." Jesus tells Thomas to struggle with belief. Scriptures, hymns, and sermons remind us again and again to be faithful—not to principles and ideas and moral codes and dogmas but to Christ and the struggle of living the Christ-life in our time and place. And that is why Jesus so highly commends those who see without signs. They must truly struggle toward belief, and their resulting witness is ardent.

Prayer: *Just as I am, though tossed about*
with many a conflict, many a doubt,
fightings and fears within, without,
*O Lamb of God, I come, I come.*Amen.*

---

*From "Just as I Am, Without One Plea" by Charlotte Elliott.

Wednesday, April 22   Read John 20:30-31.

Most biblical scholars believe that these verses in today's lectionary reading are the original ending of the Gospel of John; thus, it is important to try to understand these verses as their original readers understood them.

Let us first note that this passage summarizes the teachings of this Gospel. John's Gospel is about the love of God, who sends the Son to reveal himself through signs and discourses which lead to belief. The One sent from God suffers and dies, rises, and sends the Comforter to believers who have the life which belief makes possible.

Although this statement of purpose successfully summarizes the Gospel, it misses the outward force of the commissioning service we looked at on Monday. By adding the inspired ending on caring ("Feed my sheep," v. 17), the early church gave impetus to the commissioning and presented further Resurrection appearances.

It is possible for John's version of the Gospel, like Easter itself, to leave us with an inner glow, to lead us to bask in the personal dimension of new birth. But we need to be reminded that birth involves movement into the world. Those who dwell on personal salvation have never left the womb. To be truly born again is to be sent out of comfort and security into a world of doubt and care. We are born to be witnesses.

Prayer: *Not for ever in green pastures do we ask our way to be, but the steep and rugged pathway may we tread rejoicingly. Not for ever by still waters would we idly rest and stay, but would smite the living fountains from the rocks along our way.* Amen.*

---

*From "Father, Hear the Prayer We Offer" by Love Maria Whitcomb Willis.

Thursday, April 23   Read Acts 5:27-32.

In this passage the apostles stand before the Sanhedrin much as Jesus did (see Luke 22:66-71). Their use of the image of a tree for the cross is a reference to Deuteronomy 21:22-23, which explains that a person who has been hung on a tree "is accursed of God" (KJV). Thus, that God raised this Jesus who had been hung on a tree was an even stronger condemnation of those responsible for Jesus' death.

In his appearance before the Sanhedrin, Jesus set an example of courage for the apostles. The apostles, in turn, set an example for the whole church.

Their example serves little or no purpose if it does not inspire us to live as they lived. And we deceive ourselves if we believe that we live in "Christian" times, free of persecution. In much of Western culture our persecution is not overt as was that of Jesus and the apostles. Ours is insidious—a culture which uses our religious language but does not bear the fruits of that faith; a society where materialism, consumerism, and individualism are the leading values. If we dare to live the particularity of the gospel in front of our neighbors, we may experience what Paul meant when he said that the gospel is a stumbling block and an offense (1 Cor. 1:23).

A religious poster out a few years ago asked, "If you were on trial for being a Christian, would there be enough evidence to convict you?" We are on trial. We are Christians. Does anyone know?

Prayer: *O Lord and Master of us all, what'er our name or sign, we own thy sway, we hear they call, we test our lives by thine.* Amen.*

---

*From "O Lord and Master of Us All" by John Greenleaf Whittier.

Friday, April 24   Read Psalm 2.

We can use the psalms to reflect on other scriptures. I invite you to meditate upon this psalm. Read one of the brief scenes described below and fix it in your mind. Once you have done that, read the psalm. Then, reflect upon the question at the end. You may do one or more of the three scenes.

1. (Based on Jeremiah 5:4-6) Imagine yourself a citizen of a walled city. For many decades the citizens of your city, including you, have accumulated great wealth and power until they feel invincible. Churches are empty. "There is no need to bow to God's authority," the people say. "Look what we have accomplished on our own." But now your walled city is surrounded by enemies, waiting to destroy anyone who would venture outside the gates. Read Psalm 2 and reflection on the question in the "Suggestion for meditation."

2. (Based on Matthew 3:13-17) Imagine you are observing the baptism of Jesus by John the Baptist. Jesus comes out of the water, the clouds open up, you see a dovelike shape on Jesus' head, and you feel within you the voice of God saying, "This is my son, with whom I am well pleased." Once this scene is firmly placed, read Psalm 2, and then reflect on the meditation question below.

3. (Based on Acts 4:23-30) Imagine you are part of a group of Christians who have banded together to oppose turning a natural bog near your town into an industrial park. You and other members of your group have received hints from the zoning commission that your small businesses will face zoning problems if you continue your opposition to the industrial park. Once you have this image in mind, read Psalm 2, and then reflect on the meditation question below.

Suggestion for meditation: *Ask yourself, "What must change in my life to make me an Easter witness?"*

Saturday, April 25   Read Revelation 1:4-5*a*.

Christ Jesus is "the faithful witness, the first-born of the dead, and the ruler of the kings of the earth." Before Pilate (John 18:37), Jesus said "I have come . . . to bear witness to the truth." What truth?

The truth to which Jesus bears witness is that God alone is Sovereign of all the universe. By his acts of healing and making whole, Jesus witnessed to the fact that God's sovereignty is greater than all human-made power that breaks and hurts and destroys. By his courage in the face of threats and violence from religious authorities, Jesus witnessed to the fact that God's sovereignty is more mighty than human-derived power that oppresses, dispossesses, and alienates. Through his willingness to suffer and die and through his resurrection, Jesus witnessed to the fact that God's power ranks above even the power of death.

By his making all things new, Jesus gave witness that all the earth is the Lord's. By his care for the weak and the dispossessed, Jesus gave witness that all things come from God.

Before the throne of the one "who is and who was and who is to come" are "the seven spirits," who may be angelic beings. Or, these "seven spirits" may refer symbolically to the gifts of the Lord's spirit of which Isaiah wrote (Isa. 11:2-3): wisdom, understanding, counsel, might (fortitude), knowledge, godliness (piety), and fear or reverence of God. Listed here and later developed by the church, these gifts are given by the Spirit to those willing to take up their cross and be witnesses to Christ. Do not Pentecost and Easter belong together?

Prayer: *Come, Holy Ghost, our souls inspire, and lighten with celestial fire; thou the anointing Spirit art, who dost thy sevenfold gifts impart.* * *Amen.*

---

*From "Come, Holy Ghost, Our Souls Inspire," attributed to Rhabanus Marus.

Sunday, April 26   Read Revelation 1:5*b*-7.

Everyone will someday witness the presence of Christ. In this life or in the next, in this year or in the years to come, "every eye will see him." And that encounter with pure Light and endless Life will bring into stark contrast the contribution each one has made to Christ's crucifixion.

Every act of indifference, every abuse of position, every material gain at the expense of other created things, every pleasure which lessens personhood, all sin and wrong will be a shadow in the light of that Presence. But through grief and mourning the conquering love of the cross will break hearts of stone and create hearts of compassion and harmony.

So look on the risen Christ. Witness the Resurrection. This is the way of the true "witness," the English translation for the Greek word *martus,* from which we derive *martyr.* Witness the risen Christ and in seeing be blinded and burned and lighted and warmed. Be grief-broken and mournful and healed and joyful. For Holy Week is an integral part of Easter.

Behold! Look! See the coming Christ. Advent is an integral part of Easter. See Christ coming from the womb. Christmas is an integral part of Easter. See Christ coming from the tomb. Easter is everything. And you are a witness of these things, a martyr to complacency, a testimony to new life.

Prayer: *Soar we now where Christ has led, . . .*
         following our exalted Head; . . .
         Made like him, like him we rise, . . .
         Ours the cross, the grave, the skies, Alleluia!*

---

*From "Christ the Lord Is Risen Today" by Charles Wesley.

THE LORD, THE LIGHT, AND THE LAMB

April 27–May 3, 1992 **David G. Mobberley†**
Monday, April 27 Read Acts 9:1-9.

When God chooses to enter into human history, the action is often illuminated by heavenly light. The Lord Jesus was ushered into the human story by the hand of God under the light of a brilliant star (see Matt. 2:2). The people of Isaiah's prophecy saw a great light (see Isa. 9:2). And Paul's dramatic conversion on the Damascus road was acted out in a blinding light.

Some passages in the Bible include the word *light* to describe or to refer to the promised Messiah, to the Lord Jesus. Fundamental to the Christian faith is the principle that Jesus is the Light of the world (see, for example, John 12:46). In Paul's conversion, the blinding light actually was Jesus. The miracle that day was that Saul, although blinded by the brilliant light, "saw" Jesus. From the moment of conversion to the end of his life, Paul was an instrument of God, shedding abroad the great light that had possessed him so completely.

Is this the same light which provides the radiance flowing from the heart of God's children who follow in the footsteps of Jesus? Although it does not seem required of us that we continually undergo the great conversion experience of Paul, we can let Jesus shine from our hearts in our Christian living. And from this, Jesus accomplishes the conversion of others. Living in the light and absorbing the great truths of our faith keep us constantly aglow.

Prayer: *O Lord, help me to radiate the light of Jesus in all that I say and do. Amen.*

---

†Retired professor of biology in United Methodist colleges; resident of Englewood, Florida.

Tuesday, April 28   Read Acts 9:10-17.

In this interesting story of Ananias, the plot focuses on visions through which the Lord offers instructions. Such a vision came to Ananias, whom the Lord had chosen to restore Paul's eyesight and subsequently to baptize Paul. An absorbing part of this story is that both Ananias and Paul had visions of what the healing process was to be.

More often than not in biblical stories, visions were experienced during sleep in the dark watches of the night. I wonder what might be the physical energy that allows people to "see" visions in the darkness? Is it somehow derived from a form of inner light? Otherwise, how could one actually see visions or dreams? Could it also be the same energy that enables us to think and to grasp ideas and concepts?

Cartoonists and comic-strip artists have frequently pictured an incandescent light bulb when the caption or story line has centered on a character's grasping some idea. In real-life situations, we often affirm that an idea has come to us with statements like "the light suddenly dawned," or "I saw the light." Is it possible that energy of the same kind is involved when we have discovered another great truth in the teaching of Jesus?

A worthwhile experience is to take time to look at prints of some of the great paintings of New Testament events. See how effectively the Old Masters used color to achieve the special radiance which emanates from Jesus' face and raiment. The Renaissance renditions of scenes from the nativity, the transfiguration, the triumphant entry into Jerusalem, the crucifixion, and the ascension are particularly noteworthy in this respect.

Prayer: *Lord Jesus, let me be worthy to have you be the light within me. Amen.*

Wednesday, April 29   Read Psalm 30:4-7.

Although Psalm 30 is traditionally identified as one of the psalms of thanksgiving, some of its verses reflect moods of both hope and despair. The saints (NIV) or worshipers are being asked to praise God because the despair and darkened gloom of night have given way to hope and joy in the glowing light of the morning. We are uncertain as to whether the contrasting mood of verse 5 is describing the king's personal fortunes or those of the nation. In many of the psalms attributed to David, national interests are subjects of the poetic literature.

Nearly one third of the psalms of Israel are psalms of lament, or despair. The despair may be national, revealed in the reflections of the king deploring persecution by aggressor nations or in the reflections of a prophet lamenting the moral depravity of the people. The despair may be individual, proclaimed by psalmists whose worlds seem to have collapsed or who are being assaulted by enemies intent upon destroying them. At this point, one should note the decisive virtue of almost all the psalms of despair: "In his word I hope." Hope, when Israel was in deep despair, was the clearest reflection of the nation's indomitable will to survive and to be redeemed. In this psalm, the psalmist sees the morning light as a symbol of that hope.

In the study of world events, too little attention is given to despair, its genesis and its consequences. Despair often shapes the behavior of nations. It fashions illogical decisions, it fosters evil, and it creates frustration.

Suggestion for meditation: *How do you define despair? Do people we read and hear about in the news exhibit postures of despair? What is the Christian response to despair?*

Thursday, April 30   Read Psalm 30:8-12.

Verses 8-9 convey the image of a person who stood forlornly before the Lord in deep despair, evidently on the verge of death. For reasons which the psalmist does not tell us, the Lord had turned away. Typical of psalms of despair are verses attempting to reassure God of people's faithfulness and using rational argument in their own defense. The Pit is actually Sheol, a land of death beneath the surface of the earth. It is characterized by darkness because the shining presence of God is never seen there.

The other side of deep despair is radiant hope. And it is hope that allows faith to engender the confidence that God is righteous and kind. Some of the loveliest expressions of hope are found in the beloved poetry of the Psalms.

We should keep in mind that Israel never equated true blessedness with the total obliteration of despair. The people have always known that they must come to terms with despair. The psalms are replete with expressions of despair over humiliation at the hands of enemies.

Reeling from the sensation of absolute despair, the psalmists' cries were often for mercy and compassion. The concept of mercy appears in fully a third of the psalms. We often find it as part of a plea for God's consideration: "Have mercy upon me, O Lord " or "Be gracious to me" (see, for example, Psalm 57). God is also described as merciful and, in that sense, the emancipator and the radiant source of hope (see, for example, Psalms 25:10; 31:7; 57:10).

Suggestion for meditation: *What are some of the causes of despair among nations, societies, and cultures in our world? What are some signs of hope in the world?*

Friday, May 1   Read Revelation 5:11-14.

John of Patmos, to whom the Revelation was given, called Jesus the Lamb. John the Baptist proclaimed Jesus as the Lamb of God (*Agnus Dei;* John 1:29, 36). Otherwise, New Testament writers did not use this lovely figure of speech. Yet, it is basic to the Christian faith, symbolizing the sacrifice of Jesus on the cross as well as his sensitive nature.

For centuries, the *Agnus Dei* has been an essential prayer in the celebration of Holy Communion (the Eucharist). The prayer acknowledges that the Lamb of God has taken away the sins of the whole world. It also beseeches the Lamb to have mercy and to grant the petitioners peace.

The Lamb, sacrificed on Calvary, was the extraordinary power that has shaped two millennia of civilization. The same Lamb has also been understood to be meek and tender, having an acute perception of human need. That is the great paradox of the Christian experience. For John of Patmos, the vision of God's revelation was clear: the Lamb was worthy of highest exaltation.

This passage in Revelation has provided scriptural authority for centuries of pageantry and for the ornate and often massive edifices built by the church as houses of worship and centers of organization. Perhaps we ought to ask: Is the Book of Revelation appropriate to our time, or is there different work to do today?

Prayer: *Lord, help us to see the world's needs as you see them. And enable us through your spirit to respond to the needs of persons. Amen.*

Saturday, May 2   Read John 21:1-14.

The setting of today's reading is the Lake of Tiberias (Sea of Galilee) early one morning near the end of the forty days between Easter and Ascension Day. Its central event has been understood to be the miracle of the draft of fishes. Note that here, as in another Gospel story about the disciples' fishing (Luke 5:1-9), they were unable to net fish until Jesus came along to be among them.

But of even greater importance is that this reading is also an account of one of nearly a dozen post-resurrection appearances which Jesus made among that small company of followers who had mourned his crucifixion. It reminds us that his resurrection was an unparalleled event in all of human history.

Did Jesus know that Peter and that small company would eventually net some fish and so he lit a charcoal fire in order to cook breakfast for them? This is the Jesus of the folk, the same Jesus who washed his disciples' feet, the same Jesus who is the Savior of the world, the King of Kings, and the one who begged forgiveness for the common people as well as the religious and political leaders who had condemned, tortured, and crucified him.

Standing on the shore, Jesus was not immediately recognized by the disciples. As the first light of the morning dawned, he was there on the shore watching the disciples as if he were bringing the dawn to them. Jesus, the Light of the world, brings the light with him wherever he goes. When we trust him, the darkness of anxiety and despair gives way to a brilliant dawn of understanding. Jesus' presence is always like that.

Prayer: *Dear God, help us to meet each new day with the certainty that Jesus will illuminate our understanding if we open our eyes and our hearts to him. Amen.*

Sunday, May 3   Read John 21:15-19.

These verses relate the commissioning of Peter. Jesus first asked whether Peter loved him more than these. Not knowing what the antecedent of "these" is, we can only speculate that Jesus would not pit the disciples against one another. More likely, "these" meant the ways of the world and the life from which Peter had been called and to which he may have temporarily returned following the crucifixion. Repetition of the question of Peter's love for Jesus parallels Peter's three denials of his Lord.

Does it not seem likely that Peter was here being reinstated as the leader of the disciples? From that moment, Peter's vocation as a commercial fisherman was behind him and a new life was awaiting him.

Jesus suggested to Peter that his new responsibilities would not be easy; perhaps he was actually foretelling Peter's death as a martyr. But in response to Christ's charge to "follow me," Peter did become a shepherd, leading first a small community of believers and ultimately the whole of a growing church. The care of the flock is still the responsibility of Christian pastors and congregations everywhere.

Finding reasons to criticize the church can be easy. Its blemishes and imperfections are not hard to find. It sometimes exhibits cumbersome internal dissensions over things far less essential than loving God and feeding the "lambs." Yet we might all be helped to see the church in a more positive light if we were to seriously examine some of the historic contributions of the church as it fashioned, among other things, contours of moral worth in Western civilization.

Prayer: *Lord Jesus, help us to comprehend the full meaning of this noble commission and to become more active partners with you in feeding the lambs. Amen.*

May 4-10, 1992   **Joe A. Harding†**
Monday, May 4   Read Acts 13:15-16, 26-33.

Some amazing words were spoken to Paul and Barnabas in a synagogue at Antioch. After the readings from the Law and the prophets, the rulers of the synagogue said, "If you have any word of exhortation for the people, give it."

Consider this invitation. No doubt critics were in the congregation. Yet there were also receptive people present. It was customary to invite visiting Jews to comment on the scriptures. The leaders asked for any word of exhortation. The invitation could be heard as a request for some authentic, helpful word from God: "If you have it, say it!"—don't keep it; share it!

Exhortation is not moralisms or good advice; rather, it is a word that strengthens and gives hope and courage. The word translated "exhortation" (*paraklēsis*) is related to the word which John uses in the fourth Gospel for the Holy Spirit, *paraklētos*. *Paraklētos* means one who stands beside another to assist or encourage. The invitation Paul receives is this: "If you have any word of encouragement for the people, give it."

One of the great tasks of the church today is proclaiming an authentic word of encouragement. Most people already know what it is to have their dreams and ideals laughed at, their hopes dashed, and their self-esteem shattered. The real need is for some word that will lift the sagging spirit and the downcast heart.

Prayer: *O God, I give thanks for words that strengthen and empower your people. Give me courage and joy to speak them with conviction and hope. Amen.*

---

†Director, Evangelism and Church Growth, General Board of Discipleship of The United Methodist Church; resident, Richland, Washington.

Tuesday, May 5   Read Acts 13:16-32.

Paul was given an amazing opportunity: "If you have any word of exhortation for the people, give it!" He began by reminding the people of God's mighty acts: God made the people great during their stay in Egypt and bore them in the wilderness. God gave them judges and prophets, raised up David, and promised a Savior of David's posterity. God's mighty acts were not ended. Paul announced, "To us has been sent the message of this salvation." Salvation, *sōtēria*, means deliverance, to bring safely through. This is a recurring theme in Paul's message.

His conclusion was breathtaking, "And we bring you the good news that what God promised to our ancestors he has fulfilled for us, their children, by raising Jesus." Paul announces fulfillment, demonstrated and celebrated in the resurrection of Jesus.

This is the heart of the New Testament message. Already the word *eu-aggelion* (good news) was familiar to readers. It suggests news so powerful, so awesome in its content, that it forever makes a difference in the hearer.

Visualize Paul as he says, "We bring you the good news. . . ." Studies in communication indicate that the content of the messages we share with each other is only 7 percent verbal. Thirty-eight percent of meaning is carried by tone of voice. Fifty-five percent is relayed by body language such as posture and facial expression.

What is the nonverbal message every speaker also sends? What is the tone and body language of the congregation? Is it congruent with the good news?

Prayer: *I give thanks, loving God, for a message that is authentic good news. Make my whole being alive with the joy of your life-transforming word. Amen.*

Wednesday, May 6   Read Psalm 23.

Paul concluded his brief summary of Israel's experience of God's saving action in history by saying, "To us has been sent the message of this salvation" (Acts 13:26). Sōtēria, the word translated "salvation," suggests rescue from life-threatening danger. *Sōtēria* could mean healing from illness, a safe return home, release from fear of death—all images suggested by Psalm 23. Its effect is summed up in the psalmist's words, "I will fear no evil: for thou art with me" (KJV).

Sōtēria is not gained by secret knowledge (Gnosticism), by participation in secret rituals (Mystery Religion), or by obedience to the law (Judaism). Rather, *sōtēria* comes in receiving God's message by faith. That message is that God has acted in Israel's history and in the resurrection of Jesus Christ to deliver us from every enemy that could destroy us. This news about what God has done is the *eu-aggelion,* the good news. This message thus fulfills the shepherd's psalm and leads to the bold affirmation, "Thou art with me."

Years ago I watched a Palestinian shepherd lead his flock to a quiet stream. He spoke to his sheep, no doubt calling them by name. They followed confidently and drank freely. In those brief moments it was as if the scripture had come alive before me. My camera caught a beautiful picture. And something profound was recorded at a far deeper level within me.

Take a moment to become very quiet. Imagine yourself by the still water . . . in the presence of the Good Shepherd. Sense the deep meaning of freedom from fear and anxiety.

Prayer: *I give thanks, O God, for your presence which releases me from fear and guilt and despair. Give me courage to live and to share this good news. In Jesus' name. Amen.*

Thursday, May 7   Read John 10:22-30.

Readers of John 10 have identified Jesus with the shepherd described in Psalm 23. Jesus' words, "I am the good shepherd," and, "The good shepherd lays down his life for the sheep" (v. 11) confront us with the costliness of the shepherding mission. Verses 22-30 reveal Jesus' effectiveness as the Good Shepherd. Notice the confident assertion, "They will listen to my voice" (v. 16).

From deep within us comes the recognition that Christ's voice is authentic. We choose to follow because we understand not just the words but the tone of compassion. The one who speaks is no hireling. Jesus is not distracted, intimidated, or overwhelmed. He alone is able to confidently say, "No one shall snatch them out of my hand."

This indeed is *eu-aggelion,* good news! It is the church which has the message of hope. It is the church that can say to confused, scattered, and broken people, "We bring you the good news that God has promised" (Acts 13:32, AP).

Notice particularly the great goal of the shepherd. It is as if we see a lone shepherd on a hillside looking into the distance as Jesus says, "I have other sheep that do not belong to this fold. I must bring them also, and they will listen to my voice. So there shall be one flock, one shepherd" (John 10:16).

Prayer: *Create in us anew, O Lord, a sense of awe and excitement and urgency as we realize the privilege that is ours to share the best news ever to be communicated on planet Earth. Let the power of the message transform us and, through us, touch the world you love. In Jesus' name. Amen.*

Friday, May 8 Read Revelation 7:9-17.

The good news (*eu-aggelion*) is grounded not in human accomplishment but in God's mighty deeds. And the great deed which far surpasses all God's other acts is the resurrection of Jesus. Revelation 7 depicts the universal response to God's victory of salvation. A great multitude beyond number, from all peoples, tribes and tongues, stands before the throne of God with the Lamb, crying out, "Salvation belongs to our God who is seated on the throne, and to the Lamb!"

The church that shares the *eu-aggelion* is to move forward in the world without losing the vision of God's victory. Its dreams, purpose, program, and strategies are informed, above all, by this vision. Response to *eu-aggelion* is worship which transcends every barrier and affirms victorious faith. It is worship that rejects every idol and bows only before God. It is worship that transcends time and space, that lifts and transforms the worshiper. Such worship affirms, "For the Lamb at the center of the throne will be their shepherd." It is worship that praises in words beyond words, "Blessing and glory and wisdom and thanksgiving and honor and power and might be to our God forever and ever!" Such worship enables the church to convey the *eu-aggelion,* to stand in awe before the incredible truth, "To us the message of this salvation has been sent" (Acts 13:26).

Prayer: *O God, let our prayers and praise unite with the great company of the faithful. Inspire and transform us. Empower us by your spirit that we may share the good news with such hope and confidence that those we meet may come to praise and serve you as the living God. In Jesus' name. Amen.*

Saturday, May 9   Read Revelation 7:9-12.

There is something thrilling about a vision of the future that sees all peoples brought together in a fellowship that transcends every obstacle and barrier that has separated them. That is the exciting picture which John shares with a persecuted and discouraged church. He described a great multitude, "that no one could count, from every nation, from all tribes and peoples and languages" standing before the throne and before the Lamb. The focus is upon the living God who acts in saving power in Jesus Christ. All voices are brought together in praise and worship.

Places in the Heart is a film that concludes with an unforgettable scene of people from a bitterly divided community brought together in worship. As they share in Holy Communion, they are transformed by a love greater than human hatreds. Such a vision of the future inspires new confidence in facing problems that could be overwhelming. Such a vision becomes real in the here and now as we grasp the mystery and wonder of the good news.

Reread today's lesson. Take a few deep breaths, relax, and imagine the scene described by John. Notice the faces of the people. Listen to the song of praise. Visualize yourself relaxed and radiant, joining in the chorus of praise. See yourself with a white robe and palm branch, saying with a loud voice, "Salvation belongs to our God . . . and to the Lamb!"

Prayer: *O Lord, give us such a vision of that which is not yet that we take new courage for the task that can be accomplished by your power here and now. In Jesus' name. Amen.*

Sunday, May 10   Read Revelation 7:13-17.

The details of this picture are important. Look again at the scene described in Revelation 7:9-17. Notice not only the diversity of the gathering nations and tribes but also the unity. All attention is upon the throne of God. They "worship him day and night." All wear white robes and carry palm branches, not black robes with gavels. They wear the garments and carry the signs of victory, not of judgment. The image is of an exciting victory celebration.

Then the description moves away from the crowd as John observes, "For the Lamb at the center of the throne will be their shepherd." Clearly, the victory of faith is not a fleeting celebration that is soon ended. Because the Victor is no conquering general but rather the Good Shepherd, not just the present moment but also the future is assured. No sorrow can overwhelm. "God will wipe away every tear from their eyes." No fear of abandonment can terrify. The future offers continued renewal and hope, for the Good Shepherd "will guide them to springs of the water of life.

Again take a few minutes to become very quiet. Relax and breathe deeply. Focus on the face of the Shepherd. Visualize yourself drinking deeply from the springs of the water of life. Experience the empowerment and renewed faith God wills for your life. Are there tears to be shed? Don't be afraid to shed them. For "God will wipe away every tear from their eyes."

Arise now—comforted, strengthened, and inspired.

Prayer: *Thank you, O God, for the power of the vision of faith. I lift my voice and join the song of hope:*

> *Thanksgiving and honor*
> *and power and might*
> *be to our God forever and ever! Amen.*
>   Revelation 7:12

TRUST THE BASIC DESIGN

May 11-17, 1992   **Folke T. Olofsson†**
Monday, May 11   Read Psalm 145:13*b*-21.

The reading for today is the latter part of an alphabetic psalm. In the Hebrew original every letter from the *aleph* to the *tau* opens a verse of praise and thanksgiving to the Lord.

The sounds of nature praise the Maker: the quiet rain, the roaring sea, the song of the mockingbird at dawn. More than sounds were given to those created in God's image and likeness. God gave to humans God's word. The world is intelligible and utterable because it has a Creator. As God's creation, we know something about our Maker. We have the Word in common. In praise and prayer we return our words to our Creator.

Missing from the Hebrew, but preserved in most versions, is this: "Always true to his promises Yahweh shows love in all he does" (JB). We image God as having an ear, a hand, a heart. God is a listening God, a helping and loving God. Such is God's eternal dominion, and God's kingdom that lasts from age to age.

In praising the Lord we fulfill that for which we were created, giving the glory to God. Through praise we enter into the reign of God, founded on God's promises, wrought out through God's bleeding love, realized in the consummation: the new creation.

Sounds and words praise the Lord, who through the divine Word made the worlds. Praise is the warp and woof of life. Trust the basic design!

Prayer: *We praise you, . . . we worship you, we glorify you, we give thanks to you for your great glory, O Lord God, heavenly King.* * *Amen.*

---

†Priest in the Church of Sweden, rector of Rasbo; docent in theological and ideological studies at Uppsala University, Uppsala, Sweden.
*From the *Gloria in excelsis.*

Tuesday, May 12   Read Acts 14:8-13.

"The gods have become like men and have come down to us!" (TEV) No wonder the startled crowds wanted to offer sacrifices to Paul and Barnabas! Before their very eyes a lame man had been healed. That is exactly what one expects from gods: a vindication of the basic design.

The man lame from birth embodied the thwarted design. Being unable to walk, he reminded everybody of what life should and should not be. He recognized in the words of the apostles the Word of love and power, reflecting the love that stands behind, sustains, and fights for the basic design. He trusted the Word and was healed.

The crowds rightly gave the event a religious interpretation. Yet, they needed the apostolic preaching and teaching to reveal the real significance of what happened. They mistook the messenger for the One who sent the message. They did not plumb deeply enough. They did not see the Giver for the gift.

Religion without revelation ends in worshiping idols made by humans. The good news leads to the adoration of Jesus Christ, true man and true God. What the crowds in Lystra marveled at, shouting in their Lycaonian language—"gods" coming into their midst— God had already done once and for all: the Word was made flesh in Jesus Christ. Trust the basic design!

Prayer: *God, you did what we cried for but could not believe: you came down to us and became one of us. Immanuel, we praise your healing presence and your holy name! Amen.*

Wednesday, May 13   Read Acts 14:14-18.

A wonder-full event had taken place, and praise belonged to someone. But the crowd's enthusiasm is met by the apostles' horror. Sacrificing to men! "Turn from these empty idols to the living God who made sky and earth and the sea and all that these hold" (JB).

Paul and Barnabas pointed away from themselves to God. They wanted the people to see through them in order that the people might see the One who worked through Paul and Barnabas: the living and life-giving God.

Not creation, but the Creator, is to be worshiped. This Creator may be unrecognized, but not unknown. Nor is the Creator far away. The whole creation abounds with evidence and proofs for those who are willing to see. There is a basic design: seasons come and go, sunshine follows rain, crops grow for the harvest-time while people are sleeping, food is on the table, and fellowship thrives around it. There is a gladness of heart—the joy of being alive.

Our joy at life is a reflection of God's joy of giving life. Out of the spring of divine love, life gushes forth.

The crowds wanted to sacrifice to men whom they believed to be gods. Sacrifice is the human's meet response to the One who gives life. Yet, the ultimate sacrifice has already been made by God's very self: Jesus, the Son of God and the son of Mary. "It is finished!" (John 19:30) Trust the basic design!

Prayer: *God of life, God of love, God of joy, with all your creatures we praise and worship you, offering our lives to you as you offered yourself to us in Christ. Amen.*

Thursday, May 14   Read John 13:31-33.

Someone has left the communion and gone out in the dark. Judas is not the first one. Long before Judas's going away, there is this mysterious departure. Tradition tells us of Satan's fall from the heavenly communion, a departure which lies behind all the betrayals, all the schemes to kill and destroy, all the fixed trials, all the handing over of innocents to death (see v. 27). Someone broke the original communion. Someone wanted to live for himself, seeking only his own glory. There is an enemy and his works.

How can the Son of Man be glorified in this moment and God be glorified in him? In the Old Testament God's glory killed those who came too close. In the New Testament the glory of God is revealed *in the opposite*; the eternal Word of God now resounds in the whimper of a newborn baby. God's glory is far from being glorious. It is the glory of the homeless couple, of the stable, of the exile, of the silent years, of the rejection by the people, of the desertion by the disciples, of the darkness at noon; it is the glory of the cross.

How can I trust the basic design, seeing what I see in myself and everywhere around me: an abyss of darkness and evil?

Another has gone out in the dark outside the camp and borne it all, once and for all. There is no place where Christ has not been; there is no time where he was not. He went out to be present to all. God's absence is only temporary. Trust the basic design!

Prayer: *Lord Jesus, you have gone out in the dark to vindicate the will of God for all things created. I trust you, and I wait for the hour of glorification. Amen.*

Friday, May 15   Read John 13:34-35.

What Christ said and did his last evening with his disciples showed his love for them. By washing their feet he was their servant. In the meal he shared with them he gave himself.

Love is at the heart of life. Sometimes this is very hard to believe. God knows it. Therefore, the glorification of God in Christ starts from beneath and turns all upside down. In the outstretched arms and the open hands on the cross God becomes most visible. And yet, there is no place where God is so utterly hidden. This is the foolishness and wisdom of God: in the execution of a "politically dangerous" religious outcast, the promises of God are fulfilled and the love of God has become manifest: I AM WHO I AM and I AM THERE (see Exod. 2:14).

"Love one another, even as I have loved you." Here is the pattern: the basic design in the process of restoration. The Word through whom all things were made, visible and invisible, cries with all those who are suffering and are forsaken: "My God, my God why have you deserted me?" (Matt. 27:46, JB) The Word who became flesh now prays, "Father, forgive them" (Luke 23:34). The Eternal Word who cried as a helpless baby now calls out, "It is finished!" And the source of all is love: "Love one another, even as I have loved you." Love makes God visible. All is encompassed in love. Trust the basic design!

Prayer: *Everloving God, there is so little love in me for you, for my brothers and sisters in Christ, for my neighbor, and for myself. Cleanse my heart through the precious blood of your Son, Jesus Christ, my Savior, and fill it with your love. Come Holy Ghost, giver of life and love! Amen.*

Saturday, May 16   Read Revelation 21:1-6.

"Don't cry! Everything is going to be all right!" With these words we try to comfort the little child who has fallen. With words like these we try to hearten afflicted friends. Are they just verbal bandages or hollow phrases which we all know, unfortunately, to be untrue? No. They spring from the basic design of life. There is a trust within us that will never let itself be uprooted. There is a trust that all will be well in the end, a trust that nobody or nothing can annihilate.

This trust comes from a presence. God's holy name, the unspeakable, which we render I AM WHO I AM, also means I AM HERE. Yes, it is God's presence which is the ground and source of all trust. As God is present in pain, failure, and shame in all the places and times of crosses, so God is present at the end. As God was present in the Tent during the walk in the wilderness, as God was present in Mary's body when she was pregnant with Jesus, as God is present in the Body, the Church, so God will be present as the ultimate One in the redeemed and renewed creation. It is all over, and yet it has just begun.

God is there. God is here. God's pierced hand is open to wipe away all bitter tears. Don't cry! It's going to be all right! Trust the basic design!

Prayer: *Almighty God, your will shall be done on earth as it is in heaven. Nothing can take away our trust and our hope, for you are the Lord of the future and of all. We praise your saving presence and we magnify your holy name. Amen.*

Sunday, May 17   Read Revelation 21:5-8.

"It is finished!" (John 19:30, KJV) These are the words of a king. The notice nailed to the cross with him told the truth (see Matthew 27:37). The cross is the throne where God's glory becomes manifest. The crucified king is the victor and consummator. Far from telling that the failure now is total, his words proclaim: the *eschaton* (the end time) is here. The final word has been spoken; the ultimate deed has been done. What has already happened makes all the difference in the end.

"Behold, I make all things new!" (KJV) "It is finished!" What Jesus accomplished on the cross is now being manifested in the whole cosmos. There is no newness for novelty's own sake. It is a newness of quality. The creation has become what God wanted it to be: resurrected into eternal life.

The beginning and the end are contained in Christ. So are all the life stories of humankind between the *alpha* and the *omega*. Everyone will confront the final Word: God's yes and God's no, eternal life or the second death. Yet, he who sits on the throne still wears the marks of the cross. They will remain forever. Pierced hands do not strike.

Many things will come to an end, but our thirst for life never ends. God made us so. God gives us the drink we thirst for: God's very Self! Be true to your thirst! Trust the basic design!

Prayer: *Glory be to the Father and to the Son and to the Holy Ghost; as it was in the beginning, is now, and ever shall be, world without end. Amen.*

May 18-24, 1992   **Bill Cotton**†
Monday, May 18   Read Acts 15:1-2, 22-26.

The story of the church is the story of a people who experienced the saving vision of Christ's freedom only to have the vision muddled, and sometimes distorted, in each generation. How are we to keep the vision clear?

The conference in Jerusalem had a major issue to clarify: Are these new Christians (Gentile males) acceptable without undergoing the rite of circumcision? Do they need some sign to prove their faith? Because of disciples like Paul and Barnabas, the church was able to keep its basic foundation stone in place: namely, we will be saved through the "grace of the Lord Jesus Christ" (v. 11). Outward signs are valuable, but they are not necessary for salvation.

In the life of the church, we seem always to be trying to "divide the camp" into the good and the best. Jewish Christians who were there felt a bit superior to those Gentile "come-lately" Christians. This is an example of how the community has struggled with pride and sin. Paul's letters reveal that he spent much time trying to expunge the issue of whose faith experience is best. From its beginnings the church has been a mixture of sin and grace.

So often people look for a "proper reason" to exclude others from the community. Paul and Barnabas fought hard battles for the sake of an inclusive church based on faith. I wonder who is willing to take up that fight in the new church that the Spirit is building in our time.

Prayer: *Dear God, let your church be open and freeing because we have experienced the vision of Jesus the Christ. Amen.*

---

†Senior minister, Grace United Methodist Church, Des Moines, Iowa.

Tuesday, May 19   Read Acts 15:27-29.

It has seemed good to the Holy Spirit and us.

In the early church, change was a process of seeking discernment by the Holy Spirit. Luke's writings demonstrate for us that no part of the Christian life can escape the necessity of being guided by the Holy Spirit.

The historical issue in Acts 15 was whether a person must first become a Jew in order to be a Christian. But Jesus Christ opened up a new possibility for faith that negates the need to *prove* one's faithfulness with outward signs. The verdict is given with the preface "It has seemed good to the Holy Spirit and us. . . ." To determine that the new male Gentile Christians would not need to undergo the rite of circumcision was a radical shift. By the power of the Holy Spirit the young church gradually moved from burdensome nonessentials to develop a central core of faith. The Holy Spirit lively in our midst creating dialogue enables the church in every age to be freed from burdensome custom and thereby to be available to love.

At a congregational meeting a heated discussion was raging around a matter of great concern. At the point when polarization threatened, a member asked, "Can we stop this discussion and read the scripture and pray silently for five or ten minutes? I believe it might help." Ten minutes later the same group of people was able to resolve the conflict. The Holy Spirit invited into that meeting gave power to think, speak, and act in love. The Holy Spirit lively in our midst converts our bias, opens closed minds, and moves us out to break new ground.

Prayer: *Dear God, by the power of your spirit, guide us away from all things that would hinder love. Come and meet with us to disarm our fears so that we might be free to act. Amen.*

Wednesday, May 20   Read Psalm 67:1-4.

The Lord bless you and keep you; the Lord make his face to shine upon you, . . . and give you peace (Num. 6:24-26).

These words were learned on Sunday evenings in youth friendship circles. In that prayer we grew and matured. Last Sunday after youth fellowship in our church, the youth recited this same prayer and then exuberantly left to go home. I was reminded again of the value of the tradition of the church.

Today when I hear these words of blessing, I think of my teen years and those first experiences within the saving community. Spiritual formation begins simply. Someone repeats words they heard and remembered that were passed down to them by a previous generation. These words faithfully recalled, repeated, and interpreted within a context of love form the cradle for faith. The words get into our heads and hearts; when we need them most, they can be recalled and reclaimed. Through those words, God's word is experienced and believed.

Tradition is the way one generation connects with the next. Prayers and formula learned in youth become the skeleton for later mature faith. Adolescence can be a time when God touches us in ways that may be forgotten for a season but reclaimed as we reach maturity. A sign of these uprooted times is the street youth, who have not been gathered by the church. Most of these youth have not heard the stories that create faith.

To gather the young to "tell the old, old story"* within a context of love is still the work of the church. Those of us who value the future will do well to teach young people prayer and the story of God's love.

Prayer: *Dear God, put into our hearts your living word that we might create a future from the past. Amen.*

---

*From the hymn "I Love to Tell the Story" by Katherine Hankey.

Thursday, May 21   Read Psalm 67.

God, our God, has blessed us. May God continue to bless us; let all the ends of the earth revere [God.]

Why would the lectionary serve up a Thanksgiving psalm in May? The psalmist knew that thanksgiving is rooted not in the harvest of nature but in the discovery that God is at the heart of everything. So in all times and all seasons it is a good thing to praise God. The psalmist also has a way of ruining a comfortable psalm by putting in the words "let all the ends of the earth fear God." The NRSV softened the phrase by substituting *revere*. Either word will do, because the Hebrew word *yirah* means both fear and awe. Our concept of fear is a product of ego-centered faith. The biblical sense of awe (fear of God), however, means that we stand out of our fears and allow wonder to invade our being. A sense of awe is a sign of the love of Christ in one's life that drives out all fears. Awe is also the gift of God that creates a grateful heart.

"Let the peoples praise you, O God; . . . Let the nations be glad and sing for joy." The nation that is able to sing for joy and praise God is a nation that has rediscovered what is forgotten in every age, that God is the ruler of the nations. The psalmist always teaches the nations a proper sense of respect. This psalm announces that God guides the nations. We are part of a community of nations. To sing the psalms is to be connected with that part of the tradition that saves us from nationalism.

Prayer: *Dear God, remove our anxious care that we might love you and magnify your holy name. Amen.*

Friday, May 22   Read John 14:27-29.

Peace I leave with you; my peace I give to you . . . not . . . as the world gives.

John 14 is often associated with death. With this chapter we bury the dead. As I read the words I smell carnations and see fake green grass covering a freshly dug grave. And I fear that the word of peace offered in these lines is too much associated with the cemetery. North American culture defines peace as tranquility, calm, peace of mind, quiet, harmony, conformity, armistice, pacification. These are forms of peace that the world gives. Surely there is a peace different from these.

The church in the power of the Holy Spirit has been called to be God's instrument for peace. Too often we interpret peace as the quiet calm of the cemetery. At times I think that we have become the church at rest, a monumental church. The peace that Christ gives grows out of passion and struggle, pain and growth. The very word *shalom* means "all of the fullness of life." The church as an instrument of peace ought to have great vitality and a sense of powerful presence in it. To mix metaphors a bit, perhaps we ought to define peace like a river. Rivers that appear calm are usually deep. The river shines and sparkles in the sun and sings its way along; but the river is also unpredictable, sometimes raging but lifegiving.

The peace of Christ is not the absence of struggle. There surely will come a time when the church will be the church at rest, but in the meantime we are to be God's lively instrument of peace that will challenge the powers and make this old world less afraid.

Prayer: *Dear God, we ask for peace that only you can give. Give to each of us all of the fullness of life. Amen.*

Saturday, May 23   Read John 14:22-26.

We will come to them and make our home with them.

John 14 is part of the farewell discourses. Jesus is going away. How will the faithful survive the absence of Jesus? Collective memory is not enough. Memory fades. Everything moves into the past and is finally forgotten and lost. John provides an answer: "Those who love me will keep my word, and my Father will love them, and we will . . . make our home with them."

Each first day the community of the faithful does something that the world has never understood. We gather some people, break some bread, tell an old story as best we can, and in the process One comes to dwell in the midst of us, making it possible for us to be sent forth to love again. Those who love Jesus and keep his word will not need to rely upon memory. In the act of being the church, God's presence is with us. By the power of the Holy Spirit Jesus is our contemporary on the journey.

Each Tuesday at 5:15 p.m. I go to a covenant group meeting. Six of us gather to share each other's progress in faith and to invite the Holy Spirit to make a dwelling place among us. Members of the group often speak of promptings of the Spirit that they have felt during the week. One member was moved last year to help a neighborhood develop a project for the homeless. Others in the group have found ways to organize their time better. Some are paying greater attention to family. The group was formed out of our common hunger to find a way for God to make God's home with us. John 14 reverberates Jesus' promise that when two or three of us gather in Jesus' name, God will come to us (Matt. 18:20).

Prayer: *Dear God, come and fill this empty place within us that only you can fill. Amen.*

Sunday, May 24   Read Revelation 21:10, 22-27.

And in the spirit he carried me away.

Revelation often can be described only in metaphorical language. How else does one describe the final Christian hope in words that will benefit faith? So John pictures God and the slain but victorious Lamb, who will finally remove all darkness from our lives. In that bright city there will be no temple. God the Almighty and the Lamb have become all in all. Whether we experience this scripture as something realized in our lives daily or find ourselves among those who wait for the victorious time, the word is clear: God in Christ has become all in all.

John is preaching the Easter faith to us in cosmic dimensions. There is no vision to come. God is all in all right now. When the church lost interest in the doctrine of the Holy Spirit, the vision of God as One who is all in all got pushed into a "someday you will know" future. The church caught up in the power of the Holy Spirit knows that the time of God's reign is always now. Nations and kings are to be called to judgment now. If the Lamb has a book, it is open now. If falsehood and abomination are to be cast out, now is the time. Without a lively sense of the Holy Spirit, Easter faith is stillborn and we are left only to speculate about a time when God will even the score.

People reading this text disagree on whether it refers to now or to a future time. Both positions can be found within the tradition. However, the church caught up in the power of the Holy Spirit is always *already* experiencing both the judgment and mercy of God. John experienced God as all in all for his time. My hope is that as we read John's text it will enable each of us, in every age, to experience the fullness of God.

Prayer: *Lord God, catch us up in a vision that we might know that today is the day for our judgment and our salvation through Christ our Lord. Amen.*

SOMETHING'S HAPPENING!

May 25-31, 1992   **Deborah K. Cronin†**
Monday, May 25   Read Psalm 97:1-6.

It's happening! Heaven is proclaiming God's righteousness.

I am always surprised to discover that some pastors don't preach from the Psalms. Perhaps they don't know that the Book of Psalms is a rich biblical treasury which both helps us understand the nature of God and contributes to our understanding of the human relationship to God. Psalm 97 is a great "preaching psalm."

Psalm 97:1 calls us to worship. Verses 2-6 describe the appearance of God. The first part of verse 2 is reminiscent of the Sinai appearance ("clouds and thick darkness") while the second part reminds us that righteousness and justice are the building blocks of God's sovereignty. Righteousness (*sedeq*) is God's plan of salvation for humanity. *This* is what is "right" about God!

Those who are uncomfortable with the language of violence may find themselves uncomfortable with verse 3. Here God is depicted as fire-bombing his enemies. The stupendous power of God is revealed in verses 4 and 5. God is so powerful that earth trembles and the mountains melt in God's presence. Verse 6 tells us that not only the earth but heaven as well proclaim God's righteousness and the peoples behold God's glory. Thus, the first part of this psalm reveals that God is both formidable and fair-minded.

Prayer: *Holy God, help me remember that your capacity to destroy evil is matched by your capacity to rule with righteousness and justice. Amen.*

---

†Pastor; Executive Director of the Western Small Church Rural Life Center, Filer, Idaho; clergy member of the Western New York Annual Conference, The United Methodist Church.

Tuesday, May 26   Read Psalm 97:7-12.

It's happening! Light is dawning for the righteous.

The second half of Psalm 97 continues to explore God's relationship to people. Verse 7 tells us that God is superior to all gods and, therefore, worthy of our trust. Verses 10 and 11 are perfect examples of the exquisite, meaningful poetry of the Psalms. Verse 10 tells us that the Lord

—loves those who hate evil.
—guards the lives of the faithful.
—rescues them from the hand of the wicked.

Verse 11 tells us that

Light dawns for the righteous,
and joy for the upright of heart.

There is a cause and effect relationship between verses 10 and 11. Because of what God does for those who love God, their response is one of spiritual insight and joy! The irony of Psalm 97 is that though we live in a world of evil, we cope because of the promise of God's love, guarding, and rescue. Verse 12 closes the psalm with an invitation to rejoice and to give thanks to God.

Prayer: *Thanks be to God for the witness of the psalmist who tells us the truth about God and calls us to believe that truth. Amen.*

Suggestion for meditation: *Reflect on a time in your life when God has proved worthy of your trust. How does the memory of this event reinforce your faith today?*

Wednesday, May 27   Read Acts 16:16-18.

It's happening! God's message is setting people free!

The background for this passage is the response of the missionaries Paul and Silas to the call to come to Macedonia (Acts 16:6-10). In years past the United States sent missionaries to many lands. However, today in the United States we are beginning to receive missionaries from other countries such as South Korea. Missionaries, wherever they go, are those who have responded, as did Paul and Silas, to a call to come and witness.

The man who appeared in Paul's vision pleaded and said, "Come over to Macedonia and help us" (v. 9). By "us," he evidently meant to include women, because upon arriving in Philippi, a city in the district of Macedonia, Paul and Silas encounter two women. The first is Lydia, a cloth trader of means. Lydia receives the gospel and, in turn, introduces her household to the message which Paul and Silas have shared with her.

The second woman the missionaries encounter is a young girl possessed by a soothsaying spirit. Even though the spirit correctly identifies Paul and Silas to the crowd as God's messengers, the spirit is a nuisance and greatly annoys Paul. This causes Paul to cast the spirit out of the girl in the name of Jesus Christ.

From what false spirits can the missionaries coming to us today help free us?

Prayer: *Help me be open, God, to your servants who come to free me from those false spirits which seek to possess my will and my life. Amen.*

Thursday, May 28   Read Acts 16:19-34.

It's happening! God's power to save and rescue is present!

I once served two churches that were located near three state prisons, including Attica Prison in New York. While serving these churches I came to know prison guards and workers as people whose jobs are incredibly difficult. I remember one prison supervisor who told me that only a daily miracle keeps the prisoners from taking control of the prison away from the guards. Prison work takes an emotional, physical, and spiritual toll on these people. Both the staff and the prisoners are victims of the penal system. The high stress endured by prison guards often causes them to suffer from health problems, family tensions, and spiritual doubts. The memories of what I learned from those guards haunts me as I watch more and more prisons being built across the rural sectors of this country.

The story of Paul and Silas and their imprisonment overflows with images of divine protection which results in salvation breaking into a seemingly hopeless situation. The result is not just the rescue of Paul and Silas, but the salvation of the jail-keeper and his family. God's outrageous power to save in unexpected places and ways is revealed in this story. Do we believe today that the gospel has this kind of power?

Prayer: *God, it sometimes seems that this world is full of hopeless situations. We seek world peace while conflicts continue around the globe; we worry about the environment while threats to our planet seem to grow each day; the homeless and hungry are still with us; men and women still languish in prison. We sometimes feel discouraged and powerless. Rescue us, the way you rescued Paul and Silas and their jailer. And help us trust your power so that we might rescue others in your name. Amen.*

Friday, May 29   Read John 17:20-26.

It's happening! We are held within God's love!

Several themes run through this passage. Jesus, like any caring spiritual leader, prays for his disciples. But there is more. We should not overlook the use of the word *in*. In the New Testament Greek the word is *en* and, in this context, translates better as "within." (Thus, we believe "within" the love of God.) The word runs through the passage like a golden thread through a beautiful tapestry.

verse 20—The relationship of the disciples to Jesus is not an external one. Their belief exists within the power and majesty of the risen Christ.

verse 21—Jesus and his heavenly Father dwell within each other. Jesus' prayer is that his disciples might have the same indwelling relationship with the Father and with Jesus himself.

verse 23—The in-dwelling presence is not just for the fellowship of the believers, Jesus, and the Father. The purpose of the in-dwelling is to reveal God's sending of Jesus and God's love for the world's people.

verse 26—The purpose of the in-dwelling presence goes beyond the acquisition of knowledge about God's name to the love of God being shared with those who believe.

Prayer: *Your love, O God, is the golden thread in the tapestry of our lives. Help us to share that love with your people. Amen.*

Suggestion for meditation: *Meditate on being within the love of Jesus and God. How does this transform your life and living?*

Saturday, May 30   Read Revelation 22:12-14, 16-17.

It's happening! Jesus is coming soon!

It's easy to forget that the Book of Revelation was a real letter written to real people in real churches in the first century. This passage begins with the promise of the Risen Christ, "I am coming soon." This word of assurance was comforting to the oppressed people of the first century, even as it is comforting to us today. We do not know what is meant by the word *soon*. (Jesus said, "It is not for you to know the times or periods that the Father has set by his own authority," Acts 1:7.) But we are sure that the Risen Christ will come again.

"Those who wash their robes" is a reference to those who wash themselves in the atoning blood of the Lamb. Their blessing is twofold: they shall have access to the tree of life, and they will be allowed to enter Zion.

The passage is rich in Revelation's symbolic language. Jesus is the "bright morning star," the powerful symbol of God's new day.

> O Morning Star, how fair and bright
> thou beamest forth in truth and light,
> O Sovereign meek and lowly!*

We, and everyone else who reads or hears these words, are invited to drink the water which represents salvation.

How soon is *soon*? Only a Christian life lived with expectancy and disciplined urgency will enable us to answer that.

Prayer: *God, I can wait patiently, but I am thirsty. Give me the water of life. Thank you. Amen.*

---

*From the hymn "O Morning Star, How Fair and Bright" by Phillip Nicolai, trans. by Catherine Winkworth.

Sunday, May 31   Read Revelation 22:20.

It's happening! The day of judgment approaches.

This passage begins with the same promise which began yesterday's text: "I am coming soon." The words *Come, Lord Jesus* (*marana tha* in Aramaic, Jesus' native language) formed an early Christian prayer. But this prayer was not just for the early Christians. It is a prayer for all times and occasions, including our own.

It is important to remember that the first Christians prayed this prayer to a Lord they understood to be risen from the dead. The Apostles' Creed, written by the first followers of the risen Christ, proclaims:

I believe in Jesus Christ . . .
[who] was crucified, died, and was buried;
he descended to the dead.
On the third day he rose again;
he ascended into heaven,
is seated at the right hand of the Father,
and will come again to judge the living and the dead.

Christ's coming will be a time of judgment for all people, including the faithful and good (v. 14) and the unfaithful and evil (v. 15). *Marana tha! Come, Lord Jesus!*

As we join with the early Christians who prayed these words, we should be aware of what we are praying for. In other words, be careful what you pray for. You may get it!

Prayer: *Come, Lord Jesus, to my birth. Come, Lord Jesus, to my living. Come, Lord Jesus, to my dying. Come, Lord Jesus, and give me the peace which only you can give. Amen.*

THE FORMING POWER OF THE SPIRIT

June 1-7, 1992   **Ronald S. James†**
Monday, June 1   Read Genesis 11:1-9.

From confusion to community

It is not an accident that the confusion of tongues at Babel immediately precedes the calling of Abram in Chaldea. Apparently ancient tribes migrated to a rich and fertile plain, settled down, merged into a nationality, and began to construct a civilization. Pride in their power, a desire for fame, the hunger to be great—these passions led them to build "a tower with its top in the heavens." This many-tiered pyramid, this ziggurat with its shrine at the top, is a monument to human ingenuity, affluence, and force. "Nothing can stop us; even God is within our control!" It is the penetrating judgment of the writer of Genesis that this kind of arrogant pride, this self-reliance unbounded by humility, is rebellion against God. The attitudes at Babel can result only in division within the human family. To that fact our interminable wars bear awful testimony.

Pentecost, with its emphasis on the many tongues becoming one in praise of God, demonstrates the universal scope of the Bible. To unite the whole creation in love of God, to bring community from confusion, this is the work of the Holy Spirit.

That is why God singles out Abram and Sarai, progenitors of a new race. The human penchant toward arrogant power that characterized the event in Genesis 11 is to become faithful reliance on the power and loving purpose of God, which is at the heart of the biblical story.

Prayer: *God of the covenant, God of Jesus Christ, bring unity to my own heart, that I may bring your peace wherever I am. Amen.*

---

†Senior pastor, First Presbyterian Church, Stamford, Connecticut.

Tuesday, June 2   Read Psalm 104:24-34.

From chaos to order

Perhaps the greatest contribution of the Hebrews was to declare the unity of the world under God. In unforgettable language Genesis pictures the spirit of God, the forming power of God, moving over the unformed world. Into the abyss of nothingness, into the black and lifeless chaos, God speaks an everlasting, "Let there be light!" Because one Breath animates the whole creation, it is a unity. However divided the people, however turbulent the events of history, however opaque the divine purpose to human eyes, the spirit of God is still "moving over the face of the waters" (Gen. 1:2, RSV).

Knowing this core belief of Israel, one reads Psalm 104 with fresh feeling. What a joyous hymn to the creation! How the psalmist revels in its beauty, catalogues its orders of life—its springs of water, its grasses and trees, wind and rain, beasts great and small, sea teeming with life, birds filling the air. With a similar rapture Wordsworth wrote, "My heart leaps up when I behold / A rainbow in the sky." One feels a beauty in the world deep enough to break the heart, a mystery beyond the power of human telling, and an irrepressible instinct to say with the psalmist, "Bless the Lord, O my soul!" (Ps. 103:1).

For the psalmist the whole creation springs from and moment by moment is sustained by the creative breath of God. "All look to thee, to give them their food in due season. . . . when thou takest away their breath, they die . . . (RSV). When thou sendest forth thy Spirit, they are created." Breath creating all that is, breath sustaining our todays, breath forming every tomorrow— God ordering the chaos.

Prayer: *Creator and Sustainer, I rejoice and rest in you. Amen.*

Wednesday, June 3   Read Romans 8:14-17.

From fear to family

These are golden verses! "All who are led by the Spirit of God," says Paul, "are children of God." Open to the truth of the Spirit, in the flow of the Spirit, under the blessing of the Spirit, tuned to the voice of the Spirit, all such persons are children of God. The Spirit is forming in them a new relationship with God. No longer slaves, not subject to fear, they are adopted into the family of God. This is the biblical declaration.

Paul is a Roman citizen. He knows the legal procedure for adoption and uses it to illustrate the bond formed between an individual and God by the work of Jesus Christ. The father had absolute power over his son, as he did over his slaves. The son, however, was free, and all that the father had was his. Though the control of slave and son was absolute under Roman law, the relationship was utterly different. Paul states powerfully that the slave, subject to fear, can become son and heir of all that the father possesses, can move from slave quarters and slave mentality into the father's house. What a transformation in consciousness!

We mortals, looking into the endless abyss of space, feeling the insignificance of our lifespan measured against the ages, are subject to fear. What a puzzle our human lives, how prodigious the mysteries we face, how appalling the ambiguity, how dark and divided our own hearts! But the Spirit, who brought order from the chaos of the unformed world, who breathed life into the creation, who confirmed the truth of Christ in the Resurrection, confirms in us our adoption into God's heart and home.

Prayer: *Spirit of God, form in me your light and love. Amen.*

Thursday, June 4   Read John 14:8-17.

From isolation to union

Some passages in John are like an inner sanctum. This is one of them. We feel like taking off our shoes. The passage includes a brash request from Philip, "Show us the Father!" and an indelible response from Jesus, "Whoever has seen me has seen the Father." We can close the discussion by observing, "Ah, the divinity of Christ!" and move on to other things, or we can ask, "What does this mean?" The nature of our reply tells a lot about who we are. Yes, scripture needs the microscope of critical scholarship, but rational inquiry misses much. Here in John 14 Jesus talks about his union with the Father. There is such a consonance of spirit, such a clarity of communion, such a harmony of will, such a rightness of action, that Jesus' oneness with God is self-evident. So Jesus says to Philip, and so the world has always sensed it, for Jesus stands like a mountain set apart, throwing into obscurity the lesser peaks. Here is a man whom no human categories can contain, and yet one who shows us what it means to be truly human. He does not remain in lofty isolation but is one in whom the Father dwells, one in union with God. As such he knows only one purpose, to lead us from isolation to union.

John records the promise and the reality which has carried the church across the centuries, "I will pray the Father, and he will give you another Counselor, to be with you for ever, even the Spirit of Truth." The Greek word behind "Counselor" is *Paraclete*, the one who takes our part, the Advocate, the one called alongside to help; and not just alongside, but one who is within, in union with us as Christ is in union with God.

Prayer: *Spirit of God, make my heart your home. Amen.*

Friday, June 5   Read John 14:25-27.

From perplexity to peace

Bereft of Jesus by the shattering event of Good Friday, distraught that they had forsaken him and fled, heartsick disciples are lost in despair. They huddle behind locked doors, fearing a fate similar to that of Jesus. Cleopas and friend on the Emmaus road voiced the perplexity of the Jesus event, "But we had hoped that he was the one to redeem Israel" (Luke 24:21). Too bad that dreams have a way of dying.

But look at them not many days later: Fearless Peter preaching that mighty Pentecost sermon which launched the church like a ship on the ocean, sails filled with the winds of God; Peter and John, no longer behind locked doors but healing and preaching in the Temple, that most public of all places in Jerusalem. When arrested and prohibited from such witness they say, "We cannot but speak of what we have seen and heard" (Acts 4:20).

What explains such a dramatic change in consciousness? The coming of the Spirit! Jesus had promised the Counselor would come to them, sent in his name by the Father, to teach them, renewing in them his transforming words. It was a promise richly realized. Jesus' love and power, present in the Spirit, gave to them a peace without parallel in the world, a peace not dependent on outward circumstance, for the young church in the New Testament pages is buffeted by storm and conflict. It is a peace breathed into the disciples by the Spirit, carrying the fragrance of the eternal kingdom, forming in them serenity of soul.

Prayer: *Gracious God, in my passing days, and in all the circumstances of my life, I long to hear more deeply in my own spirit Jesus' promise, "My peace I give to you." Amen.*

Saturday, June 6   Read Acts 2:1-21.

From explanation to experience

In its essence the experience of God is beyond language, for, as the Latin sages taught us, God is the *mysterium tremendum,* the ineffable mystery. This mystery only deepens when we think of God present in our world, the Transcendent One immanent. Hebrew scripture felt this profoundly: Moses trembling before the burning bush, Isaiah hearing the summons, "Whom shall I send, and who will go for us?" and replying, "Here am I! Send me" (Isa. 6:8). Israel's faith was permeated with the wonder of this God, the eternal I AM.

Pentecost is one of the Bible's ineffable experiences of God. "Tongues as of fire, distributed and resting on each one of them," so says the account. What does it mean? To the mind of that day fire was not a destroying but a transforming element. The leaping, dancing fire changed everything it touched into something else. More a transforming force than a thing in itself, fire was an elusive mystery. And wind—what better symbol of the invisible energy of God? "The wind blows where it wills," said Jesus, "but you do not know whence it comes or whither it goes; so it is with every one who is born of the Spirit" (John 3:8).

There is a sense in which the Bible is the lengthened shadow of great experiences of God. Such experiences, while they do not submit readily to explanation, point us to the God who, as the mystics say, is hidden in plain sight. Pentecost brings a fresh dimension: The Spirit comes not simply to visit but to abide, forming in us the likeness of Jesus.

Prayer: *Gift-giving God, always beyond reach of our human words, stretch all my horizons by the presence of your Spirit. Amen.*

Sunday, June 7 (Pentecost)
Read Acts 2:5-13.

From private to public faith

"When the Church Goes Public" wouldn't be a bad sermon title. The Spirit's baptism at Pentecost spilled those early disciples out of their meeting into the street. Private quarters could no longer contain them, intoxicated as they were with the touch of God. One imagines faces flushed with the fire, hair and clothing blown about with "the rush of a mighty wind." Everything was in motion, nothing was quiet, enthusiasm reigned, as joy broke in the Jerusalem street. Yes, and they began to speak, all at once it would seem, "telling . . . the mighty works of God" (v. 11, RSV). One thinks of Amos, often God-intoxicated himself, crying out, "The lion has roared; who will not fear? The Lord God has spoken; who can but prophesy?" (Amos 3:8)

There is, of course, a profound dimension of faith in which we enter a private place, shut the door, and pray to the Father who is in secret (see Matt. 6:6). This communion is life itself for the believer, for our human face is changed in beholding the face of God. Yet those times when we feel the embrace of God are inevitably times when a commission is placed in our hands. We rise from our knees to express in a public way whatever bliss we know privately. We bear witness, we serve our neighbor, we tell the story, as the Spirit gives us gifts for ministry.

How easily our institutional structures in the church seem to domesticate the Spirit, until we know no wind and fire, until the institution we have built confines the Spirit, until our carefulness and propriety no longer spill into the street to tell "the mighty works of God!"

Prayer: *Mighty God, always wanting to breathe your life into our lifelessness, awaken all my slumbering sensibilities, until your Love Incarnate is at home in me. Amen.*

IN SEARCH OF THE SPIRIT

June 8-14, 1992 **Lawrence C. Bobbitt†**
Monday, June 8 Read Proverbs 8.

We strive to accumulate material goods and sometimes we do not even appreciate what we amass. In an age when for many people materialism is like a god, the need for wisdom is great. Wisdom comes from God, and in a sense, wisdom is the will of God making itself known to us. Wisdom is not the property of a select few; it is available to anyone who seeks it.

Proverbs 8 is a perfect Bible passage for a man and woman to read together long before their wedding day. There is so much to get ready. So many costs and decisions. How much for the ring? More than for the honeymoon? Shall we invest in housing? Or shall we fill our apartment with treasures?

And in the background come the quiet words, "I am Wisdom, I am better than jewels; nothing you want can compare with me" (v. 11, TEV). Wisdom is not just a trait. Rather, wisdom is an ingredient of the nature of God touching human relationships. And wisdom can bring love, companionship, and joy to those who recognize its existence.

As we prepare for lifelong relationships, such as marriage, we do well to reflect on God's Spirit, on God's wisdom. Long before the material matters of the world were created, the spirit of wisdom was there. And long after the material goods surrounding a relationship begin to corrode, that same Spirit will be a strong support to our knowledge and insight.

Prayer: *May our spirits be united, O God, in your Spirit of wisdom. For only you can give us clear insight into the meaning and value of life. Amen.*

---

†Pastor, Saint Andrew Christian Church (Disciples of Christ), Dublin, Ohio.

Tuesday, June 9   Read Proverbs 8:22-31.
                                       John 1:1, 14.

The scriptures reveal one God with three aspects: Creator (God), Wisdom (Spirit), and Savior-Son (Jesus Christ). This is our spiritual foundation for everyday life, a God who comes to us in three manifestations of being. But sometimes we don't recognize the Spirit in our midst, God who comes to us fresh each day.

When I was a seminary student, my church history class visited a monastery. What an eye-opener for me! "It is possible that Thomas Merton, the renowned Trappist monk, will be our guestmaster (host)," the professor informed us.

After thirty-six hours at the Abbey of Gethsemani, near Bardstown, Kentucky, we drove back to Lexington. The silence, the chanting of the monks, the simple meals, the austere sleeping quarters, and the profoundly hospitable guestmaster, Father Louis, all gave us the message: *God is near.*

My only disappointment? "Not to be with Thomas Merton," I blurted out as we drove home on that snowy evening. Because of the vow of silence, I had kept this feeling too long within me. "Oh," said our professor, "didn't you know? He was Father Louis."

Sometimes, like persons we fail to properly identify, God is there all the while. But somehow we are not fully conscious of that Presence.

Prayer: *God, you come to us in surprising and unexpected ways to touch our hearts with your truth. Help us not to miss your spirit in our midst. Amen.*

Wednesday, June 10   Read Proverbs 8:27-30.

Proverbs 8 is at the heart of wisdom literature in the Old Testament. In it wisdom is described as a primary ingredient of God, the first of God's works, a companion in the creation of the universe.

When we witness that creation in the drama of a full sunrise or sunset, we may experience God's majestic power which keeps on re-creating, day after day and night after night.

For five days, my wife and I watched the sun rise off the South Carolina coast. And every day it was different. One day brought no clouds. Other days we witnessed different cloud formations. Pelicans dotted the horizon at times, in changing configurations as their wings churned above the water. The sky produced a changing panorama from black to purple to orange to yellow each day, always in a dynamic progression.

Wisdom was present at Creation beside God, like an architect. A footnote in some Bible translations offers an alternative phrase for *architect*: "a little child" (Prov. 8:30, TEV). An architect, like a little child, is free in expression and is totally caught up in creation. Joy is the result of that free expressive creation because there are no negatives and no impossibilities in God's creating acts.

And so we marvel yet today at the horizon which stretches across the ocean, the mountains, the plains, and the cities. It serves as a daily reminder of the joy in God's creation. As we share in that joy, we are sharing the creativity of God in our lives and we are made one with the Spirit.

Suggestion for meditation: *Find a place where you can view the horizon (or sky) for a few minutes. Ponder the thought that God is continually re-creating before our very eyes. Close this time with the prayer: O God, may your Holy Spirit create in me a sense of your dynamic presence that I may be an advocate for your kingdom. Amen.*

Thursday, June 11 Read Romans 5:1-5.

The lay ministerial candidate met with the regional Commission on the Ministry. She unfolded the story describing her faithfulness to the church as a child, and then as a youth. She spoke of the impact ministers, student ministers, and faithful lay persons had made upon her life. She explained her willingness to be a youth leader when she was asked. Then she became secretary of the church. Now the church was asking her to be Director of Christian Education.

Though this spirit-filled woman is married to a police officer of a large city, with all the stresses inherent, she feels called to this new challenge. She is impelled to grow deeper in the Spirit and in service to God's church. As the mother of three teenagers, she has already proven her endurance, an essential type of strength required for ministry. By the power of the Holy Spirit, she radiates hope.

The Apostle Paul describes this modern follower of the Christian faith in the early verses of Romans 5: Our faith in Jesus Christ brings peace (v. 1). Then the living spirit of God brings love into our hearts (v. 5).

Now this woman's congregation witnesses that love poured out through her faith. And in the Commission's interview, its members witnessed the same outpouring.

The Holy Spirit brings God's love to the believer. The Spirit is indeed a gift to us, available to each of us, something we are called to seek in our day-to-day living.

Prayer: *God, on this new day you have given us, make us open to your Holy Spirit. Then, give us the desire to act upon our findings, for we seek to glorify you as we fulfill our calling to be faithful. Amen.*

Friday, June 12   Read Romans 5:5.

In the fall, when most parish ministers preach at least one sermon on stewardship, this minister had based his stewardship sermon on the significance of love, love of God and love of neighbor. And the central message proclaimed was that we need to love *more*.

The Apostle Paul describes the work of God's love in terms of the Holy Spirit. That is, the Holy Spirit is God present and active in our midst today.

What is the Holy Spirit doing? Filling us with God's love so that we can *be* a blessing or *give* a blessing to someone else. And if the Holy Spirit is God's gift to us, then we should look for ways in which our lives can be a gift to others. We should be free with our blessings, for God in Jesus Christ has been free with us.

Two years ago, our congregation sponsored a refugee family from Ethiopia. The young parents and their two sons quickly adapted to the joys and difficulties of American life. Their modest apartment is fully equipped with love gifts from the church.

This past summer another Ethiopian couple arrived in our community. They had moved from another U.S. city and were no longer under sponsorship. The family we had sponsored showed great love and concern for these new sojourners in our midst. When I asked Tafere, the young father, why he was so concerned with helping these "new arrivals" he answered simply, "God's love."

May the blessing of love we receive be the blessing we pass on. For the love of God poured out in the world is indeed the hope that does not disappoint us.

Prayer: *God of transforming love, help me to be a blessing to every person I meet today. Amen.*

Saturday, June 13   Read Psalm 8.

As I read this ancient psalm I visualize this image: The psalmist has been caught up in the glorious creation of the universe—the earth and its creatures, the heavens and their contents, the sea and its inhabitants. He has had an encounter with the living God. And God, in this cosmic plan, has placed humankind in charge. We are the caretakers and caregivers of this universal project. And we decide each day what kind of stewards we will be for God's creation.

The message of the psalmist is twofold: first, the majesty of nature reveals God's greatness. Breathing in that revelation, we breathe out praise of the handiwork of God's power in all the creation. And secondly, humankind is most precious in all this universal scene. The value God places on each of us is indeed remarkable.

Jesus, a thousand years later, confirmed the psalmist's insight when he said, "For God so loved the world that he gave his only Son, that everyone who believes in him may not perish but may have eternal life" (John 3:16).

God's message to each of us is this: You are loved! You are of great value in God's masterful plan. May we live faithfully with that remarkable message!

Thought for today: *As a part of God's master plan, how will my actions today enhance this world in which I live?*

Sunday, June 14   Read John 16:12-15.

After the worship service, a little girl cautiously approached the minister in the narthex of the cathedral-like church. He was tall and impressive in his black, flowing robe, clearly a living statement of authority in that setting. She looked up into his face and courageously asked "Are you God?" He knelt down quickly and looked into her eyes and answered: "No, my dear, I am not; but I know God very well." She was reassured and she smiled back as she bounced away.

Sometimes in the church we get confused as to who the Holy Spirit is. Is it God? Is it the resurrected Jesus? Is it the spirit of Christ? Like the little girl, we are confused about divine identities.

The Jesus of John's Gospel offers us the reassuring message that all the persons of the Trinity work as One for the good of humankind. As Jesus prepares his disciples for his physical absence in the future, he brings the comforting word that the disciples' spiritual needs will be met by the continuing, consistent power of the Holy Spirit.

In these days of earthly confusion, we need to hear again that the Spirit "will lead us into all the truth and bring us knowledge." The Spirit is in full communion with the Creator and the Savior. They are one God.

Jesus not only reveals that there is more revelation to come than they now know. He also announces that the Spirit of God is to follow and that Spirit will provide the disciples with all the truth necessary for the fulfillment of God's purpose for their lives.

Prayer: *O God, make us as little children, eager to know who you are. Strengthen our fragile spirits, that we might be faithful and productive as we witness to your presence and your unending love for each of us. Amen.*

DISCIPLES TOGETHER IN CHRIST

June 15-21, 1992   **Stefanie Weisgram, OSB†**
Monday, June 15   Read Galatians 3:23-25.

This week our readings show us what it means to be in Christ. Being free from the Law and clothed in Christ brings its obligations, its challenges, but also its strengths. As members of Christ, we recognize that we belong together. What we do, we do together because in Christ we are all one. And this is only one aspect of the joy and the cross that falls on disciples of Christ.

In today's short verses from Galatians we see from where we have come: the Law. In upper-class Greek and Roman families it was commonplace to assign a tutor, disciplinarian, or custodian, usually a slave, to male children. This person was charged with seeing to the child's rising, schooling, studies, and general behavior. Although this was only a temporary authority on the part of the custodian, it was all-encompassing. According to Paul, himself a person of the Law, this was the role of the Law in the life of a Jew. But now there is a change.

The Mosaic Law was the custodian only until Christ came. Now that Christ has come, fulfilling the Law, we enter, through faith, into spiritual maturity and become adult sons and daughters in God's family. No longer is external compliance what guides us but inner faith. What can this mean for us today when the Mosaic Law seems so foreign to our experience? When fully detailed laws either comfort or put us off but fail to engage us as whole persons?

Prayer: *Christ our guide, show us your way. Lead us beyond a rote observance of law that we may walk in your steps. Amen.*

---

†Benedictine sister of St. Benedict's Convent, St. Joseph, Minnesota; Collection Development Librarian, The College of Saint Benedict and Saint John's University, Collegeville, Minnesota.

Tuesday, June 16   Read Galatians 3:26-27.

All that we have become as sons and daughters of God we have become through Christ Jesus. The Law can no longer be a threat to us or make us anxious. Christ's coming makes it possible for us to move beyond all that. This movement into freedom begins in baptism. Just as the baptismal candidate outwardy puts on a white garment symbolizing a new existence, so do we inwardly through baptism clothe ourselves in Christ.

Ideally, this means that anyone who sees us should clearly see Christ. And as we see others so should we, with clear vision, see Christ: Christ beheld and Christ beholding. But in our human fraility and sinfulness, we mar the vision or see with blurred sight. On the other hand, if we have entered into spiritual adulthood and have become mature sons and daughters of God, we will recognize that while Christ may choose to be seen in and through us, his presence is not dependent on us. Christ Jesus is among us whether we recognize him or not, whether we model him or not. To use our fraility or imperfection as an excuse to escape the challenge of showing Christ's face to each other won't work. Given the challenge, what does clothing ourselves in Christ mean realistically?

One meaning is that we become members of a community of believers. Another is that we enter into a realm of free choice. Still another is that we enter into a relationship with God as sons and daughters who are loved in their humanity. And what all of this means is that the grace of God is everywhere within our touch. Where we fail to make Christ visible, Christ can make himself seen. Where we are blind, Christ can make himself felt. Where we sin, or are sinned against, Christ is ready to forgive.

Prayer: *Christ Jesus, clothe us with your being so that we may be Christ beheld and Christ beholding. Strengthen our weak faith. Amen.*

Wednesday, June 17   Read Galatians 3:28.

What is Paul saying now? What does it mean that there is no Greek or Jew, no slave or free, no male or female? We surely know differently! There are lots of us out here, and we are all different. At the same time, we also know that we all belong to the same humanity, are all sons and daughters of the same God, are all loved dearly. And maybe that is what Paul means. We all have equal access to salvation, to the grace of Christ in whom we are one. We may all be different, but our differences are irrelevant before God because we are all one in Christ.

This says something about unity. If at a previous time the Law caused divisions among people, with Christ's coming we have a redefinition of God's people: we are united through our fellowship with Christ. And Christ is indeed the key to our unity. In Galatians we see that in Christ we are children of God, are baptized into Christ, clothed with Christ, one in Christ, and belong to Christ. Our being is in Christ. Not just my being, but your being and her being and his being and their beings.

The challenge here is, of course, in accepting our unity in Christ. When our greatest temptation is looking out for ourselves first, foremost, and always, the demands of unity get in our way. If I accept my oneness with you in Christ, I have to look out for you, perhaps even before I look out for myself. It means I am also one with the person hated by the world or laughed at or made marginal. It means I am also one with the person so much more generous, more prayerful, more honest than I, that I feel shamed. On the other hand, of course, our oneness rests in Christ whose grace, forgiveness, and love are offered to all.

Prayer: *Ever-loving Christ, increase our awareness of our oneness in you. Show us how to appreciate the variety we bring to this oneness. May we grow in your image. Amen.*

Thursday, June 18   Read Galatians 3:29.

If we belong to Christ, and we know that we do, then we are heirs to the promise through him. By this promise from God to Abraham and affirmed in Christ, God brought into being a new people. We are this people if we live by faith. What amazing grace!

Equally amazing is what this involves in terms of the promise. To begin with, the promise is freely given, totally unmerited mercy from God whose love is steadfast and whose ready forgiveness is always available. Can we even begin to understand such grace, such a gift? This is nothing we can earn or deserve. Even if we should reject it, this faithful love and mercy and forgiveness remains; it cannot be destroyed.

What kind of response on our part is adequate? We can begin with gratitude. That might be expressed by a quietly grateful prayer from the heart or by an appreciative and humble counting of blessings, remembering that all we have is gift. Or it might be an appreciative word for someone else who reveals God's love, mercy, or forgiveness to us in ways we perhaps take for granted.

Another response that reflects gratitude would be to renew our efforts to be what we say we are, sons and daughters of God, brothers and sisters of Christ. We might deliberately choose to share in some way in God's faithfulness or mercy or forgiveness in how we live or work with one another.

These are challenges, as anyone who has tried to live this way well knows. But living this way in Christ is also where we find support and where God's help is most available.

Suggestion for meditation: *What can I do today to express my gratitude for God's promise of mercy, love, or forgiveness to me as I have most recently experienced it?*

Friday, June 19   Read Luke 9:18-21.

Today's reading finds Jesus at prayer. This is a signal for us that something important is about to happen. Before important events in Jesus' life he is found in prayer. Prayer both attuned him to God's will and empowered him to fulfill it—just as prayer can do for us. In this case prayer is a preparation for what Jesus as Messiah is going to be called to do. Before his announcement of what lies ahead for him, however, Jesus asks his disciples, "Who do the crowds say that I am?" The initial answers, even though incorrect, are not exactly comforting: the names of prophets who have suffered or who have been rejected. And then Peter speaks up, calling Jesus the Messiah of God.

What is a *Messiah* that Peter can answer so assuredly? It isn't surprising to hear Peter's answer. After all, he has seen what Jesus can do and knows what he himself has done in the name of Jesus, so his answer is based on personal experience. But Jesus isn't the kind of Messiah most people might expect. What they wanted was a Messiah they could await with dreams, ideals, and hope. But Jesus isn't going to bring about political deliverance or make a big splash. He won't be shaped to fit their, or our, ideas or dreams; rather, he shapes us to fit God's will, just as he was shaped to fit it.

And here is today's challenge: to be shaped to God's will instead of trying to shape God's will to our own. To allow ourselves to be open and vulnerable before God's will. To let Jesus be the Messiah of God on God's terms rather than on our own personal terms. To allow Jesus to shape us by his example, his gospel.

Suggestion for meditation: *If today Jesus said to me, "Who do you say that I am?" what would my response be? Who is Jesus in my life? What, if any, difference does he make in my life?*

Saturday, June 20   Read Luke 9:21-22.

Jesus, realizing that his disciples have some understanding of who he is, immediately insists they tell no one. He knows he is not the Messiah of popular expectations, so why arouse the people's expectations before they can understand? Instead, he tells the disciples what they can expect for him, what it is that the Messiah "must" do, what his prayer is preparing and empowering him to do. The Messiah, or in his term, the Son of Man, must "undergo great suffering, and be rejected by the elders, chief priest, and scribes, and be killed, and on the third day be raised."

The stumbling block, of course, is seeing the Messiah of God in the light of the cross. This is the only way to see Jesus. This is what he came to do. This is his expression of the depths of his love for us. This is what proves we are cherished by God. And this is our "must," to see Jesus in the light of the cross, just as for Jesus his "must" was to undergo the cross. This is no easy task for us. It is difficult to associate the Messiah, Jesus, with suffering, rejection, and death. Yet how can he be raised up unless he first dies? And how can we celebrate Easter without first knowing his suffering, rejection, and death for us?

And if seeing Jesus in the light of the cross is not enough, we must go another step. We must recognize this: if we accept that Jesus is a suffering Messiah, then we must also accept that we are a suffering messianic community. If we claim that we are baptized in Christ, are clothed in Christ, are one in Christ, if we acknowledge that we belong to Christ, then we must also be like him, personally and together. This means we are a suffering messianic community as well as a graced community.

Prayer: *Christ of God, you endured suffering, rejection, and death as you followed God's will. Be with us as we face our own suffering, rejection, and death and show us how to support each other. Amen.*

Sunday, June 21   Read Luke 9:23-24.

All of us are called to discipleship, and all are free to accept or reject it. If we accept, Jesus tells us we must deny ourselves and take up our cross daily and follow him.

Basically, taking up the cross means a freely chosen denial of ourselves in service of God. This is giving up some control over our destiny and opening ourselves to true self-knowledge so that we might give up some of our illusions about the world, about messiahship, about power. It means letting ourselves be shaped by Jesus. And the context of all this is the family, the church, the neighborhood, the nation, and the world.

We don't go out seeking the cross, but we know that following Jesus in service of God—which involves meeting human needs—involves walking on a path that has crosses, prices, pain, and hurt that must be accepted. Sometimes our true crosses are difficult to recognize. I might think my cross is a chronic disease when the true cross might be accepting my loss of independence or control over my life. I might see my cross as loneliness when my true cross is giving up the insatiable demand for attention and affection that controls my life so that I miss the loving attention given to me daily. Or I might reject the crosses that come my way because I am so taken up with the crosses of others. The hardest thing is to carry my own cross. If I cannot carry what is uniquely mine while I agonize over the pain of others, am I a true disciple? If I really want to form a bond with those who suffer oppression of any kind, must I not first, or at least simultaneously, suffer my own pain, whatever it might be?

And as always, just as Jesus carried his cross for all of us together, so we carry our crosses together.

Prayer: *Christ, we face your challenge and call to discipleship daily. Raise us up in trust and hope in your loving care for us. Keep us mindful that we are bound together in you. Amen.*

VOCATION: LIVING GOD'S GRACE

June 22-28, 1992
Monday, June 22

Jack L. Seymour†
Read 1 Kings 19:13*b*-17.

God called Elijah out of hiding to return to the land where his life was endangered and to set in motion the activities that would restore true worship. Elijah's call is preceded by God's appearance in the still, small voice—by God's grace (see 1 Kings 19:9-14).

Elijah's call fits the pattern of Hebrew prophecy: (1) God's presence and *grace* (2) calls one to a *new vocation* and (3) the person responds by living a *new law*, a new way of life which fulfills the call. This pattern is instructive for our own experience. God's call begins in *grace*, that is, God's presence. Grace invites us to new life. Daily life is no longer the same; old patterns and expectations are revised. From grace we receive a *new vocation*—new tasks which lead us into the world for God and others. Yet, to fulfill the new vocation, we must live in new ways. A *new law* shapes the way we respond.

This pattern is present throughout the readings of the week. Vocation begins in grace—God reaching out to us. Our lives are transformed by grace. Commitments and relationships are reshaped by this experience. Through it we receive a vision of a new vocation, a new way of living. Let's explore God's call in the grace in our lives.

Prayer Suggestion: *For today's prayer, name experiences where God's grace has broken into your life. Meditate on how your life was changed by God's call. Note changes in your commitments. Thank God for being the gracious presence.*

---

†Professor of Religious Education, Garrett Evangelical Theological Seminary, Evanston, Illinois.

Tuesday, June 23   Read 1 Kings 19:15-21.

The call to Elijah was dangerous. Elijah had been warned by Jezebel that his life was to be forfeited because of his challenge of her priests. Elijah ran to the mountains to protect himself. With self-righteous self-pity, he pleaded with God. Expecting power, he was surprised by God's grace that came in "the sound of sheer silence" (19:12). But its power and conviction were clear.

Elijah was called to be the vessel of God's restoration, even if he was not to be its agent. Moreover, God challenged Elijah's self-righteousness by noting that Elijah was only one of 7,000 faithful people.

The pattern of grace, call to vocation, and new way of life are clearly present in Elijah. *Grace* came in the "sheer silence" from God that answered and challenged Elijah's pretentions. *Call to vocation* came in his orders to set the restoration of true worship into motion by finding new kings and a prophet. The *new way of life* came as God challenged Elijah to see others who were faithful and to live in the midst of the people trusting in God's guidance.

The stories of the Bible are filled with reluctant and fearful prophets. One of the greatest, Elijah, is no different. Yet, Elijah's encounter with grace was sufficient to reshape his life: Elijah did return to the people and went about the work to which he had been called. He found Elisha and passed on his mantle. Grace gave Elijah the strength and authority to set out on the pilgrimage for God.

Suggestion for meditation and prayer: *Let us move our meditation from moments of grace to the call to vocation. Take a particular exerience of God's grace, describe the experience, and name the call of God to you which came through this experience. Thank God for standing beside us as we seek to respond to the call.*

Wednesday, June 24   Read Psalm 44:1-22.

This psalm is a lament probably used in worship on a day when the king returned in defeat. Through it the people reached out to God for support and care. Because of the defeat, the people wondered about the truth of their ways, the insightfulness of their leaders, and their own future. In the first part of the psalm, the Hebrew people reflect on their present in light of their past.

Remembering the past is crucial to understanding the present. Yet, the recollections of the past can control what is seen in the present. While the people recounted how God had led them to victory, they also missed *new* ways that God reached out to them.

Through the psalm, the people claimed they knew that their destiny depended upon God. Never did their own swords or bows result in victory, for it was God's power that surrounded them. Yet even with this *claim* of trust, they did not trust. The rest of the psalm shows them pleading for victory. They want to restore the past. They even defended themselves by denying that they were responsible for the defeat because of a lack of either skill or righteousness.

We should not quickly assume that the presence of God's grace *automatically* results in people claiming the new vocation. Often we fight God's new grace. We are unwilling to accept the release and the call that it provides because we know that the structures by which we live must be changed. The psalm reminds us of the struggle to see and accept this grace and of our attempts to bind God's grace to our will.

Suggestion for meditation and prayer: *Meditate on difficulties you have in accepting God's grace. Close by saying a few times this paraphrase of verse 8: "Only in you, O God, can we boast. We give thanks to you forever."*

Thursday, June 25   Read Psalm 44:23-26.

The conclusion to Psalm 44 helps us understand God's grace. It reveals the people's attempt to coax God into their way of thinking. Moreover, it reveals their intimate connection to the Holy One.

The tone is accusing: "You are asleep! You hide from us! You who were so great to the people of old have forgotten us!" (AP) The pain of the people is great. Afflicted and oppressed, they cry out in despair: "Rise up, come to our help. Redeem us for the sake of your steadfast love."

Too often when we hear the word *grace*, we think of a relief— something that comes easily when we are in the midst of pain. We turn grace into a solution rather than honest communication with a God who cares and suffers with us.

One of the most profound treatments of grace is in Shusaku Endo's novel *Silence,* the story of persons in Japan martyred for their faith and of a priest who cries out to God to deliver them *because* of their faithfulness. Endo's conclusion is that grace is the gift of God being with us, of God standing beside us.

Grace is not an easy conclusion that we deserve. Grace is an experience of the presence of the Holy One who knows, shares, and struggles with us in our pain. The Holy One is steadfast. The joy of living is finding those to walk beside us as we enter into pain. When we find the gift of God's grace in the midst of fear and pain, we are reborn to re-enter the struggle. The old ways have changed. Our need for control is given up in the midst of a relationship.

Suggestion for meditation and prayer: *Hear again the cry of the people and remember when it was your cry: "Rise up, come to our help. Redeem us for the sake of your steadfast love."*

Friday, June 26   Read Luke 9:51-62.

Jesus "set his face to go to Jerusalem." With these words of commitment, Luke begins what has been known as the travel narrative, the section in Luke's Gospel describing the movement of Jesus from his ministry in Galilee to his witness, suffering, death, and resurrection in Jerusalem.

With the words of the call, the command of fire to come from heaven, and the desire to bid farewell, Luke reminds a reader who is familiar with Hebrew literature of the call of both Elijah and Elisha. Moreover, note that the travel narrative is preceded by the transfiguration with its visions of Moses and Elijah (9:28-36). In Jewish tradition, Elijah was to return at the end time, the time of the Kingdom of God. Through the imagery Luke uses, he portrays Jesus as fulfillment of the expectations about Elijah. Thus, Jesus ushers in the kingdom.

The imminence of the kingdom calls the people to a new way of life—radical discipleship. Those people Jesus meets on the road encounter the importance of the call of the kingdom and the life-style it demands. For Luke, radical discipleship is how the church is to live as it proclaims the power of Jesus the Christ.

Here is expressed both a radical trust in the Holy One who stands beside *and* a radical commitment to alter one's life. Grace comes in the midst of life. Grace is the recognition that God is present, that God struggles beside us. Luke reminds us that the presence of grace calls us to *re-enter the world* with a new attitude and with new goals and to live trusting in God.

Suggestion for meditation and prayer: *Think back to an experience of grace in your life this week. Think of how this experience communicated to you God's presence in our world. Ask God to help you see how that experience calls you into the world to share and witness with others.*

Saturday, June 27   Read Galatians 5:1.

The Letter to the Galatians has been a transforming power throughout the history of the church. It was instrumental in shaping Luther's commitment which led to the Reformation. Galatians is about freedom and grace *and* the way of the Christian in the world. Paul wrote to a Galatian community in strife. Members within the community who had once experienced the new life of God's grace were again under the influence of other teachers who sought to return them to old patterns of living.

Paul's tone with the people is filled with sarcasm: "My little children, for whom I am again in the pain of childbirth until Christ is formed in you, I wish I were present with you now and could change my tone, for I am perplexed about you" (4:19-20). Paul proclaims to the Galatians that the grace of God in Christ is sufficient for them. Prior to his preaching they had worked to fulfill the demands of other faiths—the demands of the law and the expectations of the mystery religions. Each of these demands made the people constantly work to *prove* themselves worthy. Paul reminds them that the grace of Christ freed them from such proof—freeing them to enter the world in service.

As we have seen this week, that is what grace is like. Grace is the radical acceptance of the One who stands alongside. Through grace we are freed to stop trying to prove our righteousness and are called to re-enter the world sharing, proclaiming, and living graciously. To Paul, that some Galatian Christians returned to seeking the comfort of the law meant that they were not really free to be with others in love and service.

Suggestion for meditation and prayer: *Think about the things you do in an attempt to prove your worth. Ask God to help you accept the gift of grace. After reflection, pray the following paraphrase: "Help me know that Christ has set me free for service. Help me stand firm and accept the gift."*

Sunday, June 28   Read Galatians 5:13-25.

On the surface this beautiful description of life lived under grace appears to contrast the body and the spirit, but it means much more. The body is not denied in Paul's writings. Rather, what is denied is our attempt to live by the law of self—to seek to control, define, and secure our destiny by our own efforts. When we seek either to prove our worthiness or to secure it through our own individual effort, we forget that all life is a gift of a God who cares and stands beside us.

The acceptance of grace leads into vocation in the world. We can trust and we can risk because we know that Another is with us. Paul makes a claim for living. Life lived with faith and trust calls us to new ways of living. Life lived with trust opens us to others, invites us into community, and challenges us to risk living with patience, peace, kindness, generosity, joy, and love.

Great biblical patterns continue throughout time to help us understand the journey of faithfulness. That is certainly true with the pattern of the prophetic call. Through God's *grace,* God touches us with acceptance, challenge, and a steadfast trust. The experience of grace calls us to a *new vocation* of living new commitments with others and of witnessing to the power of the One who stands beside us seeking to remake the world. Out of the joy and release of acceptance and trust, we live *new ways*, showing our openness, trust, and love of the world that God also loves. We know the difficulty of trusting, but we also know its freedom. We know the invitation of entering life fully and of seeing possibilities and rebirth.

Prayer: *O God, we praise you for your steadfastness, for your grace and love that reach out seeking to transform the world. Help us trust your gift of standing beside us in the midst of the world. May we touch others with your gifts of love, joy, struggle, faithfulness, generosity, and peace. Help us to work to understand your call to us. Amen.*

CLAIMING GOD'S YES TO US

June 29–July 5, 1992   **K. C. Young, OP†**
Monday, June 29   Read Psalm 5:1-3.

Asking others to listen to us is a common experience among humans. Sometimes we are eager to express an idea; other times, it is our very person that we wish to have heard. The psalmist today very directly asks God to listen to specific words and to listen to the sound of a sigh.

Both listening and praying are perceived to be quiet actions. Yet often when I come to prayer, I experience within myself a noisiness. Sometimes this is a way to avoid deeper union with the Holy One; other times it is the price of living in a complex world. At such times intercessory prayer becomes almost an insistent "Listen to me, God." The psalmist assures us that God not only listens but considers our plight.

We, too, could learn from considering our plight. This consideration might entail a simple breathing in and out or letting our bodies picture what our plight is. Such consideration helps us acknowledge who we are this day, what our reality is, and the power that the Sacred One provides. Is our sigh nervous, harried, sad, eager, angry, lonely? Is it expressed in ill health or in the fullness of life? We ask God to heed these sighs, but do we pay heed? A sigh can tell God who we are, can express why we stand in need, can underscore our surrendering "yes" to God. The psalmist writes of this heeding God who is considerate and knows us through and through. We can with great trust let our sighs be our daily act of love and trust.

Prayer: *O heeding God, may I pledge to you this day the sighs of my being and those of the global family. Amen.*

---

†Director of Campus Ministry, College of Notre Dame, Belmont, California; member of the Sinsinawa Dominican Sisters.

Tuesday, June 30   Read Psalm 5:4-8.

"There but for the grace of God go I" is a common phrase we all have said or thought. The psalmist this day challenges us on this comparative prayer. This psalm clearly notes that God does not participate in evil and falsehoods. More often than we realize, the hardships and sufferings that come upon us and those we know we link with love as divine punishment.

As we enter more into the understanding that God loves us and does not ever harm us, we enter in a more conscious way into the temple where Holiness dwells. Unconditionally, God accepts us and draws us into life. Made in the image and likeness of God, we are, in part, God's dwelling. Do we treat with respect and reverence this place wherein lies the Holy?

On a high school retreat one of our teachers, a Roman Catholic, genuflected before the twenty of us. He let his actions express that God dwells within each of us. Such an act of reverence was his way of acknowledging that we are made in God's image, that God dwells in us, and that we are recipients of God's love. Our challenge is to accept this unearned, warm embrace from God. Until we find ways to grow in self-acceptance, we will only be admiring God's architecture from the outside. We will not see or experience the inner beauty of this emerging work of art that we and those around us are.

Some might perceive this to be inordinate self-love. We need only remind ourselves of the words of the psalmist: "through the abundance of your steadfast love." We are who we are not of our doing but of God's.

Prayer: *Here, because of your grace, O God, am I. I give you thanks for the wonder and mystery of your love and grace. Amen.*

Wednesday, July 1　　　　　　Read 1 Kings 21:1-3, 17-21.

The Israelites placed great importance on family inheritance. For them it was a way to continue the family line and to experience enduring life. Legal and religious custom forbade the kind of land transfer that King Ahab proposed to Naboth (see Leviticus 25:10, 23-24, 34). Naboth endured false accusation, rejection by friends and neighbors, and eventually death so that the inheritance would remain in his family.

Today, inheritance in the Western world often means civil-court battles. Although the legalities emphasize what happens to house, property, and money, doesn't it go much deeper than this? Inheritance is one way a person knows that he or she belongs somewhere. Inheritance indicates that in the recent past we were valued enough to be given a portion of the deceased's livelihood. An inheritance is the passing on of an identity. An inheritance acknowledges those persons who have helped us become the unique individuals we are. Usually an inheritance is a link to those who loved us. What is our family, cultural, societal inheritance? In what ways do we accept or shun this inheritance?

Can we name the inheritance that has been given to us by the God who loved life into us? Is it a living faith, a hunger for truth, a capacity for compassion? Do we value our inheritance? Do we hide it away, or display it and put it to use? Do we take time to acknowledge our inheritance?

Suggestion for meditation: *Take time today to list what you have inherited. Note how you value this inheritance. Write up a will from God to you, listing all that God wills unconditionally to you.*

Prayer: *O God, show me how to live out the inheritance of your endless love. Amen.*

Thursday, July 2   Read Galatians 6:7-18.

Many of our actions are done not out of altruism but with mixed motives. We make some of our choices to give the "right" impression. In the letter to the Galatians, Paul is quite critical of this impression management. He has known how easily religious fervor can snag a person. They do "the right thing" but place the focus on their own goodness, ambition, or power.

This entire passage invites us to live life intentionally. To be more and more aware of "why I do what I do" will allow us to uncover what motivates us. God calls us to move beyond some of our self-deception and not be fooled by what motivates our choices. Can we move from our delusions into a more conscious way of making choices?

Initially, idealism is probably a strong motivator. Yet, closer examination will uncover that more than our idealism motivates us. The writer to the church at Galatia acknowledges this idealism and challenges us further to move beyond that which first motivated us in order to make a freer choice for God.

Paul himself had an abrupt conversion moment which caused him to reorient his values and objectives. Paul did not have only one conversion moment. He kept that initial experience fresh by meditating on the marks of Jesus he bore on his body. How do we keep our conversion fresh in our memories and in our lives? The historical event of Jesus' suffering and death reoriented Paul's values. Ask yourself: Does the suffering and death of Jesus clarify my motives and reorient my values? Paul was urging this for the Christians at Galatia. A Spirit-guided life will gradually reorient our values. The fruits will be mercy and peace.

Suggestion for meditation: *Recall what first motivated you to serve another. Have your motives to be of service changed?*

Friday, July 3   Read Luke 10:1-4.

Luke is the only Gospel writer who relates the mission of the seventy disciples. Even with a shortage of workers, Jesus sends the seventy out in groups of two rather than alone. Pairing is important in ministry. In twos we can have mutual support. In twos we bear strong witness to the truth. In twos we can live out the reality of being bread that is blessed, broken, and shared with one another.

Early in this passage we read of our need for mutual support. The mission is not easy. Jesus tells those he sends to have courage. They/we are like lambs among wolves. What danger! Certainly, mutual support is vital as we face our fears and the indifference and criticism of others. We will need to encourage one another. At times we need to buoy up each other's faith.

We witness to truth together. One dimension of this is in living simply. The paired disciples are to take no purse or bag or sandals. We are invited to trust that God will provide for our needs on this missionary journey. Can we pause and remember the ways that God has provided for us in our needs?

This missioner dependency is indeed a witness of radical trust. It is a countercultural value. It takes mutual courage to live this out. We are to be an embodiment of the Christ whom we are proclaiming. The Jesus of history was willing to lay down his life in service and mission. He knew fatigue. He knew frustration when his message was misunderstood. Yet he continued on. This is the embodiment we are challenged to live out together.

We do not proclaim the gospel alone. This Jesus who sends us will follow us and go all the places where we have been.

Suggestion for meditation: *Reflect on those you have been paired with in ministry. How did (and do) you share mutual support? What has been your witness to the truth? How have you together embodied Christ?*

197

Saturday, July 4   Read Luke 10:5-12.

Some Brazilians believe that whenever a guest visits their home Jesus has entered. They are so convinced of this that they attempt to convince the guest that the guest, invited or not, is Jesus incarnate in their midst.

In Luke hospitality is synonymous, for Jesus, with ministry and it plays a dual role. The words of Jesus addressed to the seventy on mission can also be heeded by those who offer hospitality. One dimension of hospitality is an openness to receive the offered gifts. The minister comes and proclaims peace. Can the host be open to receive this gift? This passage states that the peace will remain there if peace prevailed in that household already. The minister brings peace; the receiving household offers peace.

The gospel proclaimed is like a suitcase which needs to be unpacked. The minister is admonished not to move from house to house but to stay while this gospel is unpacked and appropriated. In receiving hospitality, the minister better understands the gospel proclamation. Those offering hospitality receive the gospel proclamation through the act of giving.

"The Kingdom of God has come near to you." In the context of this passage we hear that God is near whenever hospitality happens. Brazilians know this. Two of us serving as pastoral ministers in a *favela* (slum) visited an elderly woman who had heard that her son had died. We went there to extend our sympathy. As we left she offered us an egg which her only chicken had laid. It was to have been the evening meal for her and her husband. Not to receive each other is to turn away from the nearness of God's reign.

Suggestion for meditation: *In what ways this day do you experience that those you serve and those who serve you are the incarnate expression of God? Does this change how you encounter others?*

Sunday, July 5   Read Luke 10:17-20.

The first journey is over. The seventy return, and as they debrief they are filled with joy. They experience a sharing of the Spirit's power. They call on the name of Jesus. This is a new experience of authority. With it comes a heady feeling. In calling upon the name of Jesus the seventy find their lives are changed. But Jesus tempers their missionary zeal.

Each of us remembers first fervor in relationship. There is joy, elation, and energy. Jesus cautions his followers that there is something more engaging than this first fervor exposure to ministry. This joy is to be savored but not possessed. How long do we remain captivated by this first zeal for proclaiming the good news? It varies for each of us. Yet, we can take heart even if that first fervor has waned.

There are stages in ministry. One day we experience joy in someone's openness. Another moment we experience courage as we challenge the "snakes and scorpions" of greed and selfishness. Jesus points us further on the missionary road. Jesus urges us to take heart in knowing that the ministry we participate in is a part of a whole.

At the beginning of today's passage the disciples are heartened that they can call upon the name of Jesus. But Jesus tells them not to rejoice over their power; rather, rejoice because their names are to be written in heaven. For our names to be written, we must go through this first fervor. We must experience the headiness of having influence over another person, but we must be rooted in the fact that truer zeal and authority come solely from God. Ministry deepens this awareness. In ministry and in relationships, in zealous times and ordinary times, we will be transformed and our names will be written on God's heart.

Prayer: *O God, I give you thanks for the joy and honor of serving your people. Amen.*

EYES TO SEE

July 6-12, 1992   **Catherine Gunsalus González†**
Monday, July 6   Read 2 Kings 2:1, 6-14.

Elijah had been a great prophet. Yet no prophet is forever. God had said that this day his ministry was complete. Elijah did not seem worried. Long before, God had told him to anoint Elisha as his successor, and it had been done. Elijah was ready for God to send for him. Elisha, however, was not so ready. How could he ever fill the role of Elijah? How could he be sure God really had chosen him for such a role?

Israel had had to go through such times before. How could they go on without Moses? But they had. And Elijah clearly had been in the line of Moses, for he had parted the water and crossed on dry ground. But Elisha was worried. So when the old prophet asked if the young one had a last request, Elisha asked that Elijah give him "a double share of your spirit," that is, that Elisha might have twice as much of Elijah's prophetic spirit as anyone else, the heir's proper portion.

Times of transition are difficult for God's people. We cling to the old and are sure the new will not suffice. But our confidence is not in things as they are but in God's faithfulness which we see in the raising up of new leadership. And if we are that leadership, our confidence is not in ourselves but in God's work through us.

Prayer: *Eternal God, forgive our fearfulness when your church is caught in times of great change. Keep our faith in you, and cause us to be your willing instruments for the sake of the world you love so much. Amen.*

---

†Professor of Church History, Columbia Theological Seminary, Decatur, Georgia.

Tuesday, July 7   Read 2 Kings 2:9-14.

The miraculous chariots of fire cannot be seen by human eye, yet Elisha is permitted to see them and is thereby confirmed in his role as Elijah's successor. Stephen sees the heavens open and Jesus at the right hand of God. By this vision, as he faces those who stone him to death, Stephen is empowered with forgiveness of his persecutors and great confidence (see Acts 7:54-60).

God's power surrounds us, but most of the time we walk by faith and not by sight. Yet those glimpses into the work of God which we see in the lives of others give us courage also. We are surrounded by God's power and glory, though it is usually hidden from our eyes. Faith goes on in the strength of that knowledge, rejoicing whenever glimpses into that vast glory that surrounds us break in upon us in brief moments of confirmation.

Elisha had seen the chariots of fire. He knew that the prophetic spirit of Elijah was now on him. In that knowledge, he took the mantle of Elijah and struck the water, calling on the name of God. The waters parted for him as they had for Elijah. The transition to new leadership was complete.

Faith has its moments of confirmation, its glimpses into the glory of God that sustain us. But often these are not seen by others, and the moments are gone before we can capture them. Yet such moments are transforming. The life of faith does not consist of these moments of confirmation but of obedience. The life of obedience sometimes has such moments, and they bring courage to all the household of faith.

Prayer: *Gracious God, for the unexpected moments of joy that the world can neither give nor take away, we give you thanks. Amen.*

Wednesday, July 8   Read Psalm 139:1-6.

We can celebrate the occasions when we have glimpses into God's power and glory that surround us, but the reverse side of that is that God is continually aware of us. The psalmist is astonished at such knowledge. Nor is God an observer of our lives from the outside: God is intimately aware of our thoughts before we utter them, of our hidden motives, of our most secret emotions. God knows us better than we know ourselves. We cannot fool God even though we can fool ourselves.

It is one thing to hold a theoretical view of the power of God. Then it can be talked about and debated. The psalmist is not giving a lecture on the attributes of God, however. It is quite a different thing to experience the searching knowledge of God, to know that we stand in the presence of One who cannot be fooled, to whom no lie can be told, no excuse given, One who rips away from us every feeble attempt to cover up our fears, our sins, our hopes and dreams. The psalmist speaks from such an experience of God's knowledge.

Knowing that we stand in the presence of such a God is both frightening and comforting. It is frightening because there is much we would hide. It is comforting because ultimately there is One who knows us thoroughly, who understands us even more than we can understand ourselves, and who still claims us as children of God.

Prayer: *Your knowledge, O God, is too great for us to comprehend, yet we know that in that knowledge is our hope for redemption. Let us not be afraid of being known by you. Amen.*

Thursday, July 9   Read Psalm 139:7-12.

We have all had the experience of wanting to run away from something. Perhaps we were afraid of responsibility that we had taken on, or we felt guilty, angry, or misunderstood. No solution seemed possible. Most of us outgrow the child's actual plan to run away from home, but even as adults we find less conspicuous forms of running away.

The psalmist is aware of such feelings, and the psalmist is also aware that in regard to God, we cannot run away. There is no height or depth, no distance east or west, no darkness that can hide us from God. We cannot run away.

This may sound very negative. In human situations, because of evil in the world, running away may be the only healthy thing to do—running away from abusive home situations or from political disruptions that torture and kill dissidents. But in regard to God, running away is never the healthy solution. Ultimately, having no place to hide from God is a gracious statement. Only by turning to God, rather than running away, can we find redemption. The fears and anxieties, the guilt and anger must be faced and dealt with. There is no escape, and that is good.

Human maturity depends upon facing what must be faced. God will not let us avoid that task. The psalmist's awareness of no hiding place—that God sees through all darkness and distance and will not let us hide—is both a judging and a redemptive word.

Prayer: *We thank you, O God, that even when we have given up on ourselves and the possibilities for our lives, you will not let us go. Amen.*

Friday, July 10   Read Colossians 1:1-10.

If we are serious about the life of Christian discipleship, we may often feel that we are isolated islands in the midst of a culture that lives by very different values. Indeed, serious discipleship may seem an impossibility. But surely it was no less difficult in the Roman Empire of the first century. Christians then clearly could feel isolated and up against impossible tasks.

But this letter to the Colossians has a very different spirit. Paul has eyes to see other Christians whom the Colossians have never seen. There is no isolation. And even in the midst of great odds, Paul can rejoice in the fruit that the gospel is bearing all over the world.

Perhaps because we have grown accustomed to a culture that has been strongly influenced by the church and that could claim for centuries a dominant role in Western civilization, the unmistakable loss of that status makes us feel more isolated and weaker year by year. In order to overcome our sense of isolation we need eyes to see: to see across national and cultural borders to other Christians we do not know. And we need to see in unexpected places the gospel bearing fruit and growing throughout the world. Then we, too, could be thankful rather than fearful, and pray for the church worldwide, knowing ourselves to be part of that great company of faithful who also pray for us.

Prayer: *You have made us part of your one body, O Christ, and given us the task of being your witness in the whole world. Renew in us the vision of our unity and mission, and empower us to be the witnesses you need us to be. Amen.*

Saturday, July 11   Read Colossians 1:11-14.

We often think that redemption is a future goal, earned on the basis of what we do now. When we remember all the issues of the Reformation about salvation by works or by grace, we may amend our view and remind ourselves that we cannot earn salvation—it is a gift. But it remains a future gift for which this life is preparation and trial.

But the New Testament sees redemption as a process that is occurring now. Granted, it will not be complete until the fullness of the reign of God dawns, but there is redemption *now,* in *this life*. The Colossians are reminded that God "has rescued us from the power of darkness and transferred us into the kingdom of his beloved Son." This has happened. To be part of the body of Christ now is to have been delivered and transferred in this fashion. The Colossians are called to remember who they are.

We, too, need eyes to see the present redemption taking place in our lives—now. We have been freed from the dominion of darkness. We have been transferred into the kingdom of Christ (v. 13). This has happened. This is who we are. All of our obedience and faithfulness proceeds from what God has done to us and for us in such a transformation.

It takes faith to see this present redemption. But where it is seen, then God's power and might are present realities for us. Then we can be thankful and joyful and patient, even in the midst of the evils and difficulties of this life.

Prayer: *Help us to live our lives, O God, on the basis of what you have already done for us and in us, and not out of our own strength alone. Amen.*

Sunday, July 12   Read Luke 10:25-37.

Yesterday we looked at the meaning of redemption as even now being transferred from the kingdom of darkness into the kingdom of Christ. Today, in this famous parable, we can see what such a transfer means in action. It involves creating in us the heart of a neighbor.

The redemption that God has begun in us gives us eyes to see God's power around us, God's presence that cannot be escaped. It also gives us eyes to see where we are called to work in the world. We are to be neighbors—that is part of the work of redemption in us. To be a neighbor means to see those who need a neighbor.

The priest and the Levite did not see themselves as neighbors, so they could pass by on the other side. The unlikely Samaritan did have the heart of a neighbor and therefore saw the poor man in the ditch. The Samaritan, against all expectations, is the neighbor. He sees the man in the ditch—with eyes that see as God sees. The act of the Samaritan, therefore, is an act of redemption. It is redemptive not only to the one in the ditch, in that it is God's own action toward him; it is also redemptive for the one who acts as God's instrument.

The grace of God changes us into neighbors, able to see with new eyes. The question asked was, "Who is my neighbor?" Jesus answers, "You are to *be* the neighbor."

Prayer: *We have been redeemed by you, O Christ. Cause us, therefore, to be the neighbors you have called us to be. Amen.*

THE EVER-PRESENT GOD

July 13-19, 1992
Monday, July 13

Loretta Girzaitis†
Read Psalm 139;
John 14:15-20.

As we look at this week's readings, we note that the theme of God's presence permeates them. We see how God interrupts us to gain our attention and how that presence invites us to capitalize on the power of the Spirit so that we, too, may be present to others. John, in today's reading, highlights Jesus' promise not to leave us orphans but to be present with us always.

Elijah, full of the Spirit and God's power, has passed this power and Spirit on in double measure to Elisha, who as his protégé continues the task of making God's presence felt by others (see 2 Kings 4:8-17).

Psalm 139 emphasizes God's presence in our lives from the moment of conception. God knows us, is able to read our thoughts and to witness our desires.

Paul, writing to people whom he had never met, challenges the Colossians to accept the presence of God, made known through Jesus, about whom he teaches and for whom he willingly suffers (see Col. 1:21-29).

Then, in Luke's story of Mary and Martha (10:38-42), Jesus intrudes on the hospitality of these two women, filling their household with his presence and guiding them with his observations.

Suggestion for meditation: *How does Jesus become present to me through the stranger and the friend who enter my life? How have I prepared myself to recognize this presence through the study of Jesus' teachings and through prayerful reflection on his words?*

---

†Spiritual director, writer, retreat leader; director of Victorious Spirit Enterprises, St. Paul, Minnesota.

Tuesday, July 14   Read 2 Kings 4:8-13.

Elisha had been the disciple, protégé, and intimate companion of Elijah. It was while he was working in his father's fields that Elijah had come to him, stripped himself, and draped his mantle over Elisha's shoulders (see 1 Kings 19:19).

Elisha had left his home, family, and security and had given up his future to follow this prophet. He had watched him call down fire from heaven on the top of Mount Carmel and for ten years had learned from this stranger. He was ever conscious that Elijah's mantle had fallen upon him and, touched by God's spirit and power, he now had a special mission as a prophet.

In his travels, Elisha frequently stopped in Shunem, thirty miles northeast of Samaria. Although Elisha was a stranger, a wealthy woman invited him for a meal. She became convinced he was a holy man and persuaded her husband to build a room for him that he could use whenever he was in Shunem.

Elisha was eager to repay this woman's kindness and asked her what she desired. He had contacts; he would get whatever she asked for, even if it meant he had to go to the king or the commander of the army to obtain it.

Surprised, she told him that she had no special needs, and that even if she had some, she would go to her own clan who would care for her. Besides, she wasn't looking for any payment.

Within each one of us is the desire to reward those who do us good. There is also a force that leads us to risk helping those in need. It is this kind of compassionate response that is selfless, that does not seek any praise or acknowledgement.

Suggestion for meditation: *When have you experienced the desire to help someone in need? Did you respond? What motivated your action? Did you seek praise? Were you conscious at the times you were ministering to others that you were in the presence of God?*

Wednesday, July 15   Read 2 Kings 4:14-17.

Elisha would not be put off. Surely there was something his hostess needed or wanted. His servant Gehazi provided a clue. He said to Elisha, "She has no son and her husband is old" (NIV).

In biblical times, it was every woman's dream to have a son, and it was believed that the lack of one indicated God's displeasure. Sarah (Gen. 17:15-21), Rebecca (Gen. 25:21-26), Manoah's wife (Judg. 13), and Hannah (1 Sam. 1:1-28) had been great women among their people and had also been childless. But God favored them and sent each a son.

The wealthy woman was taken aback at Elisha's promise. Was Elisha toying with her feelings when he told her she would have a son? Fleetingly she may have wondered if he were an angel, a messenger from God, to whom she had ministered.

The majority of our days seem to be routine. But there are others that are interrupted in unexpected ways. It is important that we be open to whatever happens, alert to the consequences of both the ordinary and the surprising.

A kind gesture by the woman from Shunem brought miraculous results. She had not hoped for any reward. Because she had opened her home and her heart, God was unexpectedly present, affirming her love in an inexplicable way. Now she needed but to believe and to trust.

Suggestion for meditation and prayer: *Has this kind of unexpectedly wonderful event, unique to your needs, ever interjected itself in your life and made you overwhelmingly conscious of God's presence? If so, how did you respond? Share your thoughts with God, who always desires good for you.*

Thursday, July 16   Read Psalm 139:13-18.

Psalm 139 is a prayer of praise and thanksgiving which humbly acquiesces to God's personal knowledge of each of us. It helps us understand more clearly how intimately God is present to us.

The psalmist proclaims that God created him with infinite care and formed him in the divine likeness. Here and in Hebrews 4:13, the writer acknowledges God's wisdom which knows the attitudes and thoughts of the heart. God is so intimately present to us that nothing can be hidden.

For some this thought could be frightening, for it might project an ever-watchful God who scrutinizes and records all that we say and do. On the other hand, the certainty of God's presence can be joyful, for it underlines the care God has for us. Recognizing this God who is inside us nurturing us and outside us challenging us as we are enveloped by love can lead us to greatness as we live life fully and intensely.

As did the psalmist, visualize God as being present at your conception and your birth, pleased and joyful at the creation that is being brought forth. Do you feel the intensity of this pleasure, this joy, this love? Do you love yourself the way the Lord loves you?

Sometimes it is hard to see ourselves as God sees us, to love ourselves as God loves us. We have somehow learned to be afraid of God rather than to feel secure in God's presence. To love ourselves as God loves us means learning to trust that the God who created us is the One who will never let us go.

Suggestion for meditation: *Reread verses 13-18 again. Choose a word or a phrase that is especially meaningful for you. Close your eyes as you sit comfortably in your chair. Breathe deeply and slowly. With each breath repeat your word or phrase, immersing yourself in God's presence.*

Friday, July 17   Read Colossians 1:21-23.

Throughout his life Paul lives out his goal: to teach true wisdom by helping individuals become perfect in Christ. Convinced that his mission is to pass on his knowledge about Christ, Paul writes here to the Colossians. He has never visited their city, but while in prison in Rome he is informed that the Colossians are beginning to fall away from the teachings of Christ.

Paul addresses the letter to them as those who are chosen from the ages. He attempts to convince them that Christ's death is the reconciling power that draws them together in love. He urges them to set aside everything that draws them away from God so they might become holy and blameless before God.

We, too, have been chosen from the ages to be holy and blameless before the Lord. Yet, how easy it is to drift away from Jesus' teachings. Mundane affairs crowd our days, so that if we find the time to mumble a prayer or two as we start our day or as we drift off to sleep, we are satisfied. Somehow the things of the world are more important than the things of God.

God knows us inside and out—and loves us. Can we say that we know God inside and out and that is why we love God? It is true that we cannot know God completely, for God is incomprehensible and full of mystery. Yet Jesus came to reveal his "Abba" to us. He invites us gently but persistently to learn from him. How much of a priority is this for each of us?

Suggestion for meditation and prayer: *Ask yourself: What specific steps can I take today that would lead me to know God more intimately as I journey through life? Give thanks to God for the divine love and presence extended to you each day.*

Saturday, July 18   Read Colossians 1:24-29.

Paul tells the Colossians that he rejoices in suffering for them. As he writes this letter, he is in prison waiting for judgment; so his statement carries weight. He assures them "In my flesh I am completing what is lacking in Christ's afflictions." He does this for the sake of Christ's Body. But this time he is not talking about Jesus' physical body but about his mystical body which is the church. Paul is willing to suffer because he sees himself as an instrument that brings to people the mysterious plan of God that offers redemption both to Jew and Gentile.

The tribulations and the sin in the world did not end with Jesus' death, and so we, like Paul, must continue to suffer to fill up that which is incomplete.

Most of us in the developed nations find this concept hard to accept. Jesus died, and in his death and resurrection he achieved salvation for everyone. That is true. But it is also true that he said, "Anyone who does not carry his cross and follow me cannot be my disciple" (Luke 14:27, NIV). If we are truly to be the followers of Jesus, then we must be willing to follow him to the cross.

It seems that Christians in developing nations understand and accept this concept much more readily. When they study the scripture, they see that God loves everyone, not only the rich but also the poor. So the disenfranchised and oppressed are more ready and willing to work for justice, even though it brings additional suffering through disappearances, prison, beatings, starvation, and death.

Suggestion for meditation and prayer: *List some times you have suffered, and recall your response to each experience. Are you satisfied with how you have dealt with your past sufferings? Determine how you can make future suffering meaningful in your life. Share this resolution with God.*

Sunday, July 19   Read Luke 10:38-42.

This Gospel story is a significant one, particularly for women. Girls were not permitted in Jesus' time to study the Torah, particularly with the boys at the synagogue. In fact, men were not allowed to be alone with women who were not relatives.

Yet, here Jesus is welcomed into the home of Mary and Martha, alone with friends, not relatives. Jesus is as comfortable here as in a synagogue, acknowledging the intelligence and capability of women to understand the scripture. He affirms them as he is present to them in his teaching.

Mary sits with him, attentive, absorbed in Jesus as she listens to his words. She enjoys conversation with her friend.

Martha, on the other hand, seems to ignore her visitor. Jesus has come to offer her something. Instead she is concerned about what she can offer him.

Jealous, angry, distracted, Martha turns on Mary and insists that Jesus tell her to help. Jesus responds, not to condemn Martha but to challenge her priorities.

What needs to undergird our activities, Jesus is implying, is a basic understanding of why we are "distracted by many things." Our service, when it is fragmented, distracted, focused on self, is of little benefit to others. Foundational to our serving must be a listening to and a reflecting on the Lord's words. Without loving attention to God in prayer, ministry may not be love. Prayer must signify presence, attention, absorption in God so that service might become a cooperative venture with the Lord.

Suggestions for meditation: *What are your priorities when Jesus visits you? How do you pay attention to him? When are you unaware of his presence? Dialogue with Jesus about this. What do you want to ask of him? What can you accept from him?*

July 20-26, 1992   **Ron and Patty Farr**†
Monday, July 20   Read 2 Kings 5:1-15.

People trembled at his name. Naaman, the commander of Syria's armies, gave orders and controlled the destinies of thousands. But beneath his armor, beneath his pride, beneath all his power, a disease was festering—the scourge of leprosy.

News reached Naaman that Elisha, a man of God in Israel, might be able to heal him. With hundreds of soldiers, chariots, servants, and wagons full of gold and silver; outfitted in impressive armor; and riding high on his war stallion, Naaman marched to Elisha's house. But Naaman was not prepared for what he would have to do at Elisha's humble doorstep. Elisha did not come out to greet him. Instead, he sent his servant, instructing Naaman to go wash in the Jordan. Naaman was insulted. He flew into a protective rage that exists inside most of us as well.

To carry out Elisha's instructions, Naaman would have to get off his "high" horse, take off his armor, and strip and stand naked before all his men, revealing to them the shame of his leprosy. Naaman was terrified of such vulnerability and exposure.

But this kind of unprecedented vulnerability before God is our gateway to healing and divine encounter. Without such vulnerability, God's love remains at a distance, and our wounds continue to fester. What armor do we wear? How vulnerable do we allow ourselves to be with God? Naaman finally risked nakedness in the Jordan. What are we willing to risk to encounter God and to experience health?

Prayer suggestion: *Ask this question: O God, how do I, like Naaman, keep myself from being vulnerable in your presence?*

---

†Retreat leaders; writers; co-pastors of Emmanuel Congregational Church, United Church of Christ, Watertown, New York.

Tuesday, July 21   Read Psalm 21:1-7.

I was sitting quietly in prayer with others during a retreat on Cape Cod. I remember the retreat leader saying, "Ask God for your heart's deepest desire." All at once I realized that though I had been on a journey of faith for many years, I had never really dared to ask God for my heart's deepest desire. What's more, I didn't even know what that desire was!

As I sat in the silence, I began to sift through a number of heartfelt desires: "I want to be more radical for Christ. I want to live with more joy. I want world peace. I want hunger alleviated. I want the world to be safer for our children." On and on my list went. What *was* my heart's own deepest longing? What is yours? Long after the retreat was over, this question continued to be a kind of spiritual riddle for me, a hidden gateway into God.

The psalmist proclaims to God, "You have granted [the king] the desire of his heart . . . You welcomed him with rich blessings and placed a crown of pure gold on his head" (NIV). In God's eyes we are each as noble as a king or queen. Picture God welcoming you with rich blessings and placing a crown of gold upon your head! God is wondrous, wanting nothing more than to grant us the very deepest desire of our hearts!

But we need to know what that desire is in order to ask God for it! We must go deep into ourselves to sift out all those desires that are shallow and unworthy of our souls. We must start ordering our entire lives around our heart's true desire. Are we willing? If so, we will begin to touch the place of our deepest nobility, where our souls open to God and where miracles happen. Ask God for your heart's desire, because that desire links you with the heart of God.

Suggestion for prayer and meditation: *Ask God to help you come in touch with your heart's deepest desire. Begin to live only for this desire, and watch what happens.*

Wednesday, July 22   Read Luke 11:1-4.

The disciples often saw Jesus retire into the hills to pray. What was he doing all those hours? How did he pray? Finally one day the disciples asked, "Lord, teach us to pray" (NIV). Jesus uttered the Lord's Prayer, a prayer we repeat so often we can miss its true depth. Each phrase is a gateway into God!

"Our Father." Jesus lovingly calls out to God as "Abba," a startlingly tender Aramaic address which derived from the small child's address of his or her father, rather like our "Dada."* Jesus' prayer starts with an invitation to be enfolded in God's love! "Hallowed (Holy) be your name." God is the ground of all that is holy. What feels holy in our lives? Isn't this where God is beginning to touch us and unveil every ordinary moment as itself holy ground?

"Your kingdom come." What other prayer is there than this? "O God, quietly and persistently come to us. Reign fully in our lives and in our world." This is the heart's desire for everyone who hungers for God. This is our salvation.

"Give us each day our daily bread." God is our Bread, the manna of each day. "Forgive us for we also forgive others." Abba's immense forgiveness is food and healing for our souls. It allows us to face ourselves and be human. It frees us from the prisons of our own sins. If that weren't wonderful enough, we then can become conduits of God's forgiveness to others. "Lead us not into temptation." O God, we are human and easily tempted, so we offer you our vulnerability. We hide nothing; but we rest in you.

Suggestion for prayer and meditation: *Pick any phrase of the Lord's Prayer, such as "Your kingdom come," and ponder and pray it continuously for a whole day. Let it be a gateway into God.*

---

*See Joachim Jeremias, *The Prayers of Jesus*.

Thursday, July 23   Read Luke 11:5-10.

Picture yourself walking up the darkened sidewalk to the front door of your neighbor's house to borrow an egg. You ring the doorbell. You wait politely. No answer. Feeling uneasy, you think, "Well, it is a little late; maybe I shouldn't bother them." You don't like asking people favors. You wonder if the doorbell is broken. Maybe you should knock on the door. But the thought of just walking back to the car and driving home seems appealing. In a moment you are tiptoeing back down the sidewalk, now hoping nobody will answer the door.

When we approach God in prayer, we sometimes feel as though we are standing on God's doorstep at night. We're not sure we want to disturb God. The door looks locked. But Jesus lovingly prods us to not waver or retreat but forcefully knock as if we really mean it! In Jesus' story, a man knocks on a friend's door in the middle of the night and awakens him with a request to borrow some bread for unexpected company. That took courage! Jesus says the friend finally serves him not "because he is his friend, yet because of the man's boldness" (NIV).

When we pray, Jesus instructs us not just to stand passively at God's door. There is no vitality in this. Jesus tells us to be bold with God. Like the man in the parable, we must not be afraid to knock for what we believe in. We need to knock, and knock, and knock again until the whole household of God is awake! We need to stand before God's door with our desires for healing, with our passions to make our world a better place, with our dreams that there will be bread for all. Let us come to God with confidence, and the power of God's spirit will be with us!

Suggestion for meditation: *Consider how you might be more bold with God in your actions or prayers concerning the things you feel most passionate about.*

Friday, July 24   Read Luke 11:11-13.

I remember my first summer job as a youth, working in the hot, sweaty kitchen of a fast-food restaurant. I arrived each morning by the back entrance, parked my bicycle, and then grimly faced that back door that for me held behind it endless tasks of boredom and obligation. There are some gateways we simply do not want to pass through!

Any gateway leading into God can look or feel a little intimidating to us, like that kitchen door in my youth. This is especially true when the gateway promises to usher us into more radical Christian service. When we think of serving God, part of us is afraid that God might turn out to be a relentless taskmaster. We fear that God will not respect our limits or that God's demands will be so overwhelming that our lives will go out of control.

Jesus knew his disciples had this unspoken distrust that God was more apt to drive them than nourish them. Knowing that many of his disciples had children of their own, Jesus said, "Which of you fathers (or mothers), if your [child] asks for a fish, will give him (or her) a snake instead?" (AP)

With this one penetrating question, Jesus awakens us to the reassurance we need to offer our gifts without hesitation to God. Who more than God knows how to care for us? God does not abuse us and burn us out, saying, "Go, do that, and that, and that. . . ." God nurtures us as we work, saying, "Why not go to bed? You're tired," or, "Go for a walk and relax. You're worrying too much." We do not need to fear serving God with all our heart. God knows how to balance us and give us good gifts, and all the more so when we offer God the good gift of our lives!

Suggestion for prayer and meditation: *Probe what holds you back from fully offering your gifts and time to God. Be still for a moment and allow God to tell you how you will be nourished.*

Saturday, July 25   Read Colossians 2:1-10.

Paul's heart was troubled. Under house arrest in Rome, he had received word that the fledgling Christian community in Colossae was faltering. Apparently, some false teaching was competing with the truth of Christ. So Paul penned these words to the Colossians: "See to it that no one takes you captive through hollow and deceptive philosophy, which depends on human tradition and the basic principles of this world rather than on Christ" (NIV).

Most of us can probably look back to a special turning point in our lives when, at some deep level of our being, we said yes to Christ. In that moment the gateway of our hearts opened directly to God. But as we continue on our journey of faith and are tested by the difficulties and struggles of our lives, we slip away from the wondrous power of Christ within us. We become captive to hollow and deceptive philosophies: values, standards, and laws which our culture may uphold but which distract us from our blossoming commitment to Christ.

Like the Colossians, we may stop short of fully receiving the gift of Christ. Christ, by dying, gave us tremendous freedom to live—not by fear, not by "human tradition," but by radical love. Martin Luther King, Jr., kept his eyes on this Christ of love when he chose to disobey civil law—the written code of society—in order to obey the higher law of God. You and I are also called to base our every action and decision on nothing less than Christ in the way we spend our money, raise our families, influence our government, and care for our earth.

Suggestion for prayer and meditation: *Ask Christ in the silence to reveal himself at the very core of your being. Yield to his love as it seeks to shape your every thought and action.*

Sunday, July 26   Read Colossians 2:6-15.

In *The Man Who Planted Trees* by Jean Giono, a simple peasant in rural France decides that his dream is to plant trees. Every morning, he carefully counts out enough seeds for the day's work and sets out for barren hillsides to dig his tiny holes and deposit his seeds. He continues day after day for many years. Life goes on around him. Two world wars come and go. Still he greets every morning in contented silence, leaving his little cottage with just enough seeds for the day's planting.

Over the decades what was once barren, forsaken land slowly evolves into fertile orchards and forests watered by flowing streams—a Garden of Eden now lovingly tended by the neighboring villagers, all thriving from the beneficial changes brought to their land by one man and his dream.

How wonderful to hold a vision so steadily in our hearts that we make that vision into a reality! How can we do it? Paul tells us: "Continue to live in [Christ], rooted and built up in him, strengthened in the faith as you were taught" (NIV). At some point in our journey of faith, Christ plants a powerful dream in us, such as "Feed the hungry," "Heal the sick," or "Bring peace." But as the days and years go by, we become distracted by lesser concerns and forget to *live* the dream. We forget we have the power of Christ at work within us to make that dream come true. We forget that we "have been given fullness in Christ, who is the head over every power and authority."

The man who planted trees knew the power of his seemingly small actions; he let nothing distract him from his dream. Likewise, let nothing distract us from the tender dream which Christ has planted in us to create a better world.

Suggestion for prayer and meditation: *In silence with Christ, ask, "What one step can I take today to help you transform our world?"*

The Will of God

July 27–August 2, 1992   **John W. Bardsley**†
Monday, July 27   Read 2 Kings 13:14-20*a*.

Chronic question

Knowing the will of God has been of great concern ever since our Creator breathed the breath of life into Adam and Eve. When the prophets, respected holy men, spoke, "Thus says the Lord!" people listened because these holy persons were close to God.

In today's reading, we hear of Elisha, now an old man. He has not been heard from since he sent a prophet to anoint Jehu (2 Kings 9). Though on his deathbed, Elisha must do one more act of power and might. As so many have when a leader is about to die, Joash weeps, wondering, *What will I do now?* Joash uses the exact words Elisha did when telling of Elijah's death (see 2 Kings 2:12). For Joash, Elisha is more important to the nation than all their chariots and armies.

Elisha tells Joash to shoot an arrow out the east window to show that the victory would be in the east, where Syria had taken Israelite territory. Guided by Elisha, Joash takes on power and authority he never thought possible.

People still look for leaders who represent the highest ideals of commitment and service. For believers, these ideals mean holiness—living close to God so that our acts reflect God's will and purpose.

Doing the will of God, we ride God's chariot to victory!

Prayer: *O Lord, help us know your will. Then give us the courage to do it. Amen.*

---

†Pastor, Jonesville First United Methodist Church, Jonesville, Virginia.

Tuesday, July 28   Read 2 Kings 13:14-25.

Accepting the will of God

Elisha commanded Joash to strike the ground with the arrows. Joash perfunctorily struck the ground three times without enthusiasm. Elisha was furious! He had spoken for God, and Joash had not really paid attention. "You didn't go far enough! You didn't go all the way!" Elisha said. "Therefore, the victory is limited, incomplete" (AP). A golden opportunity had been presented to Joash, and he had blown it.

How often have we gone only part of the way with God? How often have we stopped just short of the goal? God's enemies and opponents do not. To paraphrase verse 19, "Keep shooting the arrows until you've won!"

A young woman spoke about her multiple sclerosis and the effect it was having on her ability to live life as she wanted to. This Christian mother, now speaking to others in groups about her faith, said, "I would not change anything in the past year, including MS. Oh, I wish I didn't have to deal with it, but it has caused me to spend more time seeking the will of God. I should have done that much sooner."

Victory is achieved with complete commitment, persistence, determination, and enthusiasm. Joash stopped short of these. When we focus totally on knowing the will of God, the results are always surprising and boundless.

Prayer: *Lord, let me know and understand that when I work with you, we can do anything. Amen.*

Wednesday, July 29   Read Psalm 28:1-5.

The will of God sought from the source

This psalm is divided into two sections. The first portion, verses 1-5, dramatically expresses the psalmist's desperate need for God. The urgency is probably an illness caused by or blamed on certain godless and reprehensible persons.

The problem has reached such a critical stage that if aid does not soon come, the writer will end up in the pit, that is, the abode of the dead, Sheol. There is no place to turn but to God, the Rock. *Rock* is used several times in the Old Testament to indicate the strength and protection the Lord offers.

God's help is needed so the psalmist will not suffer the evildoer's punishment. We can almost hear the psalmist plead, "Listen to me, Lord! Don't turn a deaf ear to me! I don't want to end up like them!"

Then he lifts his hands, begging for help and mercy. Uplifted hands are a prayerful posture and signify a reaching out to God, eagerly awaiting some sought-after blessing. The psalmist does not wish to overlook anything that will convince God to hear him in this crisis.

In Luke 11:5-8, Jesus speaks of the friend's boldness—persistence. James says that the prayer of a righteous person is "powerful and effective" (James 5:16, NIV).

The psalmist pleads directly to God and waits confidently for a positive answer, for assuredly the will of God is that believers be saved.

When we consider God's readiness and ability to hear as well as God's love for us and willingness to answer, we find good reason to direct our pleas to the "Rock of our salvation."

Prayer: *Lord, help us realize that you have already begun to act on our behalf even before we ask for your help. Amen.*

Thursday, July 30 Read Psalm 28:6-9.

Found in answered prayer

The desire to have prayer answered is as deep as the desire to know the will of God. We hold out all sorts of promises if God will just answer our request. Implied in such promises is that the answer given must be the one we want.

Whatever the threat that occasioned today's psalm, it is now gone. God has answered the psalmist's prayer. Prayer and praise go hand in hand, and the psalmist moves rather abruptly to praising God. He responds not in any irrational emotional way but from the depths of a saving experience (v. 6). Then follows a powerful affirmation: "The LORD is my strength and my shield . . . a fortress of salvation" (NIV).

The psalmist cannot contain his joy and happiness. His heart trusts God and "leaps for joy." Our God is a great God. The psalmist offers words of gratitude and thanksgiving.

The psalms have been a help and encouragement to many and were understood and used by Jesus. We can understand the psalmist's prayer and spontaneous exultation. When the danger is removed, when the crisis is past, when we realize, once again, that God can be trusted, there is relief and happiness. A song of boundless happiness replaces the cry of distress.

Others benefit from the witness of a happy spirit and a joyful heart. The miracles of God's answers to our prayers should not be kept a secret. "Let the redeemed of the LORD say so" (Ps. 107:2).

Prayer: *O God of all, open our eyes to your miracles that come to us in our deepest need. Amen.*

Friday, July 31   Read Colossians 3:1-11.

In the resurrected life

Too often we speak of resurrection only in terms of the future. But for Paul the resurrection life begins in the kingdom of God here and now.

"So if you have been raised with Christ, seek the things that are above" is not a philosophical abstraction. It is guidance to the Colossian church, which is being threatened with dangerous doctrinal differences that would divert them from their faith in Christ as the Son of God (Col. 1:15-19; 2:3, 8-23).

The answer is to "set your minds on things that are above." This is a deliberate act, a conscious spiritual discipline. We are surrounded by much that entices us away from faith in Christ. Some tend to think that once we are saved, everything falls into its proper place. We have nothing to worry about. Not so. Paul says, "Put to death . . . your earthly nature" (NIV). This means new values, new priorities, new motives. To be "in Christ" is to be in the *real* world—now. Freed from the magnetic power of sin, the new life is now ours and we are being renewed. Resurrection begins now!

Individually and collectively we are called to live in the victory of Christ over those things that would enslave us as persons and prevent us from interacting as loving members of the human family of God.

Finally, there is no distinction of race or color in this family. "Christ is all and in all!"

Prayer: *Lord, help us put our feet, our hearts, our minds, and our spirits on higher ground. Amen.*

Saturday, August 1   Read Luke 12:13-21.

In how we handle possessions

More than once, Jesus answered a question with a teaching, a parable. In this case a man had asked about the proper division of an inheritance. But Jesus makes it clear that he is not interested in this kind of thing, or, at the least, has no time for what he considers to be trivial pursuits.

The wealth that the inquirer seeks is vain and transitory. Jesus is concerned with the lasting riches that bring abundant living. He says not a word about clever investments, only that life is more than "abundance of possessions" (v. 15). We can wrap ourselves in a big house with all the accessories, but in bad times, if we have lived only for self, we will have no soul with which to face life. We will be empty, without foundation.

Jesus turns the question around and raises an altogether different but more meaningful issue with which the man must deal. The man's mind was preoccupied with worldly or physical things. Jesus points out that life does not depend on amassing a huge fortune (v. 23). The noblest work can restrict and retard our growth and development in life if we invest our efforts in it only.

The antidote for such selfishness is Christ—his life, his teachings. "For where your treasure is, there your heart will be also" (v. 34). To be "rich toward God" is to put the heart in Christ. The practicality of Christ's teachings is awesome.

Prayer: *Lord Jesus Christ, help us keep the things of life in their proper perspective. Amen.*

Sunday, August 2   Read Luke 12:16-21.

Found when we wake up

Searching for wealth and possessions is wasted effort because death always comes when we don't expect it, despite all sorts of warnings. And it comes too soon. In the final analysis, wealth is irrelevant to entering the kingdom of God.

The rich man gathers all his possessions in one place, tearing down old barns to build bigger ones. Jesus calls him a fool because the man has focused only on collecting "things." To be "rich toward God" means living selflessly and being in close communion with God through prayer and following the example of Jesus.

If we are wrapped up only in self, our horizons are extremely limited. We may live on a high when things go well, when a project is successfully completed, when others tell us how good we are, how talented. But unless life is balanced between the physical and the spiritual—in their proper perspective—we pay for our shortsightedness with depression, obsession, and the longing for a "change"—something different to expand our narrow world.

When Jesus is Lord, we do not have to be overly concerned about taxes or money-market rates. The tragedy that Jesus pointed out was that his questioner really believed that riches consisted of what he had accumulated. Jesus was upset because that man had his priorities so out of place. What about us? Christ wants us to remember that we receive our inheritance by our God's pleasure.

Prayer: *O God, help us to live so that all we do will make us rich toward you. Amen.*

OUT OF SURRENDER, VICTORY!

August 3-9, 1992   **Robert L. King†**
Monday, August 3   Read Jeremiah 18:1-11.

I found myself at a turning point in my life and literally lived this passage. I could continue in the direction I was going, or I could try to turn my life around. But I was powerless to do either. I could neither continue nor change. Fortunately, I found a recovery program, and a fellowship of others with a similar problem, that taught me change was possible by placing myself in the hands of a power greater than myself.

I could argue endlessly whether my problem was sin or a disease, and many have died trying to make that differentiation. I do know that whether sin or disease, the results were the same; I did things that harmed me and others. I also know that on the morning of March 14, 1967, I was so badly defeated that it didn't matter what it was called; I needed help! Recovery turned out to be simple, though not easy. I first realized my lack of power, acknowledged that a power greater than myself could bring me to recovery, and then turned my life over to that power to be shaped in God's design.

God said to the people of Israel, "I can do with you as I want! If you will realize your wrongdoing, and turn to me and let me shape you, I will save you and make something worthwhile of you" (AP). When I was finally able to acknowledge my need for God and took action, God saved me and made my life worthwhile.

Prayer: *God of life and hope, form me, mold me, and make of me what you will. You truly are the potter, and I the clay. Amen.*

---

†Retired environmental engineer; layreader and chalice bearer in The Episcopal Church, Charles Town, West Virginia.

Tuesday, August 4   Read Hebrews 11:1-3.

This is the introductory section for the chapter which calls the roll of saints and heroes of the Old Testament. The author is making the point that we must rely on something we cannot see.

To those of us who have had a "prodigal" experience, the moment of turning back (or repentance) certainly requires the act of turning toward God. In my case, I felt I simply had no choice; I heard others say it had worked for them, but I certainly was not sure it would work for me. As a result, each step was taken in a kind of blind, desperate hope that God loved me and wanted the best for me. Little by little, I started to really believe. As God became real to me in little ways, I found myself willing to follow God more completely, to take more bold steps of faith.

For me, this idea is the central point in a personal relationship with God as I now understand God. If I do not have the faith required to hope for things unseen, then all the theology in the world is a waste of time. I must be willing to make a decision to turn my whole will and life over to the care of God, without placing preconditions on my fate. It would be nice if I could do this once, but for me it is a daily dying to God's will for my life and reaffirming my decision to follow God's leading.

I continue to be surprised by the fact that walking in faith gives me a degree of freedom I could only dream about when I was out there "doing my own thing." For when I really "do faith," I am free from fear, worry, anger, lust, envy, and all the other chains which restrict true freedom.

Prayer: *Loving God, we acknowledge our need for you and for the true freedom available through following you. Amen.*

Wednesday, August 5　　　　　　　　Read Hebrews 11:8-16.

This relatively short summary of the story of Abraham and Sarah highlights their journey of faith and is an example for us all. Abraham's full story is given in Genesis 11:26–25:8 and fills in the details of his life and his dealings with God.

One of the great scenes in Genesis is the point where God instructs Abraham to call his wife Sarai by the new name of Sarah, and then says he is going to give Abraham a son by her (see Genesis 17:15-16). Abraham then falls on his face laughing (Gen. 17:17), since Sarah was at that time 90 years old!

In my own journey of faith, I have many doubts and questions. I'm not at all proud of this, but the fact is that I often rebel at the direction God appears to be taking me. I need the benefit of these olden-day warriors of faith to know that while my behavior may not be correct at least I'm not the only one who has ever questioned God!

The journey of faith may require that I put my hope in things unseen. However, through reading scripture and sharing with other Christians who are trying to make the same journey, I can be assured that I'm not the only one with questions as I grope my way along the journey. For as I get older, I believe it to be less important that we find the answers to our questions and more important that we continue to search for the proper questions to ask. There are no simple answers; if there were, we wouldn't need to walk in faith.

Prayer: *Thank you, Lord, that in my walk in faith, I have the example of Abraham, Sarah, and others to help light the way and to console me in my confusion. Amen.*

Thursday, August 6   Read Hebrews 11:17-19.

Recently my thinking about this passage was greatly influenced by a newly ordained Episcopal priest who had left the Northwest to come to Virginia Theological Seminary in Alexandria, Virginia, a suburb of Washington, D.C. One evening she talked about the concern she had for the effect of the move on her daughter as she decided whether to attend seminary, and it struck me that, in her own way, she had been required to "sacrifice" the interests of a loved one in order to answer God's call to her to enter the priesthood. The trauma of a major geographic change, as well as a change to living in a metropolitan area is not the same as that of sacrificing a child as a burnt offering, but the element of questioning the potential long-term effect is still a part of the picture.

All of us face such questions in our lives in some form, at some time, and at some level of intensity. The issue may be a career change, a geographic change, or it may be the heartrending decisions regarding the end of a failing marriage, surrendering custody of children (or of withdrawing life support equipment from loved ones who are dying. Recently, another friend was faced with that particular decision in the case of her daughter.) We are called to make decisions which have an effect on some other person in our lives for whom we care very deeply. The question is whether we too can move with faith, trusting God's leading when God's will is in our decision.

Prayer: *Thank you, Lord, that in my walk in faith I can know you will truly sanctify the sacrifices I make in your name and turn them into victories for you. Amen.*

Friday, August 7   Read Luke 12:32-34.

I have a car with over 150,000 miles on it which I dearly love to drive. It's a very comfortable car; I like the way it rides; there is an absolutely perfect place to put my commuter coffee cup as I drive; it is *my* car, so I don't need to worry about keeping it clean for others. In short, I treasure it and wouldn't trade it for the world!

But one of these days, it isn't going to want to start in the morning. Or it's going to cough, wheeze, and die on the way to or from some important function, and the cost of repair is going to be so much that it won't be worth fixing. Then, no matter how much I treasure the old red car, it's going to have to go to the great boneyard for cars. With a sad and heavy heart, I'll wave good-bye to it and turn to another car which, I will hope, will soon become as comfortable. In fact, I may soon wonder why I put up with the old red one so long, and begin again to treasure the perishable!

Too often, we put our faith in real estate values, bank accounts, jobs, cars, sports teams, and in people, only to be disappointed when they fail us, wear out, or are stolen. But we who have surrendered our will and our lives to God, and committed ourselves to following Christ, have found a power that *never* fails, or wears out, or can be stolen from us. That power is truly our source of victory!

Today, allow yourself to relish in the thought that surrender to God has allowed access to a treasure like none other the world has ever known. It is yours if only you agree to accept it.

Prayer: *Lord, as I surrender to your will, let me know the joy of your kingdom which never fades away—and never fails. Amen.*

Saturday, August 8   Read Luke 12:35-39.

My friend Heidi is an 8-year-old German shepherd. Notice I don't refer to her as *my* dog, because it's not clear who "owns" whom. In the last year, Heidi and I have become fast friends because we can spend so much more time together. She is a real example of the intent of today's reading.

Heidi loves to be involved in my activities. She loves to ride in my old car, planting herself dead center in the back seat and sitting up as if she were a queen. If I go upstairs, Heidi is with me. If I go outside for wood, Heidi is with me. Generally, she is so close that I can scarcely move, so my favorite expression is "Look Out!" When I'm away from her, I feel strange because I haven't said those two magic words. Twenty-four hours a day, Heidi is waiting for the action, whatever it may be. It is almost embarrassing to be loved so deeply by any animal and to know how vitally interested she is in my activities.

Watching how Heidi relates to me, I've learned some valuable lessons. First of all, because of her eagerness, I tend to let her do more things with me because it's clear she thoroughly enjoys the involvement. And I like to be with her because she is eager to be involved in my life. Because of her eagerness, I tend to make sure she's well taken care of. I really enjoy being with her and lavishly spoil her.

As we go through our days, it may be helpful to consider Heidi's example. How eager are we to please God? How eager are we to spend time with God, in God's presence doing God's will? How lavish are we in our praise of God and God's goodness to us?

Prayer: *Lord, as I surrender to your will, let me know the joy of responding eagerly to your call. Amen.*

Sunday, August 9   Read Luke 12:40.

It is a chilly December 7th as I write this. Heidi and I have brought in wood for the stove, since mixed snow and rain is forecast for the night. As you read this some twenty months later, it's hard to remember what snow is like, isn't it? As I write, today is the 49th anniversary of Pearl Harbor, but we are all much more deeply concerned about events in Iraq than in remembering that day 49 years ago. As you read this, it's possible that the events of Iraq will be only a distant memory. When you read this, the red car will have finally given up for good (it wouldn't start this morning), and Heidi and I will be walking a little more slowly.

Some 2,000 years ago, a certain relatively young carpenter from Nazareth, considered a radical by many, but in fact the long promised Messiah, allowed himself to be captured by authorities and to be wrongly tried. But through that surrender, he achieved a victory so stunning that its effects have been felt throughout the world ever since—much longer than the Hitlers, the Idi Amins, the Saddam Husseins, and other fleeting leaders in our history.

Today, as you worship in your church, many of you will recite three critical phrases: *Christ has died, Christ is risen, Christ will come again*. Say those phrases out loud right now! Feel the wonder of those phrases. Say them again, but add "for me" after each. Spend the day in wonder at the promise that Christ will come again, for you. Right now, ask yourself if that fabulous possibility isn't worth being ready for. Then decide what being ready really requires—and do it!

Prayer: *Lord, as I surrender to your will, let me know the joy of victory over sin and death. In the name of Jesus Christ. Amen.*

THE TENSIONS OF FAITH

August 10-16, 1992   **Bruce Mitchell†**
Monday, August 10   Read Jeremiah 20:7-10.

For most people, life offers moments of deep discouragement. For some, these may be moments of abject despair. So it was for Jeremiah.

This man of God had cried out against injustice, immorality, and deceit. With deep conviction, and with all the power he could muster, he challenged the priests and people to change their ways or they would find the temple destroyed and the people cast to the ends of the earth.

And what was his reward? Jeremiah found himself placed in public stocks, exposed to the ridicule and abuse of all who passed the temple court gate. Bound firmly, all Jeremiah could do was endure this time of despair, wondering if, despite his deep faith, he had been deserted by God.

Few, if any of us, have endured this sort of persecution or can even visualize what it would be like. However, for those who are true to God there will be moments much like the one experienced by Jeremiah. Occasionally there are tests of life—and faith—when, like Jeremiah, an individual can feel he or she has been deceived by God—moments when an individual may feel moved to cry out to God, "Where are you when I need you?"

We, in our human weakness, need to remember that it is in times of trial more than any other time that God comes closest, giving strength to face today's dark times and providing hope for tomorrow's possibilities.

Prayer: *O Lord, in the dark moments of life, remind us that there is light and hope in Christ. Amen.*

---

†Associate pastor, Trinity United Methodist Church, Bradenton, Florida.

Tuesday, August 11   Read Jeremiah 20:11-13.

In the past fifty years we have been subjected to a continuing picture of prisoners being released from prison camps. We have seen the gaunt faces of individuals who have suffered human privation beyond anything we, in our day-to-day existence, can understand.

Who of us can ignore or forget the horrifying pictures of Holocaust death camps and the faces of the living dead who somehow survived the unbelievable human cruelty and social injustice that were part and parcel of concentration camp existence? We cannot disregard seemingly incredible stories of God responding to prayer and of long-forgotten passages of scripture being recalled during solitary confinement. Time and again released prisoners have testified that God's power alone empowered them to survive an inhuman imprisonment.

Jeremiah shares this in today's passage. Sometimes called "the weeping prophet," Jeremiah prayed and meditated, consistently exhibiting an inner spirit of faith. Despite his persecution by priests and other leaders who paid mere lip service to God, Jeremiah continued to address the sins of the nation and the unwillingness of the people to repent.

In 1979, Vladimir Poresh, a Russian Christian, was arrested and put on trial for anti-Soviet activity. When he was sentenced to imprisonment and exile, his friends sang "Christ is risen." It is in this same vein that we can experience today's scripture passage, a testimony by someone in anguish, grief, and tears—yet one filled with certainty that faith in God would ultimately carry him to a personal victory.

Prayer: *O God, through Christ, put a victory song in our hearts, especially when things seem the worst. Amen.*

Wednesday, August 12   Read Psalm 10:12-15.

"If God is a loving God, why does he allow bad things to happen to good people?"

The question was asked in a small group by the mother of a young woman robbed and murdered in a shopping center parking lot. In a way, it is the same question raised by the psalmist in today's scripture passage.

The psalmist's plaintive cry is echoed in many ways in today's society. As a death-row murderer is led to the gas chamber or the electric chair, people cry out for justice to be done—for punishment of the convict. But what is justice in the eyes of God?

Is it possible that humankind at times takes justice into its own hands? Is it possible that forms of justice are developed that are inconsistent with God's viewpoint of justice? Is it possible that humanity at times experiences a tension of faith when it seems, on the surface, that God may not act in circumstances that seem dreadfully inconsistent with God's expressed wish for a world of peace and justice? Perhaps our greatest fault is losing patience with God and taking initiatives of our own that, no matter how well intentioned, may be inconsistent with God's plan for the world.

Likewise, it may be that, in the pressures and self-centeredness of our own lives, we forget God has already provided us a response to the psalmist's cry:

> He has told you, O mortal, what is good;
>   and what does the Lord require of you
> but to do justice and to love kindness
>   and to walk humbly with your God?
>
>   Micah 6:8

Prayer: *Give us, O Lord, hearts that are sensitive to injustice and hands that are willing to address it. Amen.*

Thursday, August 13   Read Psalm 10:16-18.

One of the top secular songs of yesteryear was one that proclaimed musically " I did it my way." In a sense, that's part of the modern human ethic—if something is to get done one has to move ahead and do it, often with individual initiative and without consultation with others.

The psalmist reminds us that God will not endure the wicked indefinitely; ultimately, God's will overcomes evil. In today's passage the psalmist expresses the prayer that justice would be quickly extended.

In our lives we can approach our desire for justice in two ways. First, with faith in God's power to bring peace and justice into the world, we can develop and maintain a strong prayer life emphasizing the need for justice. Secondly, we can respond to God in tangible and personal ways so that we become God's vehicle in making peace and justice happen.

As Christians, as people trusting in the power of God, we can pray for God's intervention. We can develop and nurture a strong faith that even in the most desolate of situations God is with us. We may feel tension when things do not go as we feel they should, but faith and prayer keep us in tune with God. In stressful situations, especially in dire times in our lives, prayer and faith in God's power bring us closer to God. Ultimately, we will find ourselves brought through God to a deep inner peace in the face of adversity.

Prayer: *Remind us, God, that in every situation you hear and respond to our faith-full prayers. Amen.*

Friday, August 14   Read Luke 12:49-59.

For me, the Ingalls family on the television series "Little House on the Prairie" was the model of a family who faced everyday hardships with deep faith. They, like many frontier settlers, did not have an easy life. They contended with crisis after crisis; but always the Ingalls met every challenge, joy, and tragedy as a family faithful and close to God.

Though the Ingalls family is an idealized portrait, they nevertheless did face the tension of survival with deep faith. Today's family also faces tensions and stresses that can divide it. Often both parents must work. Parents are on the run transporting children to and from school activities, sports practice, or dancing or music lessons. At home there is the tension of homework and the influence of television, video games, secular concerts, and entertainment heroes and heroines. Where does God fit in?

A stress of faith is part and parcel of our everyday contemporary life. Certainly, there are families in the 1990s every bit as cohesive and every bit as involved with the church as was the Ingalls family of book and television fame. But there are many others where children have rebelled against their parents' values, against the church, against Christian faith, and against God.

If we are to take Jesus' admonition seriously, we need to recognize that division can be part of family life. Jesus calls us to be faithful to God, even when those close to us choose not to be. Though we may find our faith challenged, God continues to work through Jesus Christ.

Prayer: *God, in the face of pressure and division, keep my heart true and faithful. Amen.*

Saturday, August 15   Read Hebrews 12:1-2.

Have you ever seen the start of a major marathon? Hundreds of runners crowd together at the starting line, muscles tensed for the starting signal.

As the starter's pistol sounds, this mass of humanity surges forward. Hours later, one by one, individual runners cross the finish line. However, not everyone who starts the race finishes— the physical stress of the long and arduous run takes its toll.

So it is with the race of faith God has set before us. Life itself presents challenges, some of which are very difficult to contend with. Physical limitations, illness, job reversals and broken relationships—all make our human race to the finish line of life more challenging.

For some, winning the race, at any cost, is the only goal. For others, the joy is in the race itself. For all, the race requires the determined desire to move forward.

The writer of Hebrews alluded to many individuals in biblical history who had "run with perseverance the race set before us." Their victory was centered in remaining faithful to what God had placed before them. They could have dropped out of the race at any time they chose, but their faith in God gave them spiritual strength and stamina to face with assurance the stress of every adversity.

Though many of the people were not delivered *from* adversity, they all were delivered *through* adversity by God's consistent presence in response to their faith. So it is for each of us: we may not find release from life's stresses, but through Jesus Christ we can find the daily power to handle them.

Prayer: *Merciful God, when it seems easier to give up, provide the faith and strength for me to go on. Amen.*

Sunday, August 16   Read Hebrews 12:12-17.

Jeremiah, the psalmist, the author of Hebrews, and Jesus Christ, all shared a common conviction: we cannot deal with the tension in our lives apart from God. Though our faith cannot remove the tension that exists, and by its demands may even add to the tension, our faith can provide the means to handle every day-to-day challenge we might face.

What are the ways we can maintain a strong faith in the face of adversity?

First, we can try, as best we can, to retain an air of optimism. Not everyone can display optimism in the same way or at all times in life. The attitude of one senior pastor who was near death was an unusual example of optimism in all things. When his associate pastor asked him if there was anything special in the church that needed to be emphasized, he smiled and whispered, "Keep the ministry upbeat."

Second, we need to maintain a disciplined prayer life—always turning over to God the burdens and victories of our lives. And we need to believe that, in God's own way, God will respond.

Third, we need to pattern our lives after Jesus Christ, trying in every way possible to reflect Christ in all we say and do.

Finally, all of these need to be nurtured in the fellowship of other people. Never has an individual been able to resolve the stresses of faith in isolation.

Today may be the most challenging day you have ever faced. The miracle is that God has provided the means to handle that challenge—through faith and through God's presence in all things.

Prayer: *O God, I do not ask for my stressful moments to be removed; I only ask for the strength, faith, and wisdom to face them squarely. Amen.*

THE CHALLENGE OF DISCIPLESHIP

August 17-23, 1992   **Beth A. Richardson**†
Monday, August 17, 1992   Read Hebrews 12:18-24.

The readings this week are not for the "faint-of-heart Christian." They are rated PG-13. The passages present the challenges and responsibilities which accompany the benefits of discipleship—not easy things for me to hear some days.

Today's reading refers to the scene at Mount Sinai (Exodus 19) where the Hebrew people, washed and scrubbed, stand before God and accept the covenant without even knowing the terms of the contract. It is a dramatic and fearful scene: fire, trumpet blasts, a mighty voice in the thunder, the earth shaking.

The writer of Hebrews draws the parallel for the followers of Jesus—Mount Zion and "Jesus, mediator of a new covenant."

Underneath the passage is a sense of awe, respect, and even fear. "What is this 'fearing' God?" my modern sensibilities ask. There is plenty to fear in the world besides God. Nuclear weapons, natural disasters, disease, criminals with guns—all seem more threatening to me than God. Isn't God supposed to be supporting me instead of adding more stress to my life?

It seems strange to fear God when there is such evil in the world that children are abused by the ones they trust and national leaders make decisions based on money rather than human lives. I want a God who will comfort me in distress and reduce my fear, a God who will take care of me and the world and not demand too much. I want to see the fine print before I sign the contract.

Suggestion for meditation: *Reflect on the expectations you bring to your relationship with God. What do you expect of God? What does God expect of you?*

---

†Diaconal minister; assistant editor of *alive now!* magazine, published by The Upper Room, Nashville, Tennessee.

Tuesday, August 18   Read Hebrews 12:25-29.

We followers of Christ have received "a kingdom that cannot be shaken." God's mighty voice sifts away everything that can be shaken, that is, everything that is not essential to our lives in the Spirit. God, the consuming fire, refines and purifies creation that all may point toward God's kingdom.

Following God involves a process of refining. Earlier in chapter 12, the author of Hebrews says that God will discipline us as children, "for our good, in order that we may share [God's] holiness" (v. 10). God challenges us to live by certain standards and then holds us accountable.

In my own journey, this refining has been like peeling away layers. The outer layers were easy—crusty bits of things that I had outgrown. They were not important to me. I walked away from those shed layers with a lighter step and a confident smile.

The next few layers were a bit more tricky. These parts were cumbersome, but they were also an integral part of my functioning. To shed these, I would have to adjust to new ways of doing things, new ways of looking at life. It wasn't that I did not want to be changed. But those ways were comfortable and familiar.

Shedding the inner layers is the most difficult. These layers are closest to my core. These are things which feel essential to my way of being and functioning in the world. Peeling them away is like removing a cast which has been on for a long time. It comes off painfully, and the new skin underneath is tender and soft and vulnerable. As these inner layers are removed, I am tender and soft and vulnerable, pliable in the hands of the Creator who is shaping me.

Prayer: *God who is a consuming fire, temper me with your flames that I may be a cornerstone for your kingdom. Remove from me those parts of my life which can be shaken and then soothe me with your healing balm that I may be molded to your will. Amen.*

Wednesday, August 19   Read Luke 13:22-28.

This scripture and others like it scared me when I was young. In fact, they still leave me with an anxious feeling. How will I know which door is the right door? Which door is narrow enough? What if I can't find it?

There are many confusing signals for today's traveler on the spiritual way. I've seen no signs pointing to the narrow door. There are many that show me the "true" way, or the most efficient way; the narrow way is not so popular.

I imagine that the narrow door is off the beaten path, that we have to do some searching to find it. We may be alone on the journey much of the time, but there are others who have gone before us and who leave us hints and markers. I wonder what are some of the signs that help us find the "narrow doorness" of life.

Compassion. The world is close to us today with instant news reporting. There are wars and famines and murders in our living rooms. It seems impossible to enter the way of compassion and not be overcome by it. The way of compassion means not so much generating our own compassion as opening ourselves to be channels of God's infinite compassion.

The unbeaten path. Going along with the crowd seems easier and safer. (Could so many be going the wrong way?) The unbeaten path leads to places of quiet and pain and solitude. It may mean working for peace while the crowd is screaming, "Nuke them!"

Self-examination. Self-examination on the spiritual path means setting ourselves against God's plumb line to see where we need to be shored up or evened out. Entering the narrow door may mean choosing to enter a difficult process of healing old wounds or giving up self-destructive behaviors.

Suggestion for meditation: *Reflect on your journey. What are the narrow doors through which you have passed? Which are facing you?*

Thursday, August 20   Read Luke 13:29-30.

Jesus turns the world order upside down. "People will come from east and west, from north and south." There will be all kinds of folks at God's banquet. There won't be just the folks we usually see. And the head table will look different too. It won't be the usual bunch—the ones with power and money and friends in high places. Some of these will be the last ones in line, and some of "the least" will be sitting at the head table.

"The least" of Jesus' day included the poor, the sick, the widows and orphans, the Gentiles, the women. Who are "the least" of today? They are many of the same as in Jesus' day—the poor, the sick, the women, those who are culturally/racially different from the ones who hold power. They also wear names such as: the children, the homeless, the addict with AIDS, the refugee, the gay or lesbian person, the poor of other countries.

When I look inside myself, I see that there are parts of me which are the least and which I must honor and protect: the new-found gifts which must be nurtured and tended, the wounded places which need time to heal, the needy and anxious parts of me that cry out for constant care and attention. These are the parts of me which I would sometimes rather leave by the side of the road. They embarrass me and slow me down.

Jesus asks us to honor and protect the little ones, the parts of our society and of ourselves which are weaker, which are the disliked and the outcast. Set the table for some extra folks. Stand at the end of the line and enjoy the beauty of God's messianic banquet, of God's rainbow of people.

Suggestion for meditation: *Sit quietly and imagine sitting down to dinner with Jesus. Look around and see who is there. What are you feeling? Jesus has something to say to you. Listen to what Jesus has to say to you; listen to what you have to say to Jesus.*

Friday, August 21   Read Jeremiah 28:1-9.

The setting for the Jeremiah passage is a suffering Judah, caught in the middle of a regional battle between Egypt and Babylon. Jeremiah proclaimed that God's will was for Judah to submit to the rule of the Babylonian ruler, Nebuchadnezzar. The prophet Hananiah prophesied the opposite, that Judah would be restored within two years.

Hananiah's message of peace was good news to those who held out hope that God would save Judah from a difficult servitude. Hananiah was a prophet with a popular message— good news! But Jeremiah challenged Hananiah for prophesying peace when the Lord was calling for the yoke.

People prefer to follow those who predict good news. In economic or global-environment forecasts, it is easier to listen to promises that everything will be okay than to hear anticipated dire outcomes.

Earlier in the Book of Jeremiah God cries out, "They have treated the wound of my people carelessly, saying, 'Peace, peace,' when there is no peace" (6:14). Wounds, whether physical or spiritual, personal or national, must be treated seriously and with care.

Jeremiah brings a message of truth to those who follow God. Sometimes things have to get worse before they get better. Healing involves pain. An abcess has to be cut open and allowed to drain before it will heal. Following God means discerning the way to healing when others are calling out, "Good news! You can get well without pain." Following God means being willing to be remolded into the vessel which will best carry God's message. It is a process of refining, sometimes painful and challenging to us as individuals and to the community of faith.

Prayer: *God who challenges and heals, grant us shalom, wholeness. Make us vessels of your peace. Amen.*

Saturday, August 22   Read Psalm 84:1-8.

Psalm 84 is a pilgrimage hymn. We can imagine it was sung by those on the way to the Temple to worship God. Some came from far away—from Egypt or from the north—to bring their firstfruits of the harvest to dedicate before God, to celebrate a festival with a special sacrifice. The journey was long and probably on foot.

The pilgrims carried with them food and shelter for the journey. They carried the water they would need to get to the next desert spring or well. The pilgrimage itself was an act of dedication to God.

My life does not seem to include such a strenuous act of faith. I drive to church and back in a couple of hours. But when I see my life as the place where God dwells, when I see each day as a part of my faith journey, I realize that I too am a pilgrim.

My journey is through deserts of fire as God burns and shakes away that which is extraneous to my life of faith. It takes me down thorny, little-used paths to narrow doors. My journey confronts me with decisions that challenge me and pit me against the status quo. My journey bids me to follow the true path, even if it is difficult and others have found an easier way.

And, as the psalmist sings, that which leads me on through the desert is my longing for God. "My heart and my flesh sing for joy to the living God." Even the littlest ones may find a place close to God—the sparrow, the outcast, the vulnerable parts of me. Written on my heart are the pathways that will lead me to the place where God lives. And God is the source of my strength for the journey.

Suggestion for meditation: *Breathe deeply and feel your heart and flesh sing for joy to the living God. Close your eyes and imagine your pilgrimage. Where are the dry, rocky places? Where are the cooling springs of water? How is God's strength evident in your journey?*

Sunday, August 23   Read Psalm 84:9-12.

God is the source of strength we need for our journey in faith. God sets challenges ahead of us. It is not easy to follow the path of discipleship. False prophets will call out that they have the way to peace, the simple way, the certain way. But God calls us to see with the eyes of faith the way that we should go. God equips us with the tools we need to live as faithful disciples.

God is our shield. God shelters us from the searing sun, from the swords of the enemy, from the blinding, sandy winds. God calls us to difficult tasks, but promises that we will have what we need to accomplish the tasks. God will not lead us into a wilderness we cannot survive.

God is our strength. God equips us with food and water and companions for the journey. God holds us in tender arms when we are in pain. God carries us on eagles' wings when we are too tired to go any farther. God is our Encourager and Sustainer.

God is our sun. God lights the way through the darkest, longest tunnel. Even when the forces of darkness surround us, we are not alone, for the Light reaches there too. Our deepest wounds are healed as we expose them to the healing light of God's love and care.

God calls us to a difficult road. And then God walks with us on the way, encouraging and protecting us. We are challenged to find the narrow door, to peel away the layers of ourselves which hinder our ability to serve God. But we are not alone. We walk together with each other, with the communion of saints, and with God's loving and protecting spirit.

Prayer: *Loving and protecting God, send us on our way with strength for the journey and joy in our hearts. May we follow the pathways to you which you have written on our hearts. And may we remember that we are never separated from you and your love. Amen.*

EVERY LIVING SOUL BELONGS TO ME

August 24-30, 1992   **David C. Davis†**
Monday, August 24   Read Ezekiel 18:1-4.

In response to God's particular way of caring for people, Israel complains and continues a discussion regarding corporate and individual responsibility. Israel was suffering, so they believed, because of their forebears' sins. Here is an emphasis on a theme found throughout the lectionary lessons: "Who has a part in God's kingdom?" People in all ages have raised questions about who will eventually be a part of God's kingdom. The lessons for this week seem to provide an answer. Ezekiel attempts to get God's message across to the people in spite of their previous ways of thinking, including the use of proverbs. God's message is simply, "Know that all lives are mine." God is an all-inclusive God. This was quite disturbing to a people who thought they were exclusively God's people, which, in their minds, made them the assured inheritors of the Kingdom. They became so complacent in their position that they thought they had the right to complain and even to confront God.

This week's lections will provide us a brief listing of various persons who may be viewed as the people of the Kingdom. It will be important for us to remember those words of God through Ezekiel, "Every living soul belongs to me" (NIV).

Prayer: *Dear Lord, your chosen people forgot the purpose for which they were chosen: to be messengers to all the people in your created world. Help me not to become so obsessed with being your child that I forget I am but one of your children, all of us much loved by you. Amen.*

---

†United Methodist minister; Chaplain and Director of Pastoral Care, Carle Foundation Hospital, Urbana, Illinois.

Tuesday, August 25   Read Ezekiel 18:5-9, 25-29.

Ezekiel continues to provide God's message to the people. He speaks about a righteous person, one who does what is right and just. Even though much emphasis is placed on what a righteous person is not, there are two types of persons who seem to be very important to God; namely, the hungry and the naked.

There are many persons living in our own time who lack food and adequate clothing. We often read and hear about those who live in other parts of the world where there are famines or an inadequate distribution of food and other essential supplies. Perhaps some of us try to do our part by donating a little money which will be used to purchase basic necessities for such persons.

But we often overlook the hungry and naked who may be living in our own communities. We may take pride in supporting local relief organizations which attempt to meet the physical needs of such persons in our communities. But do we let our support for these worthwhile agencies excuse us from personal involvement with God's people who are suffering from a lack of basic necessities?

Prayer: *Dear Lord, it is easier for me to give money to organizations which will distribute it in a more systemized manner than I have time to do. However, I realize that you would have me be involved in the lives of others. Please help me as I try to get more involved in the lives of your people in need. Amen.*

Wednesday, August 26   Read Psalm 15.

This psalm provides, according to many scholars and theologians, one of the best descriptions of a person of God. In this particular scripture such people are identified by the manner in which their speech affects their relationships. It seems peculiar that the way one speaks may identify that person as one of God's people. Yet, this seems to be important to the psalmist. There are two main focal points in this psalm: first, that a person is to speak plainly in order to be understood; and second, that a person is to be careful in what manner speech is directed towards others. This includes living up to standards set by scripture, speaking the truth, not being slanderous, not being insulting, not rebuking, honoring God-fearing persons, and being honest and fair in business dealings.

It may be difficult to find someone to fit this listing of standards. The psalmist does not allow for "good intentions" or "striving for perfections." He puts it simply and in a practical manner, "Here is the way in which you are to relate to other people." It reminds me of a saying I have heard many times in different ways, "What you say may be important, but how you say it will determine how important it is to the hearer." A simple concept, but one of great value!

Prayer: *I come to you, O God, my Creator, knowing that I tend to make some simple concepts into complex theories and principles. Help me to relate in a simple and honest manner to all peoples. Amen.*

Thursday, August 27   Read Hebrews 13:1-2.

The writer of Hebrews reminds us that "mutual love" is the basis of true friendship among people who are a part of God's kingdom. I see this lesson as a continuation of the psalmist's message. Perhaps the Hebrews' author does not take to heart the exhortation of the psalmist to use simple speech. But at the core of the Hebrew writer's message are mentioned persons who are important to God and are to be recipients of one's love and hospitality: strangers.

Strangers have always had a special place in the rules and laws followed by the Israelites. They connected strangers with "holy persons" who might be sent to them by God, almost in the sense of being God's inspectors. Could this be one way that God "checks up" on the chosen people? This line of thought takes something very simple and turns it into a judgmental standard. But if we look at it simply and honestly, it greatly resembles the "golden rule" which speaks plainly of treating others in the same manner we would like to be treated. If one is wandering about in the desert there is always the likelihood of needing food, drink, and shelter. Such provisions are representative of all such things which come our way from our God, the Creator. It is a matter of sharing with others what has been given to us.

Prayer: *O Lord, you who are friend to all, be with me in my efforts to befriend the strangers who come into my life. Be with me as I begin this effort today. Amen.*

Friday, August 28   Read Hebrews 13:3-8.

The writer of Hebrews continues the exhortation to be aware of other persons who are important to God's kingdom: prisoners and those who are oppressed (ill-treated). Both of these probably have one profound feeling in common—loneliness. We are challenged to find ways of dealing with the loneliness we perceive in the lives of others. Loneliness is probably the worst kind of hell one can experience in this life. Some studies have indicated that people do not fear the actual event of death so much as they fear being alone when they die. Those who are lonely—and in the case of our reading, prisoners and oppressed—experience loneliness prior to dying. Again, we are reminded to follow the "golden rule," providing to others what we would like for ourselves. After all, are these persons not a part of God's kingdom?

The writer goes on to speak of principles applying to marriage, immorality, adultery, love of money, and being content with what we have. But I would rather focus my attention on the writer's last admonition for this study, "Remember your leaders." He seems to be saying, "Our leaders drew our attention to the great leader, at least pointed us in that direction, to Jesus Christ." If they point us in the right direction, are we not also to steer others towards Jesus Christ? We may then become aware that such messengers (leaders) are a part of God's kingdom.

Prayer: *I am so sorry, my Lord, that I have not always recognized all of your children who belong to the Kingdom. I have overlooked the prisoners, the oppressed, and those who are my leaders. Help me to look beyond the symbols and titles, to see the persons who live beneath them. Amen.*

Saturday, August 29   Read Luke 14:1,7-11.

Jesus went to dine with a Pharisee. This must have been quite a shock for some of Jesus' followers. In scripture we read that Jesus spoke out rather harshly against the rulers of his day, political and religious. And yet, one of the Pharisees finds a place in Jesus' heart, enough so that Jesus openly acknowledges his friendship by going to dine with him. It is pretty difficult for many of us to think that a political-religious leader could be a part of the Kingdom. Yet, this lesson specifically spells it out for us. It is not what we have or what we have become that assures us a place in the Kingdom.

It may be particularly difficult for many of us to realize that some very politically minded people are a part of God's kingdom. We put together Jesus' words about being humble with what he said about the rich and what the scripture says about the simple folk understanding more than the wise, and we could conclude that only persons with a particular background can enter God's kingdom, can carry God's message of love. Of course, there are persons from many educational, geographic, cultural, and economic backgrounds who carry God's message. Those who believe in Christ and who follow Christ's teachings are a part of God's kingdom, are recognized as God's people, and are called to invite and welcome others into the Kingdom.

Prayer: *I am so limited, O Lord, when I attempt to think in your terms. My human limitations keep me from seeing the broad expanse of your creation which includes all people. Please help me to expand my way of thinking so that I can see all persons more nearly as you see them. Amen.*

Sunday, August 30   Read Luke 14:12-14.

Jesus' story of a marriage feast focuses on the selection of seating patterns that we may be tempted to follow. Jesus speaks of people competing to get one of the seats of honor. In very plain language, Jesus instructs his hearers to think of themselves in a practical manner rather than to think too highly of themselves. They should not take the seats of honor where they might be asked to move in order to make room for someone else. The person who considers himself or herself to be "above" others may be humiliated by discovering other persons are equally important.

This reminds me very much of God's message to the people of Israel when they began to take God for granted, complaining and even blaming God for their sins. In today's scripture reading, Jesus instructs the host to give some additional thought to whom he invites to his house for a meal: the poor, the maimed, the lame, and the blind. Notice that Jesus said nothing about what possessions, privileged positions, or honored social status any of these persons might have. Thus, we are brought full circle back to the Lord's message through Ezekiel that "Every living soul belongs to me" (Ezek. 18:4*a*, NIV).

Prayer: *Precious Lord, my thoughts are so human, and so often judgmental in viewpoint. And I often attempt to apply the same kind of thinking to you. Forgive me for my overly selfish attitude, for my self-centeredness; and for trying to make you less than you are. Help me to be as inclusive of others as you are inclusive in your acceptance of me. Amen.*

SHAKY TIMES AND THE SOLID ROCK

August 31–September 6, 1992   **Larry Peacock†**
Monday, August 31   Read Psalm 94:12-19.

God's truth is a bedrock we can stand on

In shaky times, there are truths on which we can stand. These truths, rock-solid and eternal, cannot be narrowly constructed or exclusively shaped to apply only to "our kind" of people or only for our national security. Rock truths, truths which stand the test of time, are of God, who has not abandoned creation though evil seems to reign and oppression kills those on the edges of society (Ps. 94:3-7).

According to the Mishnah, Psalm 94 was sung communally on the fourth day of the week. Deep in the heart of God's people were placed these two truths: God is a God of justice, though sometimes it seems long in coming and many do suffer; and God is a God of comfort and blessing, though often we see and feel that only in the midst of troubled times.

Such truths of God give us a rock on which to stand as we struggle against such evils as racism, injustice, violence, and oppression which exhibit themselves in structures of discrimination and perpetuate themselves in fear of those different from ourselves.

Such truths also give us a rock to stand on as we call for a spirituality which connects mystery and silence with compassion and service.

Suggestion for meditation: *Recall a time you felt yourself to be in a personal struggle and God was present to help and comfort.*

---

†Co-pastor, Malibu United Methodist Church; author, spiritual director, and retreat leader, Malibu, California.

Tuesday, September 1　　　　　　　Read Psalm 94:20-22.

God is our shelter and strength

North of the San Gabriel Mountains in California there is a monastery situated in the high desert. It is a place of refuge for me. I climb the hill behind St. Andrew's Priory and search out my holy place in the midst of spiky agave plants and withered Joshua trees. There, surrounded by mountains and blue skies, and sitting on coarse, rocky soil, I take shelter in God's creation and God's love. When there were angry questions about my ministry and when I was struggling with my own doubts, I found a refuge in that barren place. When I feel worn out by the wear and tear of the journey through life, there I find rest and shelter.

The poet-prophet of Psalm 94 sees the injustices of scheming and greedy judges and knows the pain (vv. 16-17) of speaking against a prevailing practice, an accepted evil, a national scam. Yet the poet-prophet turns to God for shelter, for a rock-secure place to find time for healing and safety from the assault of the wicked.

We all need those places of refuge, whether they are actual rock-hewn shelters or not, whether we go there physically or just visit them in our minds. We trust God for the healing of wounds and memories and for the strength to enter again into the thick of plots, schemes, and maneuvers that cheat the poor and blame the victim. We can give thanks to God for our places of refuge.

Prayer: *Each rock holds the warmth of your sun, Creator God. I ask that you hold me now in your warm embrace, that you shelter me in your loving care. Be my refuge when the storms of life are raging. Amen.*

Wednesday, September 2   Read Ezekiel 33:1-11.

Rock solid truths often involve hard words

Ezekiel is to speak the hard word of warning. He is to sound the alarm to warn the nation of Israel of its evil ways. He is to blow the trumpet on individuals whose lives rip the fabric of harmony and unravel relationships. But hard words are not the only words in the story. The people are warned, and sitting in exile they begin to bend under the weight of their sins and the echo of the trumpet. They complain to God about their hopelessness, so the prophet bears the answer from God, "Turn from your evil ways and come back. I take no pleasure in the death of the wicked" (AP). God speaks words of warning and yearning.

A friend of mine told me of a time when he lived in a very close community and became convinced that someone there was acting in a way that was damaging to the whole community. My friend went to the leader of the community and shared his concern. He further said if the leader wished, he would take on the task of asking the disturbing member to leave. The leader asked my friend if he loved the offending member. After a pause and a negative answer from my friend, the leader said, "When you love him, you may ask him to leave."

The truth must be spoken, but spoken with hope and love. I am wary of those who relish the role of judge and trumpeter. Hard words, strong words come from hearts aching with love that none should perish and none of God's children be harmed. The truth must be spoken, but spoken with hope and love.

Think of a time you have had to speak a hard word and the grace given you to say it.

Prayer: *Deepen the ache in our hearts for your truth, Holy God, and shape our words to match your passionate desire that all should turn and be saved. Amen.*

Thursday, September 3 Read Luke 14:25-26.

Hold on tight to the Rock; hold on loosely to people

Jesus turns to face the crowd of followers. He speaks words hard to hear, difficult to fathom: "If any one comes to me and does not hate his own father and mother and wife and children and brothers and sisters, yes, and even his own life, he cannot be my disciple." Even with scholarship telling us that the word translated "hate" is closer in meaning to "love less" or "to put in second place," we still struggle with our allegiance to family over against commitment to God. Jesus certainly had respect for the fifth commandment, to honor our mothers and fathers, but on the way to Jerusalem he is preparing his followers for the choices of discipleship.

The question Jesus poses is whether we are willing to place our love of God above all else. Jesus knows God's love for us is eternal and everlasting. We look for affirmation and affection from our families, our friends, our relationships. Kind words, an occasional hug, a moment's recognition are important, but we are sometimes disappointed because we expect a person, a relationship to fulfill all our needs. No family member is perfect, no relationship totally sustaining.

Our families and our relationships are gifts from God, who is like a loving parent. They give us glimpses of God's complete and unconditional love for us. As much as we are able, we are to choose wisely as our mates and friends, those who know the Giver of Life, so that we may discern together the yearning and purpose of the One who turns to us with an invitation to follow with total commitment.

Prayer: *Loving God, we cherish the gift of our family and friends. But help us not to seek from them what is found only in you—our true name and our deepest calling. Amen.*

Friday, September 4   Read Luke 14:27-33.

Hold tightly to the Rock; hold lightly to things

In the winter of 1973, England was experiencing a shortage of fuel and several commodities. Stores were lit by lanterns, and rumors of food shortages cast a sober light on our holiday preparations. A story circulated around the parish I was serving that a woman had been stopped as she was walking home, pulling a child's wagon loaded with bags of sugar. When asked what she was doing, she replied, "I'm trying to beat the hoarders." We laughed but recognized the truth hidden in her words.

In so many clever ways, with lots of clever words, we try in our own ways to beat the hoarders and to avoid the words of Jesus, "Unless you renounce all your possessions, you cannot be my disciple" (AP). It is only one verse, but it echoes the story of the rich young ruler (Luke 18:18-27) and Zacchaeus (Luke 19:1-10). Jesus turns to the followers who long to be disciples and asks them to ponder the cost and face the tenacious web which possessions and money weave around us. No financial plan, no get-rich scheme, no nest egg, no saving-for-college fund is to be more important than our relationship with God.

Our obsession with security, money, and possessions not only costs us our relationship with God but gives us no real pleasure. We never seem to have enough and are constantly driven to get and to be on guard against those who would take from us what we have.

Prayer: *Gracious Giver of every good gift, be with us in our struggle with possessions. Open our hearts and our hands so we may know the freedom of trusting you in all things. Amen.*

Saturday, September 5   Read Philemon 1-7.

Stand on the solid rock and praise God

Someone has said that flattery is telling people exactly what they think of themselves. The end result of flattery, however, is often deflated egos. Praise, on the other hand, works wonders, for it rings true and lifts us to nobler efforts.

Paul has praise for Philemon. Philemon is a leader of the church that meets in his house, and his love for Christ and all the saints has traveled the many miles to Paul in his prison cell. Philemon has carried out his public responsibilities with love, and because of his love, "the hearts of the saints have been refreshed." Paul holds Philemon in his prayers and gives thanks to God for Philemon's love toward others.

In shaky times, it is a comfort to know there are some who hold us in their prayers and give praise to God for our faithful words and deeds. In one church I served, I helped lead a weekly prayer group. On one occasion, we drew the name of another in the group who had a particular prayer request. Without sharing whose cards we had drawn, we took our cards home and covenanted to be in prayer for the individual. Several years and two churches later, I met one of the women from the prayer group who said she had drawn my card and had prayed for me periodically over the years. She wanted to know if she should continue praying for what I had written or for something new. I was awed and moved to know that this woman had carried me to God in prayer over many miles and years.

We can stand on the rock of God's love that comes to us in the lives of many people, and we can praise God for fellow Christians who continue to refresh the hearts of the people of God.

Suggestion for meditation: *Remember and give praise to God for people who hold you in prayer. Pray a prayer of blessing for a younger Christian whom you know and can encourage.*

Sunday, September 6   Read Philemon 8-21.

Let us stand on the Eternal Rock together

The Book of Philemon is not a theological treatise on slavery and social injustice. It is a personal letter which doesn't question the existence of slavery but does begin to undermine its practice in the Christian community.

Paul has been instrumental in the conversion of both Philemon and Onesimus. He is their "father" in the faith. Yet he now finds himself harboring a fugitive slave, albeit a very useful young Christian, who belongs to Philemon. At the very least, in a Roman legal sense, Paul should send Onesimus back and pay a day's wages for each day that he has kept the slave.

But more than law is at work. Could not God have a purpose in this? In God's mysterious way, Paul has been helped, the church has gained a useful worker (a play on words since *Onesimus* means "useful"), and Philemon has a new brother in Christ.

Paul asks Philemon to treat Onesimus differently, not because Paul commands it, or because Philemon might feel indebted to Paul because of any part Paul might have had in his conversion. Rather, Paul urges a new relationship for love's sake.

The love of God transforms old patterns, unhealthy addictions, persistent co-dependencies, obsessive expectations. By our baptism in Christ, we move from living in isolation into the corporate Body of Christ, the barrier-breaking fellowship where all are sisters and brothers.

Paul writes with his heart, hoping, praying, and believing that Philemon will act graciously not out of compulsion but out of spontaneous love and free choice.

Suggestion for prayer: *Add your prayer to Paul's that brotherhood and sisterhood in Christ might be established on the rock of God's love and be a sign to all the world that love can remove barriers.*

September 7-13, 1992   **Ed Trimmer†**
Monday, September 7   Read Psalm 77:11-20.

The beginning verses of this psalm describe the author's concern over God's faithfulness. The psalmist faces serious problems and is very upset that God has not responded to pleas for help. In verse 11, however, the tone suddenly changes. Verses 11-20 remind us of the mighty deeds God has accomplished in the past. It was not until the psalmist remembered God's presence and action in personal and communal history that the heaviness of personal depression and problems could be lifted. While the memory of God's help in the past may not be an adequate pastoral resolution of personal hurt, it does set the momentary, individual pain in the context of what God has done.

For serious questions about God's faithfulness and presence with us to arise in times of trouble and pain is not unusual. To help us through these times it may be helpful to evoke the powerful memory of times when God has been faithful to us in the past, to remember when God has healed and been present in our individual lives and in the life of our community. This remembrance can have the power to transform the pain, and the acknowledgement of the present pain keeps the remembrance of the past honest.

Throughout history, both personal and communal, we will sometimes ask where God is in the midst of our struggles. From this psalmist comes an answer: Remember God's mighty deeds.

Suggestion for prayer and meditation: *"I will call to mind the deeds of the Lord; I will remember your wonders of old." Make a list of the deeds the Lord has done in your life.*

---

†Associate Professor of Christian Education, Methodist Theological School in Ohio, Delaware, Ohio; member of advisory board, YOUTH! magazine.

Tuesday, September 8   Read 1 Timothy 1:12-17.

While the psalmist renews trust that God is faithful by remembering God's mighty acts of the past, the author of this pastoral epistle takes a slightly different direction. In the epistle God is thanked for being faithful as this faithfulness is reflected in the story of Paul's life and salvation.

Because Paul's life is used as the typical example of God's faithfulness, even the worst sinner may take hope. Indeed God's universal saving intent in Christ ought to become obvious, because of God's saving action with Paul.

I have the opportunity to hear many revival services. Often speaker after speaker will spend great time and energy describing his or her past life of sin. In fact, they spend so much time on their past life that it is easy to miss the point of God's saving mercy.

In contrast, the author of 1 Timothy, while reminding us of past transgressions, focuses on gratitude for God's mercy. While some of us can go into great detail about past transgressions, to do so may cause others to miss the point of the universal scope of God's love. I believe we should focus more on our response to God and what God has enabled me to do, or you to do, or Paul to do—a response that is filled with thanks and praise and lives committed to God's service.

Prayer suggestion: *"I am grateful to Christ Jesus our Lord, who has strengthened me, because he judged me faithful and appointed me to his service." Pray to God for strength and continued faithfulness.*

Wednesday, September 9　　　　　　Read Luke 15:8-10.

This week's lectionary readings include two of the three stories in Luke's Gospel about God's love persistently seeking the lost and rejoicing over their redemption.

The parable of the lost coin (today's reading) focuses on the "lostness" of people and how they become lost. In this parable being lost is the result of carelessness, since the woman presumably did not intend to lose the coin. The parable of the lost sheep points to being lost by folly (vv. 1-7), and the parable of the prodigal son points to being lost willfully (vv. 11-31).

While acknowledging that these are significant issues, I would like to focus once again on God's faithfulness to us. God is faithful and searches for me even as one searches for a lost coin. Whether the coin (about a day's wages) represents a significant amount or an insignificant amount (a question of one's socioeconomic situation) is of little consequence. The point remains that God searches for us. God continues to be faithful to us, even while we are lost, and rejoices over our redemption. For this we can be thankful and rejoice!

Suggestion for prayer and meditation: *"Rejoice with me, for I have found the coin that I had lost." Spend the day remembering and rejoicing for the saints (the mothers and fathers) of the faith.*

Thursday, September 10   Read Luke 15:1-7.

Again we hear, as we read the parable of the lost sheep, the theme of God's love persistently seeking the lost and rejoicing over the redemption of even one of us. God continues to be faithful!

It often amazes me how often we who call ourselves Christian insulate ourselves from the "sinners" of the world. We want to have "Christian" yellow pages so that all of our business can be done with other Christians. We exercise while listening to Christian music in our Christian family life centers. Indeed if we want, we can spend almost every waking hour at the church or involved with other Christians.

The so-called righteous of Jesus' day, the Pharisees and scribes, were concerned that Jesus was spending his time with sinners. Why, Jesus even had meals with them! Surely this must negatively affect Jesus' own spirituality, or so the "righteous" thought. In response to their "grumbling" Jesus told a parable.

This parable may remind us that we ought to be more involved with those who are lost than those "persons who need no repentance." Even with a large flock (a hundred sheep was a large flock in Jesus' day), the focus is not on the needs of the ninety-nine but on the one who is lost. Repentance is what brings joy to the heart of God. God's mercy breaks through all human restrictions on how God should act toward sinners.

Prayer: *Forgiving God, we do not want to be numbered among the Pharisees of our day. Help us demonstrate your love and faithfulness to those around us, regardless of their earthly status. Teach us to rejoice when just one person turns to you. Amen.*

Suggestion for meditation and Christian action: *"This fellow welcomes sinners and eats with them." Invite someone to eat with you who is outside the faith community.*

Friday, September 11   Read Hosea 4:1-3.

Up until now we have been focusing on God's faithfulness; it is now time to focus on our own faithfulness.

Hosea, a prophet of God, spends these few verses condemning God's people, the community of the faithful. Hosea points to God's indictment against Israel both as individuals and as a community of faith. The prophet says that there is no faithfulness or loyalty in the land, that there is no real understanding or knowledge of God. Morality is being ignored.

Hosea was concerned with the pride of the people in their wealth and in their military power. Surely, the same can be said for many of us. If Hosea were preaching today, would he not speak similar words to us as individuals and as a community?

The indictments God has against us, that Hosea would point out, would probably concern individual morality in areas such as abuse of drugs and of alcohol, lying, swearing, murder, and gambling. Some of the indictments against corporate morality might include a life-style of consumerism, economic profit and growth at the cost of creation, acceptance of legalized gambling, the rise of individualism at the cost of community, and the racism of many of our institutions, including the church.

Hosea is concerned with the pride of the people in their wealth and in their military power. Surely the same can be said for many of us.

These verses end with a desolate picture of the suffering of God's creation. To many of us, a similar picture can be painted of God's creation today. A call for repentance is needed, a return to faithfulness.

Suggestion for meditation: *"There is no faithfulness or loyalty, and no knowledge of God in the land." Make a list, much like Hosea's, of the faithfulness or lack of faithfulness in ourselves and in our faith communities.*

Saturday, September 12   Read Hosea 5:15–6:3.

Hosea realized that God longed to find in God's people steadfast love (constant loyal devotion responding to God's own outpoured constant love) and true knowledge of God (intimate experience of communion with God, not mere information about God). What was lacking in God's people was not only religious vitality and devotion but the fundamental religious consciousness which might be expected in any people who had reflected at all upon human life and destiny.

Hosea realized that true response to God comes not from the acceptance of ideas or dogmas. True response to God concerns *the will* as well as the intellect and the emotions. True turning to God calls for both love and knowledge, separating oneself from evil and *acting justly* to affirm life and God's creation.

Hosea reminds us that if we return to God and our turning is not a false repentance, as much of Israel's was, God will be faithful and return to us. But for our repentance to occur there must be some sense of searching before the divine law, a sense of the judgment of God (not just the love of God), a sense of a loss of an *intimate* relationship which can only gradually be restored.

Hosea uses the imagery of showers to help the people understand this point. In a land and a time where rain literally meant the difference between life and death, between growth and decay, the imagery is powerful. The land was totally dependent upon spring rains. When those rains came, the land rejoiced. If we are faithful, if we return to an intimate relationship with God, our joy will be like those showers bringing us growth and life, not decay and death.

Suggestion for prayer and meditation: *"Come, let us return to the Lord. . . . [God] will come to us like the showers, like the spring rains that water the earth."* *Spend the day reflecting upon those aspects of your life that need repentance.*

Sunday, September 13   Read Hosea 6:4-6.

Hosea answers one of the age-old questions: What does God want of us? "I [God] desire steadfast love and not sacrifice, the knowledge of God rather than burnt offerings."

In churches and seminaries around the United States, spirituality has become a major focus. Fifteen or twenty years ago interest in Christian spirituality appeared to be slight among seminary students. In contrast, in the past few years seminaries offering courses in Christian spirituality have seen these classes filled repeatedly.

My initial reaction to this new interest in spirituality was great enthusiasm and excitement. *It's about time,* I thought. It was a joy to read such books as Richard J. Foster's *Celebration of Discipline*, Rueben P. Job and Norman Shawchuck's *A Guide to Prayer for Ministers and Other Servants*, and more recently *A Guide to Prayer for All God's People*. I sought a deeper spiritual life to help my faith.

But now I have some reservations. I see a spirituality developing in many congregations that often has little or no relationship to the world, a spirituality that tends to focus on the personal realm of spirituality and ignores the communal and corporate realms. Further, it tends to enable one to disengage from the real problems of the world.

Is the current spirituality of many of us today akin to the sacrifices and burnt offerings of Hosea's age? Will God say to us, "I desire steadfast love and knowledge, not personal piety and prayers"? How will our current interest in spirituality relate to being faithful?

Suggestion for prayer and Christian action: *"I desire steadfast love and not sacrifice, the knowledge of God rather than burnt offerings." Reflect upon this passage this week. Spend part of the day today or in the coming week working with the poor or disenfranchised.*

FROM SOMETHING TO SOMETHING

September 14-20, 1992 **Fred Venable†**
Monday, September 14 Read Psalm 107:1-22

Psalm 107 is a song of thanksgiving. Our lection expresses thanks for being delivered from wandering in the desert wasteland. The pilgrims were also redeemed from prisons (v. 10), hard labor (v. 13), darkness and gloom (v. 14), and illness (v. 17).

Verse 2 is the text for today:

Let the redeemed of the LORD say so,
 those he redeemed from trouble.

We who are redeemed are redeemed *from* something—we are saved *from* something. But our redemption is complete only when we realize we are redeemed *to* something.

Israel was redeemed out of desert wastes. That was literal for them; it is not literal for me. The only "desert wastes" I have known are in traveling our beloved West. I always had an adequate car, occasional gas stations, and passable roads. Not a lot of trouble; and for any trouble I did have, I found help in friendly fellow travelers.

But I know that is not what this psalm means for me or you. Inside, where our issues of life and death are settled, we all have many desert wastes and prisons and illnesses and dangers. The name for all these is sin.

From the time God called Abraham, God has been redeeming us from sin. That deserves our praise. Today let us say so!

Prayer: *Accept our praise, O God, for redeeming us. Amen.*

---

†Senior pastor, Hillsboro United Methodist Church, Hillsboro, Oregon.

Tuesday, September 15   Read Psalm 107:1-9.

> Some wandered in desert wastes,
>   finding no way to a city to dwell in;
> hungry and thristy,
>   their soul fainted within them. (RSV)

Ever since Adam and Eve were sent forth from the garden, we have looked for a city to dwell in. Exhausted in the search, our souls faint.

We have a year-old schnauzer for a pet. He has a salt-and-pepper colored coat, and around his face are strong markings of white and black. Looking from under those long eyebrows, his eyes reveal a penetrating intelligence. His name is Wise and Wonderful Rabbi. Rabbi's intelligence isn't all that great, but he has one distinct advantage over me: He is completed in his nature. I am not.

When Rabbi was a day old, his "dogginess" was complete. My humanness still is not complete here, and I am on the upper side of middle age. Rabbi never lies awake at night and asks of the darkness, *What's wrong with me? When will I ever learn? Am I okay? Will I ever become real?*

I ask those questions. I am badgered by them. Rabbi frolics in playful completeness while I continue to look for a city in which to dwell where I will be complete. I fear my hunger and thirst will cause my soul to faint within me before I reach that place.

Yet, as Rabbi's completeness is a gift, so will mine be. The first Adam got me into this; it will take the Second Adam, Christ, to get me out. It is a condition to which I was born, and on my own I am powerless to change it. The power to change comes to me as a gift. I accept it, walk with it, follow it, and find my path out of the desert wastes to wholeness and health.

Prayer: *O God, I am powerless to redeem myself from sin. Make me whole and complete. Amen.*

Wednesday, September 16   Read Psalm 107:1-9;
                                     Exodus 6:2-9.

> Then they cried to the LORD in their trouble,
> and he delivered them from their distress.

What did the people of Israel do as they wandered among the desert wastes? "They cried to the LORD in their trouble." This same remedy is repeated for each of the other distresses covered in this psalm.

This is an oft-repeated theme of the Old Testament. God called Israel to be a special people. Trying to follow God, they failed. God rescued them. Again they failed. Again God rescued them. This pattern of call-failure-rescue is repeated over and over in the history of Israel.

It is difficult for us to read this history without getting impatient with Israel for their failure to be God's people—if we do not realize that it is our history, too. Wilderness, illnesses, prisons—Israel experienced them all. So do we. God reached out and promised Israel a way out of their troubles, as before when Moses led them across the Red Sea. Yet they were reluctant to believe this word from God because of "their broken spirit and their cruel bondage" (RSV).

Spirits are broken and bondage becomes cruel when our repeated efforts fail. As Israel saw other nations strong, they wanted such strength. We want by our own strength—or wisdom or cunning—to save ourselves. But only God can redeem us. That is gospel truth.

Prayer: *Help us, O God, to set aside our pride to redeem ourselves so that we can accept your redemption. Amen.*

Thursday, September 17   Read Hosea 11:1-7.

Grace is hard to accept and hard to keep. It is difficult because grace is the opposite of most all our human activities. Our lives from the beginning are dominated by the belief that effort guarantees results. The equation of grace is that no effort guarantees results.

"The more I called them, the more they went from me," God said. They kept sacrificing and burning incense to idols. They wanted to live the belief that effort guarantees results, so if they wanted protection and a destiny, they had better do something. They found unacceptable God's offer of grace apart from any effort from them. They did not understand grace. Today, grace is still a stumbling block.

Even when we were small, we learned that certain behavior got us favors. We learned that good grades brought favorable responses from our parents. Fighting with our sister brought punishment; not fighting earned approval. When we stayed out too late, we got grounded. But the end-around run for sixty yards and the winning touchdown sent Mom and Dad into an ecstasy that lasted for months. What praise and approval we got from them! And then in church we heard, "God is like a father."

Oh! Then God accepts us for our good behavior and is distant when behavior is bad. A month's work gets a month's pay. When we try hard, we succeed.

God said to Israel, "I love you not for what you do, but because you are you." That didn't make sense. It still doesn't today. But that is grace, and our Christian faith is built upon that one foundational rock.

Prayer: *Lord God, help us accept your love freely given to us. Amen.*

Friday, September 18   Read Hosea 11:8-11.

How can I give you up, O Ephraim!
How can I hand you over, O Israel!

God declares to Hosea, "I am God and no mortal, the Holy One in your midst, and I will not come in wrath." Therefore God cannot give up on Ephraim or hand over Israel. They are God's—always have been, always will be.

And all this in spite of their unworthiness! Again, we see that stumbling block to grace, that insistent wish to make the effort, to earn the grace.

A favorite cartoon of mine shows a Salvation Army worker standing with her tambourine. Lying at her feet is a derelict. Looking up at her, he asks, "Can you save me here, or do I have to go someplace?" Our tendency is always to ask if we "have to go someplace." God will redeem me *when*—when I shape up, when I stop being so angry, when I practice spiritual disciplines, when I lose forty pounds, when I stop drinking.

No, God redeems us where we are, as we are. Being God and not human, God makes no demands on us. God's equation is not our equation.

After I mentioned going to church, an elevator operator I was talking to asked me if I was a Christian. I said, "Yes, Are you?" Just as the door closed, she answered, "No. I'm not good enough." I wasn't able to tell her she does not have to be good enough. None of us does. Israel was never good enough. Israel was shot through with unworthiness, but God loved them anyway. There is nothing we can do to make ourselves worthy of God's love, for God loves us infinitely already. We do not have to "go someplace."

Prayer: *Thank you, God, for your love we do not understand and of which we do not have to be worthy. Amen.*

Saturday, September 19   Read 1 Timothy 2:1-7.

God's grace is given with an end in view: that we live a certain quality of life. The Book of First Timothy says we are to lead a "quiet and peaceable life, godly, and respectful in every way." It is to be a life patterned after the attributes of God. It is to be the style of life which Jesus lived.

And it will require effort on our part. Grace does not mean that we do nothing; it means that the first act is God's act. Grace does not mean that we are not to be moral; it just means that we cannot obtain by being moral the acceptance we must first get by grace. Morality comes after grace. Growth means moral effort and struggle. There is a price to be paid.

Someone has written that in Christian ethical teaching, *noblesse oblige*. That means "nobility obligates." Prince Andrew visited our country in the spring of 1984 and while in Hollywood, he sprayed paint on some cameramen. Rather than apologizing, he said he rather enjoyed doing it. The press castigated him for his behavior, as well it should. Why? Because such behavior is not seen as fitting of anyone of noble birth. People of noble birth are obligated to behave better than that. We who have been ennobled by God's grace, we who have been made God's children, are obligated to act in a way that befits our right to call Jesus our elder brother.

"By grace you have been saved through faith. . . . For we are what [God] made us, created in Christ Jesus for good works, which God prepared beforehand to be our way of life" (Eph. 2:8, 10).

Prayer: *O God, may what we do this day be as close as possible in character to what you have done for us. Amen.*

Sunday, September 20 Read Luke 16:1-13.

From our desert wastes of sin God redeems us with divine grace. We are redeemed by grace not to stop but to begin to go forward. God calls us to move out into the world in new and challenging behavior patterns. Not to do this should be the exception rather than the rule.

Several years ago, a man in the San Francisco Bay area was found by one of those organizations that search out missing heirs. He was heir to a fortune of $260,000. This man had lived for years in the skid-row section of his city. He wore scruffy boots and worn-out jeans. Still, the story was not all that remarkable. Many people inherit large sums of money. A sizable number are searched out and given money they did not even know about. It was months later that this man's story was publicized around the country. That happened when someone found out he had put the money in the bank and still lived on skid row in his dilapidated room. He still wore the same boots and worn-out jeans.

That man had a fortune in the bank, but it did not change his behavior. How like some of us! We have a fortune in the grace of God, but we still live the shabby, worn-out lives of a faithless world.

Many people apply what the world gives them more shrewdly than we who are heirs of God's grace apply what God has given us. We have a fortune in God's grace. Shouldn't we this day live like it?

Prayer: *Thank you, God, for your unlimited and unmerited grace. Help us live fully this day in your grace. Amen.*

GOD'S LOVINGKINDNESS

September 21-27, 1992   **Paul Barton**†
Monday, September 21   Read Psalm 107:1, 33-43.

What is God's response to the poor and needy? Several passages in this week's readings focus on the relationship between the rich and the poor and God's relationship with the rich and the poor.

The author begins this psalm by inviting others to share in his gratitude to a God who responds with "lovingkindness." The Hebrew meaning for *lovingkindness* is "God's constant commitment to people and creation." God's lovingkindness is the expression of solidarity with God's people.

During our evening worship on Sundays and Wednesdays, women stand up "to give thanks to the Lord." They begin their testimony saying: *"Quiero dar gracias al Señor porque . . ."* ("I want to thank the Lord because . . .") In their testimonies of thanksgiving, they do not take for granted the obvious—health, work, family, and faith. Some of these same women work long hours hunched over sewing machines at a clothing factory. They have to meet an hourly quota for buttons, seams, or belt-loops. Each day they return home from work exhausted from the monotonous routine and the back-breaking working conditions. Because of their faith, these women, who suffer unjust working conditions and low wages, are able to stand up and give thanks for God's lovingkindness. They know that God is with them.

Prayer: *God, open our eyes to your acts of lovingkindness so that we may participate in them. Lift up the needy, and grant a heart of compassion and sensitivity to those in positions of power. Amen.*

---

†Pastor, La Iglesia Metodista El Buen Pastor, Kingsville, Texas.

Tuesday, September 22   Read Psalm 107:33-43.

In this psalm God's lovingkindness is expressed through God's solidarity with the poor and needy. The psalmist portrays a God who takes sides. This God punishes the wicked and executes justice on behalf of the powerless, the hungry, the needy. Here is a God who "lifted the needy out of thier affliction, and increased their families like flocks" (v. 41, NIV).

I struggle with this passage as I wonder how God goes about lifting up the needy and bringing down the wicked. In the psalmist's eye, God uses creation to execute justice. The prosperous land of the wicked becomes fallow, while the oppressed receive a land full of harvest and a city that is habitable. Considering the stewardship that humankind has practiced over creation, it seems that God does not have to do anything more than leave human beings to continue in their actions until they create their own deserts.

God also works through us to carry out justice. At some time in our lives, we find ourselves working on behalf of others who are being mistreated or who are in conditions of need. At other times, our consciousness does not allow us to be silent in the face of flagrant injustices. Many instances come to mind of the needy and the powerless throughout the world rising up to demand adequate food, housing, health, water. God provides us with the faith and the vision to realize divine justice.

God's spirit is a justice-bent spirit (Isaiah 43) that works in creation and in human beings to realize glimpses of God's kingdom. The psalmist calls forth a faith that does more than "consider the steadfast love of the Lord"; he calls forth a faith that emulates God's lovingkindness in our own lives.

Prayer: *O God of creation and justice, make us mindful of your kingdom, and give us the grace to live as its standard-bearers. Amen.*

Wednesday, September 23   Read Joel 2:23-27.

This passage begins with the call to rejoice and be glad in the Lord for the restoration of the land. The prophet Joel reminds us that God is the one who continues re-creating our world through the lifegiving elements of nature. The restoration of the land is God's way of showing faithfulness. Joel calls us to rejoice not only because the land has brought forth an abundant harvest but more importantly because God has remained faithful and gracious to God's people.

Swarms of locusts had devastated the land of Israel. Joel regarded this "army" as God's punishment toward a sinful people. Yet there is evidence that the people repented, for God brought about a time of harvest following the devastation of the land.

During a spring and summer of drought in south Texas, the land turned gray and dusty. Members of the church I pastored continued to ask for prayers for rain. They recognized, as did Joel, that our continued presence in creation depends on God's grace working through creation—harvest, rain, sunlight. The day that rain finally came, I ran outside and rejoiced in God's faithfulness. To see the rain fill the cracked, grassless earth filled my heart with gladness.

The lovingkindness of God is expressed through divine actions of solidarity with God's people and in lifegiving creation. This steadfast love is not simply sentiment, but is clothed with acts of justice and mercy. God responds not simply by bringing about justice through creation but also by fulfilling the divine promise to remain their God, to forgive them and to redeem them.

Prayer: *God, your response to us has been faithfulness and mercy. Where there is drought, let your rain fall in abundance. Where there is sinfulness, bring repentance. Where there is repentance, bring forgiveness. Where there is forgiveness, bring rejoicing. Amen.*

Thursday, September 24   Read Joel 2:28-30.

The image of pouring evokes feelings of gratitude. When water is poured upon the baptized child, or the wine is poured into the communion cup, we understand ourselves as recipients of God's love. With the promise of the Holy Spirit given, we are called to rejoice for the fulfillment of that promise.

Prior to the day of judgment, the Spirit will bring about prophecy, dreams, and visions. God's spirit will be poured out even among the "servants, both men and women" (TEV). God's spirit is given to open the eyes of young and old, male and female, rich and poor, so that all may respond to God's grace.

The reception of the Holy Spirit at Pentecost is but one instance in which this promise was fulfilled. There are many times in history in which God's spirit has been poured out to bring about repentance and deliverance. John Wesley, Martin Luther King, Jr., Sojourner Truth, and Oscar Romero were Spirit-led men and women who directed the world's attention toward justice and righteousness.

Yet God's spirit is poured out not only upon legendary men and women but on all those who call upon the name of the Lord. One of the most inspiring laypreachers I have ever heard is a 72-year-old member of my church. His preaching and witnessing radiate God's spirit.

God's faithfulness extends even to the gift of the Holy Spirit. The spirit which God gives enlightens our human spirits, so that we are able to respond to God's lovingkindness with rejoicing, thankfulness, and generosity.

Prayer: *We give thanks to you, O Lord, for your faithfulness extends even to the gift of your Spirit. Pour out your Spirit upon us, that we may live and speak your truth. Amen.*

Friday, September 25   Read 1 Timothy 6:6-19.

The passage from Psalm 107 asks, "How does God respond to the poor?" Paul's letter to Timothy answers the question, "How are the rich to respond to the poor?" The passage from Timothy places the value of material wealth within the context of generosity and life before God.

Paul tells Timothy that the rich can respond to the less fortunate with either greed or generosity. They can either make the attainment of wealth their ultimate goal or use their resources to benefit the well-being of others. The relationship that Paul advocates between the wealthy and the poor is a relationship filled with generosity and sharing.

Many of us are willing to compromise our integrity, to realign friendships, and to neglect our families for the love of money. Paul is straightforward in declaring a painful truth, that many persons have "wandered away from the faith and pierced themselves with many pains" for the love of money.

Paul encourages Timothy to "instruct those in the present age who are rich not to be haughty or to set their hopes on the uncertainty of riches, but rather on God." The response of the rich toward the poor is to be generous with their goods.

A daughter of one of the wealthiest families in South Texas, Sarita Kenedy East had a strong relationship with her church. In her elderly years, she donated her vast landholdings and wealth to her church to establish a foundation. The foundation that she began has provided millions of dollars of aid to respond to the needs of the disadvantaged.

Sarita Kenedy East is remembered for her generosity. How will we be remembered?

Prayer: *We thank you, Lord, for the opportunity to share in the lives of others through giving and receiving. Give us generous hearts in our giving and gracious hearts in our receiving. Amen.*

Saturday, September 26   Read Luke 16:19-21.

According to this passage, one of the ways that some people respond to the needy is to ignore them. The rich man confined himself within a world of wealth. If he had lived today, he might have had a wall surrounding his estate, a limousine with tinted windows, and a vast array of fine clothes and valuable collections. His concern for the finer things in life would not allow him to cross paths with dirty Lazarus.

Lazarus's standing at the rich man's gate is no different from the world's poor standing at the gates of the wealthy. I am reminded of the thousands of poor persons in the *favelas* of Rio de Janeiro who live on the mountainside overlooking the wealthy in their high-rise apartments by the sea, or the inner-city barrios encircled by elite communities in the United States. In place of the dogs licking the sores of Lazarus, the diseases of tuberculosis and hepatitis sap the life out of neglected children.

Those who are neither wealthy nor poor are offended when they must encounter the homeless on the streets. We are afraid of being attacked by impoverished youth who have taken to violence. The legal response to these persons is to make laws to remove them from public places.

Frederick Buechner wrote, "The Gospel is bad news before it is good news."* The bad news is our failure to respond to the poor with the same lovingkindness that God shows them. The good news is that God does not overlook the poor.

Suggestion for meditation: *Meditate on the neglected and disadvantaged members of your community. How does God want your community, your church, you to respond to them?*

---

*Frederick Buechner, *Telling the Truth: The Gospel as Tragedy, Comedy, and Fairy Tale* (New York: Harper & Row Publishers, New York, 1977), p. 7.

Sunday, September 27   Read Luke 16:22-31.

The message that one receives from this passage in Luke greatly depends upon his or her social condition. If a poor person had heard Jesus' words, he would have hope for justice and for eternal life in the presence of God. If a wealthy person had heard Jesus' words, he or she would hear a warning against greed and insensitivity toward the needy. Since this passage was directed toward persons in position of wealth, it must be accepted for what it is: a warning to those who have wealth not to neglect or disregard the needy.

After the rich man finds himself in the fiery furnace, does he have true repentance, or is it simply regret after the fact? In hopes that his family will repent before it is too late, the rich man wants Lazarus to return to the earth so that he may warn them of their impending disaster. Abraham reminds the rich man that his family has everything necessary for repentance: the Law and the prophets found in the scriptures.

More than just an allegory to describe what happens to selfish persons, this second half of the parable directs us to reread the scriptures so that we may better understand how we might respond to the poor. The scriptures clearly advocate compassion and generosity toward the poor. Jesus often spoke about the priority of faith over the priority of wealth (see Luke 18:18-25, for example).

Will we listen to the scriptures? Will we listen to the cries of the poor? Can we respond to the poor in the same way God has— with lovingkindness, generosity, justice, and compassion, offering hope?

Prayer: *Lord, make our eyes and ears sensitive to the suffering around us. Let not our hearts be hardened by the overwhelming demands for help. Give us instead your graciousness and generosity, so that we may hope to be with Lazarus in the life ever after. Amen.*

THE CALL OF JUSTICE

September 28–October 4, 1992   **Carolyn E. Johnson†**
Monday, September 28   Read Amos 5:10-15.

When I was a child, nothing was more fun than our neighborhood kickball games. Sometimes, we just lost track of the time and played past our deadline. Then we would hear the most ominous sound of all, a call from one of our parents, usually mine. This call was something like "Carolyn Elaine Johnson, come here!" We would look up and see one or more of our moms standing at the gate to the field. We would run to the gate and try to negotiate for just a few more minutes, pleading and promising all sorts of things.

During the days of Amos, the gate to the city was more than a point of entrance. It was the site where important business was transacted, especially the hearing and deciding of disputes. Justice was rendered at the gate. Amos reminds the people that they must do more than be good; they must *seek* goodness, a goodness interlocked with the establishment and maintenance of justice.

When my mother called all three of my names, it was a dramatic call to remembrance, responsibility, and relationship. So it is with justice. We must remember the call of conversion and commitment as a determinant of the direction for our lives. We must remember the call of the cross which enables us to remain in a faithful, loving relationship with God and each other.

Prayer: *Ever-loving God, as we hear your call to justice, let our hearts be embraced with a new compassion to seek you and live. Amen.*

---

†Senior Research Associate for the Afro-American Studies and Research Center, Purdue University, West Lafayette, Indiana.

Tuesday, September 29　　　　　Read Amos 5:6-7, 10-13.

Called to conversion

Justice demands conversion, the act of turning away from that which distances us from God's purposes and the continuing process of restoring and remaining in a correct relationship with God. The restoration of relationship and the reforming of our lives are vital aspects of conversion.

The onset of new technologies such as computer word processing has drastically changed the way in which many of us do our work. Gone are the old typing days of carbon paper, messy correction fluids, and typewriter erasers. There was a time when you could distinguish the home-typed document from the professionally typeset one by looking at the right margin. The left margin of the home-typed sheet was straight, but the right margin was jagged and crooked. Computers make the right margins straight with a function called justification, the ability to make each line fit into a relationship with the straight right margin. It self-adjusts as you type, keeping primary the task of staying in a right relationship.

We are not computers and shouldn't strive to be, yet the computer reminds us that we should be constantly trying to self-adjust as we live out our lives. Justice doesn't have to be thought of as correction after the fact; it can be a constant way of living and doing what is just. Justice means understanding that we have some responsibility for the consequences of our actions.

As a prophet, Amos was speaking both for God and before God. He reminded the people that justice was more than an end product. It was a method, a means of living.

Suggestion for prayer: *Pray about an issue which you think needs justice at the gate. Pray for a conversion in the hearts and minds of those involved.*

Wednesday, September 30   Read Psalm 101.

Called to conviction

Stories and jokes abound about St. Peter and the gates of heaven. Usually these stories focus on some aspect of behavior from our earthly lives which will determine whether we are permitted to enter the pearly gates. What are the standards by which we will be judged? What are the standards by which we monitor ourselves?

The psalmist makes a bold statement, a pledge of the ethics by which he will live. Think about the public vows and pledges you have made, such as those in scouting organizations or clubs, marriage vows, oaths of office and profession, allegiances to flag and country. These are our public statements to which we are willing to be held accountable—our pledges as an ethic, a plumb line, for our behaviors. They are statements of the convictions that will drive our behavior.

Yet we know that the words of our public pledges are often not practiced in private. The psalmist asserts the vow that his actions on behalf of God in his private settings will also prevail in the public stances he takes.

How often do justice issues seem depressing and distressing? We often focus solely on our need to work on these as part of our Christian duty. The psalmist provides for us a wonderful gem about the nature of justice—it can be a pleasurable reward. To do justice is an honor and a cause for celebration.

Prayer: *God, lead us to know your righteousness and to act justly toward all people. Amen.*

Thursday, October 1   Read Luke 17:7-10.

Called to commitment

Gertie, a retired nurse, is still active at 90. Although she wears a leg brace, she can get around well enough to do her volunteer work at the local hospital and for several charities and service clubs. Recently, she was presented with an award for 70 years of community service.

She shied away from press coverage and was upset that the award also included a special dinner in her honor. Reluctant to receive any glory, she commented, "It's just me, and the way I do things. It's nothing special; it's what I'm supposed to do—help others."

How wonderful it must be to have developed a sense of service to others so integral to one's behavior that it is "nothing special"! Paid servants have a contract and an obligation to do the task as a basis for future payment. Voluntary servanthood requires a contract of heart, mind, and will.

The gospel message reminds us that as servants of God, what drives us should not be the search for acclaim or acknowledgment but the search to find every avenue available to express our love for God and each other. We will accept appreciation humbly, because the tasks are no longer for our glory but for God's.

Prayer: *Gracious God, let your love sustain and nurture us as we strive to do justice. Amen.*

Friday, October 2   Read Luke 17:5-6.

Called to clarity

When they asked Jesus to increase their faith, perhaps the disciples were thinking, as we often do, that more is better. But in focusing on justice we must look at the power of our faith, not at some artificial measure of quantity.

On the last day of a spiritual growth class, I tried an experiment with the students. I showed them a stick of chewing gum and said that this gum was special; it was like faith and could help solve our problems. All they had to do was chew it. I asked them to chew the piece of gum I had given each of them. But they all laughed, reminding me I hadn't given them any gum. I insisted I had indeed given them gum, and I asked how many believed me. No one seemed to believe me until one student finally began to look around her seat for any sign of gum. Another student stood up, turned his chair over, and to his surprise found a stick of gum taped to the bottom. Others did the same and also found gum. They were so sure they didn't have it because they hadn't actually seen me give it to them.

We cannot see the promises God has given us, yet we must trust that no problem is greater than God's power and that we can become empowered by God. Our faith in God's power gives us clarity of vision to examine justice in a new perspective—the perspective of a power that can make a difference and can move a mountain, even if the mountain is ourselves.

Suggestion for meditation: *Do a litany by praying for several different justice concerns. Between each prayer sentence sing or say softly the chorus of "Open My Eyes" : Silently now I wait for thee, ready, my God, thy will to see. Open my eyes, illumine me, Spirit divine!**

**Hymn, words by Clara H. Scott.

Saturday, October 3   Read 2 Timothy 1:8-12.

Called to courage

Fear of suffering and shame can be a powerful threat to leading a justice-based life. And overcoming that fear can be the greatest act of courage. Participants at a meeting were asked to state reasons why they were not more actively involved in justice issues. Lack of time, lack of information, and uncertainty about their skills were the most frequently cited reasons. One woman, after she had already given one of these reasons, said those were her public excuses. In reality, she was afraid that her association with these issues might hurt her. Through her tears she explained that at one time she thought about volunteer work for a rape crisis center, but she turned it down at the last minute because she didn't want people to think that she might have been raped. She is concerned about AIDS and related issues, but fear made her reject an invitation to serve on a task force, because people might think she or someone in her family had AIDS.

In the epistle, we are reminded that the protection of self is less important than the need to be a witness to the love of Christ. For many of us, real courage is doing those things which we feel will lead to embarrassment, rejection, isolation, and/or loss of self-esteem. These fears emanate from the drive to protect self. For some, gates become not the entryway from the outside, but a way of preventing the outside from entering.

As Christians, we must seek the courage to live out our convictions, understanding that if these convictions are centered in Christ we can be sustained by his love and by the enabling power of the Holy Spirit.

Prayer: *Almighty God, grant us the courage and the wisdom for the facing of this hour. Amen.*

Sunday, October 4   Read 2 Timothy 1:1-7, 13-14.

Called to the cross

"Who me? I'm just a turtle on a fence." This piece of African-American folklore was at one time a frequent response to a compliment. The point was, if you saw a turtle on a fence, you would surely wonder how it got there. You would know someone had to put it on the fence, and someone or something had to keep it there. The saying was a way of acknowledging that our successes are not ours alone; we have been encouraged, nurtured, and mentored by people who have helped us arrive at our points of maturity. We are maintained by the love of God, support of friends and family, and a heritage of faith.

In this letter Timothy is reminded of his heritage. This remembrance is perhaps a means of recognizing that we fall on a continuum of history. We must be humble in recognizing that the way has been prepared for us, but we must also be bold and assertive in carrying on the torch of the legacy of our inheritance.

Since the creation, justice and truth have been interwined. We are called to be the guardians of truth and the facilitators of justice. The truth is that the God who calls us to conversion and demands conviction is also the God whose compassion gives us courage. The truth is that the God who gives us clarity of thought is also the God who demands commitment. The truth that the cross has made us different, made us anew, is the same truth which acknowledges that the cross is about justice; and there is no justice without the cross. The cross is the place where mind, heart, and spirit bind together for justice. Answer the call; it's time to go home.

Prayer: *May the love of truth and the search for justice be our journey home. Amen.*

BEING MADE WHOLE

October 5-11, 1992   **W. Douglas Mills†**
Monday, October 5   Read Psalm 26:1-3.

The Book of Psalms may contain the best-loved pieces of scripture, for both Christians and Jews. The Psalms are poetry, hymnody, prayers. There are some similarities between some psalms and some other parts of scripture: there are prophetic psalms, historical psalms, psalms which sound like Proverbs and psalms which extol the Law. Still, many of the psalms are different because they are, in the first place, the words and voices of people—our kinfolk—addressing God.

The psalms are the words that people just like us have used throughout God's history to speak to God. Psalms like this one express the emotions of God's people struggling with a living faith. We read, hear, and speak words of confusion, words of disorientation, words of praise, words of confession, words of comfort, and words of joy.

Because the Psalms are so honest, they are also frightening. When we read the anguish of our spiritual ancestors, we recognize that we, too, have felt that way, have wanted to say those things to God, have looked for an outlet for that kind of hard, heartfelt emotion.

We find that outlet and release when we use the Psalms as our own prayers. As the "authorized" prayers of the people of God, the psalms give us permission to search ourselves, to open ourselves to the clarifying light of God, to build our relationship with God on open and honest communication.

Prayer: *O God, test my heart and test my mind. Keep your steadfast love ever before me, that I may walk in faithfulness to you. Amen.*

---

†United Methodist clergy working in new church development, Farmington, New Mexico.

Tuesday, October 6   Read Psalm 26:4-12.

Psalm 26 may be called, technically, a lament. However, the particular misfortune which caused this utterance is not described for us. In ancient Israel, worshipers in need would go to the Temple to offer prayers for comfort, release, or vindication. Ritual cleansing, including hand-washing, was a part of the response one made before going into God's presence.

Life is sometimes like that. Concerns, afflictions, and troubles crowd in from so many sides that it is hard to describe any particular problem. Life, as we know it and are accustomed to living it, can become threatened by change and uncertainty. The fear of the unknown may be the strongest fear of all.

How do these things happen to us? What is the cause? Like the psalmist, we review our current life and decide that we haven't been keeping evil company; that we have "nothing to do with hypocrites" (TEV). We are blameless, innocent. Our integrity is intact. Yet, trouble casts dark shadows over our lives.

What do we do? How do we keep our lives oriented toward the righteousness of God? We take guidance from the psalms.

First, come clean. "Wash your hands." Prepare for God's loving but thorough inspection (v. 6). Second, enter God's presence and worship at God's altar offering a "song of thanksgiving" telling of God's wondrous ways and deeds (vv. 6-8). Finally, trust in God's unwavering support (vv. 11-12).

Suggestion for meditation: *Sit in a quiet place. Imagine yourself entering into God's presence. See God washing off the impurity of your sin. Give thanks to God for all that is left—the many blessings of life so often taken for granted. End by singing a verse of your favorite hymn.*

Wednesday, October 7   Read Luke 17:11-13.

Some of the best experiences of life—and of ministry—often occur in borderlands, boundaries where territories abut, places on the edge of other places.

Jesus was on his way to Jerusalem, passing through the borderland between Samaria and Galilee. He chose neither the route through the foreign land of Samaria nor the established route through Perea. He made his own path.

Samaritans generally had no dealings with the Jews, and the Jews felt little more than contempt for Samaritans. It was nearly unheard of to find the two living together. But here, in this boundary area between places, ten lepers met Jesus. One was a Samaritan, the rest Jews.

Need, exclusion, tragedy had united people whose national and religious identities normally insisted on separation. Ethnic background no longer mattered. Survival and safety were the only concerns.

Disasters of many forms will often bring a divided community together—in spite of differences in religious upbringing. Life, as a gift of God, is to be shared. Common needs draw us together and common affliction reminds us that we all owe our creation, preservation, and redemption to God.

In the place where I live—a border area between Anglo culture and the Native American way of life—need often brings together people who usually pretend the other doesn't exist. It is a gift and a blessing to be given border areas, where we discover our common dependence on the God of all creation.

Prayer: *God of love, you come to us in so many ways: you come in the needs of others; you come in tragedy. Open my eyes to your presence, and my hands to your grace. Amen.*

Thursday, October 8   Read Numbers 5:1-4.

In scripture leprosy includes more than we today commonly understand as leprosy. Biblical leprosy might also include psoriasis, ringworm, or even a wound with a discharge. Clothing affected by fungus was considered leprous, as were homes affected by dry rot (see Leviticus 13).

The Law required that lepers be banned from the community. Lepers were excluded. They were cast out, made to walk about calling out, "Unclean, unclean." Being banished from the community meant both emotional anguish and economic hardship. In both cases, issues of survival were always uppermost in the leper's mind.

In a way, we might consider all those afflictions which cause a separation among people to be leprous-like. For years, persons with cancer were treated as unclean. Friends and family turned their backs on the cancer patients, afraid the disease was somehow communicable. Now, AIDS sufferers frequently are treated the same way. Though the medical community has shown that there is no danger in casual contact, still the AIDS patient is often treated as an outcast, as unclean, not to be spoken to or touched.

Where is God's grace in this treatment of the leper, the cancer patient, or the AIDS sufferer? Is there a word of comfort? Can Christ's followers offer compassion, maybe even healing?

Suggestion for meditation: *We have all met "lepers" in one form or another. Close your eyes; ask yourself, "Who is the leper in my community? Who is the outcast?" Visualize them surrounded by God's love. See them comforted in their loneliness. Pray for their health.*

Friday, October 9   Read Luke 17:12-14.

Entering a village, Jesus met ten lepers. The lepers observed the sanitary and legal requirements of the Law (Lev. 13) by standing off at a distance. Yet they quickly bridged the gap by calling out, "Master, have mercy on us."

Jesus met several lepers in his ministry. In the first chapter of the Gospel of Mark, Jesus also met a leper (1:40-45). That one was bolder than these ten, for he walked right up to Jesus and said, "If you choose, you can make me clean" (Mark 1:40). Jesus did. Simon, with whom Jesus ate, was also known as a leper (see Matthew 26:6). There must have been other occasions, too, because when the disciples of John the Baptizer came to question if Jesus was the one they waited for, Jesus told them to tell John what they had seen: the blind could see, the lame could walk, the deaf could hear, lepers were cleansed, and the dead were raised up (see Matthew 11:5).

Jesus had no physical contact with these ten lepers. Almost matter-of-factly, Jesus told the ten lepers to go and show themselves to the priest. It was while they were going that they were cleansed. Without telling them of their cure, Jesus told them to go and give thanks. When they did as they were told, when they went, they saw the first symptoms of the cure which had been given.

Have you ever considered this: Healing may always be waiting for us at fingertip reach? We may need only to ask. We may not recognize healing until we go our way, take up our life again, and move on. But, to be healed, we must move on.

Suggestion for meditation: *Sing or say your favorite hymn about God's faithfulness.*

Saturday, October 10   Read Luke 17:15-18.

Passing through a village, in the borderland between Samaria and Galilee, Jesus was met by ten lepers. They begged for mercy. Jesus had mercy on them, then told them to go show themselves to the priest. As they went, they discovered they had been healed.

Of the ten, one came back to Jesus with grateful thanksgiving. He praised God. He threw himself at Jesus' feet and gave thanks for the miracle. What makes this so amazing, according to Luke, is that the one who returned to give thanks was a Samaritan.

We might expect that a Samaritan would be the last to give thanks to a Jewish leader. We would also expect that the Jewish lepers of the group would be the first to return to give thanks. But that was not the case. Ten had been cleansed, but only this one returned in thanksgiving, and that one was a foreigner.

Ministry is like that all too often. Those who serve are frequently disappointed if their expectations include receiving frequent words of thanksgiving. Few, maybe only ten percent, ever come back to offer a word of thanks. Many acts of service are never acknowledged. Many hours of work go unnoticed.

Our joy, our satisfaction, then, must come from another source. We must turn to God for our "strokes" and our recognition. We must revel in the assurance that what we do we do for the glory of God. God's satisfaction is our ultimate concern.

Prayer: *Lord God, may I be ever mindful of the grace and mercy you bestow on my life. I give you thanks today for. . . . Amen.*

Sunday, October 11   Read Luke 17:19.

This story of Jesus healing ten lepers comes in the middle of Jesus' teaching about the coming of the kingdom of God. Immediately after this incident, Luke records one of Jesus' sermons about the last days. It will be like the days of Noah, Jesus said, a day of purification and cleansing, a day after which there is no turning back.

This healing story happens in the midst of this "eschatological" talk (discussion of the end times) because healing, salvation, and the kingdom of God are all connected. The healing of leprosy was seen as a kind of resurrection. One who had been dead was now alive again, able to greet friends and live with family. National and racial barriers were broken. Disease was healed. And the healed person responded with gracious thanksgiving.

Jesus healed ten lepers; one, a foreigner, returned to give thanks. Jesus told the one to get up and be on his way, assured that his faith had made him well. In New Testament Greek, "healing" and "salvation" are closely related. Presumably, the other nine had faith enough to accept healing from their leprosy. But this one, the Samaritan, had faith enough to accept healing and be grateful. He was more than cured; he had begun the process of salvation.

The kingdom of God is like that. It is in the midst of us when we break down barriers, find healing, and give thanks, having arrived at the knowledge and acceptance of God's merciful love.

Prayer: *Break into my life, gracious God, with healing and with salvation. Pour out your spirit upon me that being made whole I may give thanks to you, loving and serving you and my neighbor in all that I do. Amen.*

GOD'S FAITHFULNESS—OUR PATIENCE

October 12-18, 1992   **Dan G. Johnson†**
Monday, October 12   Read Habakkuk 1:1-3.

The theme of the scriptures this week has universal appeal because it deals with a problem we will all face at one time or another: unexplained suffering, God's role and timing in its resolution, and our interim response to it.

He had just been told that he had cancer. The words of Habakkuk were on his lips: "How long, O Lord, must I call for help, but you do not listen?"(NIV). He felt alone, forgotten, forsaken by God. He wasn't, but that was how he felt.

I had been working for four years in a ministry in the inner city. Unemployment was at 22 percent, lives were being wasted, young children seemed to have no future. I touched one or two here and there, but my cry at night as I tried to sleep was, "Why, God?" In the words of our scripture, "Why do you make me look at injustice? Why do you tolerate wrong?"(NIV) The well-known author and rabbi Harold Kushner struck a universal nerve in his book entitled *When Bad Things Happen to Good People*. Why do the innocent suffer?

It would be tempting to hasten to an answer, for dwelling on these question marks is uncomfortable. But the Israelites did not hasten on. There is something valuable in feeling the weight of these queries. Take some time today, and remember those for whom life is not easy.

Prayer: *O God, give me a sense of empathy, caring, and feeling for the hurts of others. Come quickly and mightily to their aid. Amen.*

---

†Senior minister, Indian River City United Methodist Church, Titusville, Florida.

Tuesday, October 13   Read Habakkuk 2:1-4.

Waiting is the hardest part. "It's been three hours; the operation should have been over an hour ago." "She said she would call as soon as she arrived home. I know it is an eleven-hour trip, but she has been gone so long." Waiting is never easy.

The people of Eastern Europe had been waiting for a long time for change. When it came, it came swiftly and the Christian church was at the center of that change. Blacks in the U.S. have known what it is to wait—to wait for freedom, to wait for basic human rights, to wait for economic and personal justice. Now the dream of Martin Luther King, Jr., and Rosa Parks and others has begun to be fulfilled.

The people of South Africa have been waiting for too long for apartheid to cease and for justice to "roll down like waters" (Amos 5:24), but it is coming. The people of Israel waited in Egypt for a deliverer. During the exile they waited for someone to lead them home. For more than 500 years they waited for a messiah. You and I also know what it is to wait.

Habakkuk, burdened with his doubts about the presence, concern, and ability of God, is told to wait. "Climb the watchtower and simply wait." He is assured that an answer will come. It may linger. It may come slowly, but he is to wait.

Habakkuk is to be a model for successive generations of waiters, for the righteous shall live by faith, not by what he or she sees, not by appearances, but by faith—faith in the active goodness of God, who will never forsake God's people. The righteous shall live by faith, an active faith that participates in the redemptive activity of God so that God's kingdom of the future is always becoming more fully realized in the present.

Prayer: *O God, help me to live—to act and believe and dream—not by sight but by faith, faith in you and the coming of your kingdom on earth as it is in heaven. Amen.*

Wednesday, October 14   Read Psalm 119:137-141.

Anatoli Shcharansky is a brilliant scientist of Jewish descent. At one time he was a well-known dissident who was placed in a Russian gulag for his criticism of the Soviet regime. During his seven-year imprisonment, his wife, Avital, was able to smuggle a small copy of the Hebrew scripture (the Old Testament) in to him. It became his lifeline. Once, he was placed in solitary confinement for 130 days because he refused to part with it.

Finally, through international pressure he was released. As the guards took him to the border to freedom, they tried one last time to take away his copy of the scriptures. Shcharansky responded by falling down in the snow and shouting defiantly, "Not without my Psalms, not without my Psalms. I will not leave without my Psalms!" The guards returned them to him, and he walked to freedom.

What is it about the Book of Psalms that causes one to cherish them as Shcharansky did? What is it about the Book of Psalms that causes the great saints of Christendom to love and treasure them? It is this: The psalms express our deepest feelings. Sometimes they even say what we would never dare say, but what we nevertheless feel, such as the cries of complaint to God in Psalm 74, "O God, why do you cast us off forever?" (v. 1) They express our deep thanksgiving, our heartfelt praise, and an abiding sense of trust; and they voice our hopes and the assurances of God's promises which sustain us in the day of trouble.

That is why we can affirm the scripture today: "Your promises have been thoroughly tested, and your servant loves them" (NIV).

Prayer: *Precious God, give me a love for your word like that of the people of faith who have gone before me. Through adversity may it sustain me; through joy may it ground me; through sorrow may it lift me; and through success may it humble me. Amen.*

Thursday, October 15   Read Psalm 119:141-144.

These verses reflect the character of someone who walks by faith and not by sight. Sight would see only the troubles and distress. I know when I begin walking by sight and not by faith. I become preoccupied with myself and my problems. I let my problems interpret the promises of God, rather than letting the promises of God interpret my situation, thus, transforming it.

Two women I know each lost their husbands to heart attacks within a few weeks of each other. One became embittered toward God and life. She turned against her neighbors and friends and struck out at anyone who would try to help her. It was sad to see that her grief and troubles had blinded her to the word of promise from God, that God's presence would be with her, that in due time she could discover new directions for her life.

The other woman, after a normal and healthy period of grieving, seemed to begin to walk by faith and not by sight. She claimed the promises of God and stepped out into the new journey God had for her. She didn't drive, but she didn't let that be a drawback. She made arrangements with her rural neighbors to get a ride into town. Her faith and buoyancy became an inspiration to the rest of us. I asked her about her evenings. Weren't they the most difficult time? She said they could be, but each evening for dinner she gets out her best china, her nicest silver, and her finest crystal, and she dines in elegance.

With the psalmist, you and I ask for understanding, that we might live; for it is God's perspective that is more important than what appears to be reality. That understanding may require patience and waiting, but we know that we can trust God.

Prayer: *Lord God, help us to live by faith and not by sight, so that the way things appear does not preempt the way things can be in the providence of God. Amen.*

Friday, October 16   Read 2 Timothy 3:14-17.

There have been times when I have found it difficult to believe that what the Bible says about God is true. It was during those times that I turned to older and wiser Christians, many of whom had nurtured me, and I believed in their belief in God's word. They provided a bridge for me until I could come back to an immediate affirmation of God's promises.

When times are tough and it is difficult to see any evidence of God's faithfulness and your patience is wearing thin, those are the times when it is helpful to look to the saints and be sustained by their model. That is what Timothy is being encouraged to do. His grandmother Lois and mother, Eunice (see 2 Tim. 1:5), transmitted their vibrant faith to him. They had modeled the faith; they had lived the faith; they had prayed the faith. Timothy was the receiver not only of a written faith but of a living faith.

Some of us reading this will be, like Timothy, inheritors of a great faith. We have witnessed the lives as well as the words of our ancestors in the faith. Others of us began in faith on our own. But all of us are called upon to live the faith in such a way that those who follow us, whether in our families, in our church, or in our neighborhood, will be strengthened in their understanding of the faith by what they have seen in our embodiment of the faith. The inspiration, veracity, and value of the written word of God are affirmed.

Prayer: *Lord Jesus, may I remember that the word became flesh and dwelled among us. It was that personal dimension that was so important. Help me today to live so that others might be drawn to your written faith because of the living faith they see in me. Amen.*

Saturday, October 17   Read 2 Timothy 4:1-5.

We come to this notion of patience once again. Timothy is told to preach the word boldly and with a sense of urgency but also with a sense of patience and endurance, because the effects of God's word are not always apparent and are seldom immediate.

We have come full circle, back to Habakkuk and Psalm 119. Patience and trust and a belief in the word of God are sometimes all that we have to hold on to. We live in a world that idolizes the obvious and the immediate. But God does not work that way. God's ways are like the leaven that works quietly and slowly; like the farmer's seed, its growth cannot be perceived, but suddenly the stalk appears. The faithful follower of Jesus Christ must not yield to the pressures of this world and to the tyranny of the apparent. When trouble comes, when God seems to be distant, when prayers seem to be ineffective, when waiting seems unbearable, remember God's saints who cling to God's promise no matter what!

Timothy is given a crucial phrase: "in season and out of season" (NIV). It calls to mind the famous passage from Ecclesiastes 3: "For everything there is a season . . . a time to be born, and a time to die . . . a time to weep, and a time to laugh. . . ." Living life has to do with perspective. There are seasons; there is an ebb and flow. Not everything must happen at once. Patience, poise, and perspective are essential.

God's word to Timothy is a reminder to me to be bold in my witness to Christ but also to be patient and enduring, knowing that we rely on God's promise and God's word rather than on what may or may not appear to be results.

Prayer: *O God, forgive us for our shortsightedness and presumption, assuming that we know what you must do and how quickly you must act. Free us to trust you and your ways more than our understanding of what those should be. Amen.*

Sunday, October 18   Read Luke 18:1-8.

I am especially grateful for this last scripture reading of the week, for in the context of the prior readings it provides an important and neglected insight into the biblical understanding of patience. Biblical patience is active, not passive.

The widow is persistent in her pursuing and pleading with the judge. The judge is neither kind nor just. He has no inclination to respond to the widow. Finally, because of her persistence he relents and acts justly. The point of the parable is almost too obvious: if an unjust judge who is neither caring nor kind will respond to the pleas of an unknown widow, how much more will God, who is both loving and gracious, respond to the prayers for justice for God's chosen ones?

Jesus assures his followers that God's faithfulness is not to be doubted. God will act justly. God's rule will triumph. God's people will be vindicated. Jesus doesn't say how long the widow persisted. Once again the matter of timing is left unstated. In fact, Jesus concludes the parable with a reference to the coming of the Son of Man, the timing of which, he confirmed, no one knows.

Until God's faithfulness is fully expressed in our world, we are to be patient—actively, persistently, prayerfully patient—like the widow. I know it sounds contradictory, a bit paradoxical. Perhaps this brief excerpt from *The Sower's Seeds* by Brian Cavanaugh (Paulist Press) will help clarify this concept of active patience: "The disciple asks his master, 'What can I do to attain God?' The master answers by asking, 'What can you do to make the sun rise?' The disciple says indignantly, 'Then why are you giving us all these methods of prayer?' And the master replies, 'To make sure you're awake when the sun rises.'"

Prayer: *Dear God, help us to pray with persistence and to trust with patience. Amen.*

October 19-25, 1992   **Martha E. Chamberlain**†
Monday, October 19   Read Zephaniah 3:1-5.

We can choose to grow through criticism . . .

Or, we can resent so deeply that we strangle the ragged, fragile relationships of our lives. Zephaniah spoke of those who cannot accept correction. Although painful, confronting our error produces change and growth.

"Admit it," our thirteen-year-old foster daughter screamed at me. "Say 'I am mad at you.' Don't say you're upset. You're as mad as I am!"

She was right. But why should I take correction from her? She could lie, curse, disregard all kindness and advice, and then dare to tell me what I felt, and furthermore, that I was dishonest.

Although hard to swallow, her reprimands taught me to identify and name my feelings honestly. Now, more than twenty years later, I am thankful that I chose to listen. I feel only the deepest love for her today.

Although not responsible for another's reactions, we are accountable for our own attitude in both giving and receiving rebuke. Whether it is a child or a cantankerous co-worker, each person has a right to courteous criticism.

Unfortunately, at times we all inflict as well as suffer unjust criticism. And when erroneously chastised ourselves, we need to forgive as we have been forgiven.

Prayer: *Anoint me with wisdom and love, O Lord, that I may choose both to give and receive correction in the spirit of humility. Amen.*

---

†Former missionary nurse in Zambia; free-lance writer and author, Springfield, Virginia.

Tuesday, October 20   Read Zephaniah 3:6-9.

We can choose to change through cleansing

I recently heard a story that had been told by Robert Schuller which illustrates the tragedy of outward change rather than inward transformation. It seems that a great brown bear in a European zoo had been confined over a long period of time in a 12-foot square cage. When it was decided that greater freedom would enhance his well-being, the bear was placed in an outdoor area with trees and rocks and water. But for the remainder of his life, he continued to pace twelve feet in one direction, then twelve feet in another.

Although we may welcome new beginnings by adding to light-hearted New Year's Day resolutions or kneeling in humility at a private altar, permanent change may elude us because we do not experience inward cleansing.

"I will purify the lips of the peoples, that all of them may call on the name of the LORD and serve him shoulder to shoulder" (vs. 9, NIV). This beautiful picture of God's intervention conjures up an idyllic scene where the purified worship together and work toward one purpose.

But unfortunately we are all too much like the ancient Israelites—or even the bear—who often returned to their former ways. Warring, idolatry, and sinful alliances strongly tempted the ancient Hebrews. Our temptations are much the same, but the cleansing love of our Lord Jesus Christ can set us free from the bondage of sin.

Prayer: _Could it possibly be that even though I am set free, I fail to choose abundant life, O Lord? Help me to choose the life you offer. Amen._

Wednesday, October 21   Read Psalm 3:1-4.

We can choose to praise God when discouraged

Twenty-six-year-old Mike disappeared while flying an F-18. I wondered how his family and friends and fiance would bear the pain. But when his parents visited us four months later, although our young Marine friend had not been found, they radiated peace and victory. I wondered, *Was this simply their means of denial?* As we talked, however, his mother told of her discovery that the intentional, paradoxical "sacrifice of praise" (Heb. 13:15) had produced hope and peace.

Sacrifice does not connote ease and comfort. Rather, in the presence of pain, we can choose to focus on who God is—on God's nature, purpose, love, and presence. Then, although the *choice* to praise God in those circumstances is difficult, its result is peace.

Praising God in a maze of discouragement and pain seems preposterous. Yet the sacrifice of praise bridges the gulf from despair to hope. Fearful and heartbroken, David wrote this psalm while fleeing from his own son, Absalom (2 Sam. 15). But David chose to focus on the "Glorious One," rather than on his circumstances.

The often repeated pattern of despair and hope is not confined to the ancient poetry of the Psalms. We see the pendulum swing from the depths of anguish in Genesis to the ultimate culmination of God's plan in the Book of Revelation. And sooner or later, we, too, walk with disease, disaster, and depression. But having experienced the depths of despair, we may choose God's way to the heights through intentional praise.

Prayer: *O gentle, loving God, may I continually choose to "offer a sacrifice of praise" rather than focus on my pain. Amen.*

Thursday, October 22   Read Psalm 3:5-8.

We can choose to commit the outcome to God

Although we sometimes do not see how God is working in our lives, we can commit everything to God, assured of God's commitment to us.

The psalmist sleeps—because God is in charge. He faces the new day—because God's strength is his own. He relinquishes fear—because God fights his battles.

When we intentionally offer our lives to God, our ongoing, daily choices, though not necessarily more simple, can result in peace.

We can choose to commit to God those circumstances over which we have no control, those difficult choices between two equally good options, and those decisions of great import, whether they be choosing friends in high school, or a college major, or a spouse, or a career change.

We can also give to God our emotions and temperament, even when depression or illness or stress has created a hard-to-live-with person. God is ready to work the miracle of new life even when we least expect it.

Prayer: *May we choose to recognize your present, active involvement in our lives, even though we do not see you, as we commit everything to you, O God. Amen.*

Friday, October 23   Read Luke 18:9-14.

We can choose to see ourselves through the scriptures

Looking at ourselves through the mirror of God's word may reveal depravity, vulnerability, deviousness, pride—things we would rather not see.

Therefore, although we spend a lifetime and sometimes a fortune, trying to discover who we are, we forego the plumbline in our searching. We ignore the mirror in our looking. Or, like my friends, we use the wrong pattern.

Starting with one paper pattern, the group of women cut and sewed several hundred cloth bags to fill with toys for Mexican children. But dozens of completed bags actually measured several inches smaller or larger than the original pattern. Pieces had been cut from numerous copies of copies of the original.

We do not like to acknowledge it, but we, too, have followed wrong models. We have even prayed as the Pharisee did, "I am not like other people." To discover and admit the common denominator of our human condition is a lifetime process.

Even the disciples gathered around Jesus at the Passover meal registered sadness and disbelief at Jesus' announcement that one of them would betray hem, "and one by one they said to him, 'Surely, not I?'" (Mark 14:19, NIV)

"Finding oneself" in the most helpful and healthful sense starts with looking in the right place. In the scriptures we confront the self for whom Jesus lived and died. Then change begins and continues over a lifetime.

Prayer: *O God, give me courage to see the worst and grace to choose the best: change, cleansing, and growth through Jesus Christ. Amen.*

Saturday, October 24   Read 2 Timothy 4:6-8.

We can choose to persevere until death

In 1988 Christians in the Soviet Union celebrated the 1,000th anniversary of Christianity in that country. They understand perseverance. By choice. By grace.

Not long ago Evelina Ahukovskaya served a five-year term for teaching Sunday school to Russian children. Others from two Christian charities suffered in prison for supplying food, clothing, and conscience. A Baptist pastor and his three sons endured torture, beatings, imprisonment, isolation, and constant surveillance because of their Christian beliefs.

Timothy had begun to understand, observing the life of his mentor, the Apostle Paul, that serving God does not make one immune to human problems such as loneliness or aging. In addition, his friend Paul suffered deprivation, imprisonment, danger, persecution, hunger, torture, and humiliation, just because he called himself a follower of Jesus Christ.

How much do we know of personal suffering as a result of our faith? Oh, perhaps a momentary embarrassment may have been associated with some thought of "suffering" for righteousness' sake. But even that admission causes us to blush with shame when memory searches out Saints Paul and Stephen, or those in *Foxe's Book of Martyrs*, or the hundreds of thousands of others—even to this day—who suffer for their faith. Their ability to endure is enhanced by their active, thoughtful choice to persevere.

Prayer: *O God, may I choose to persevere even when my own human endurance gives out. And may I participate through prayer with those who truly suffer for your sake. Amen.*

Sunday, October 25   Read 2 Timothy 4:16-18.

We can choose to serve in spite of life situations . . .

Or, we can run like Jonah, refuse like the rich young ruler, complain like Moses, or legitimately beg off for our own good reasons.

Eleanor has a good reason not to be involved. She is paralyzed on one side. But she drives the community's handicapped wherever they need to go and welcomes with a hug those who enter the church door. She looks for troubles and needs—then works to try to solve them as the "shepherd" of her neighborhood care group.

Pat and Carl's eight-year-old son is blind, deaf, and mentally handicapped. But their three-year-old niece sometimes stays with them because her mother has cancer. Pat also brought our family dinner after my surgery, as she does for so many others. Recently she packed her car with three heavy boxes of food and a large turkey for Thanksgiving dinner for a needy family. Sunday mornings they teach a class, and at night they lead youth Bible Bowl.

In today's lesson the Apostle Paul was still suffering in old age not only from a bodily handicap but also other continuing difficulties. In prison again, saddened by the desertion of co-workers and working through the pain of persecution, he still could proclaim, "But the Lord . . . gave me strength."

Prayer: *Lord, you profoundly illustrated the meaning of power through service as you chose to kneel at the feet of twelve friends with a towel and a basin. Whatever our circumstances, may we choose to serve as well. Amen.*

PEACE WITH JUSTICE

October 26–November 1, 1992   **Linda Worthington†**
Monday, October 26   Read Luke 6:27-36.

There is a special focus in October on peace with justice. The annual recognition of the work of the United Nations for peace is in October. Many churches call attention to programs in housing, hunger, and jobs at home; and to disarmament, oppression, and international relations.

In this week's readings we glimpse a perspective on peace, first as nations interact in the period at the end of the Old Testament, then as Jesus instructs his disciples on their coming roles. "All the peoples and nations and languages shall serve God," Daniel says (7:14, AP). And Jesus promises, "Peace will be yours even when others hate you" (Luke 6:22). He then reminds us to love our enemies and do good to them (6:35).

All Saints' Day is at the end of the week, and it is a time to remember those who have gone before us throughout our long Christian history. Another kind of peace comes to those we remember who "heard . . . the Good News that brought you salvation." (Eph. 1:13, TEV).

Mother Teresa has embodied Jesus' teachings of bringing peace and mercy to the poor. When she came to Washington, D.C., I took a friend to meet her. We pushed through crowds of people who were trying to reach her, to touch her, to get even a glimpse of her. She, more than anyone I know, embodies the compassion that Jesus taught us to show toward others.

Prayer: *Forgive me, Lord, that I find it difficult to be merciful and loving to those whom I do not know, and even to those I do. Amen.*

---

† Editor, Chevy Chase United Methodist Church local edition of *United Methodist Reporter,* Chevy Chase, Maryland.

Tuesday, October 27   Read Daniel 7:1-3.

The Book of Daniel was written during the second century before the birth of Christ by a faithful Jew to strengthen his people during a time of persecution. The writer, trying to rekindle the faith of Israel, put his message into the mouth of Daniel, the man of God, who was a great Jewish saint of an earlier age. He is the indomitable hero of the story.

Daniel has become the spokesperson for God, the deliverer of a message, much in the same way as the prophets of the Old Testament. He came at a time when Hellenism had spread throughout the known world and a Hellenistic king, Antiochus IV Epiphanes, had set himself to destroy Judaism altogether. Antiochus instituted the first religious persecution the Jewish people had ever known (168 B.C.). However, a stalwart band of devout Jews decided to fight back. "And they chose death rather than . . . profanation of the holy covenant" (1 Macc. 1:62, JB).*

One of the ways Daniel delivers God's prophetic message is through dreams and visions. In today's reading he describes the beasts that represent the great political powers who will surely rule if the people do not remain faithful to God. God's kingdom is an everlasting one for the faithful in contrast to the kingdoms of the world, which, like the kingdoms described as beasts in the dream, will be destroyed in the course of time.

Daniel's message to us as a nation and as individuals is to be totally faithful to God. God keeps the covenant with those who love God and keep God's commandments.

Prayer: *O, Lord, I fear for my nation and for myself, for I know that we have strayed far from your commandments. Help me, and help my nation, to be your faithful servants. Amen.*

---

*First Maccabees is one of the books of the Old Testament Apocrypha.

Wednesday, October 28   Read Daniel 7:15-18.

In the midst of Daniel's vision of the beasts and destruction came "one like a son of man" (v. 13). Daniel had received this message from God, but he needed help to understand it. God sent an interpreter in the form of an angel to explain the visions so that Daniel in turn could deliver the message.

The angel indicated that the human figure amongst all the beasts/nations would be given everlasting and universal dominion over the holy community of Israel. The message continues that all nations shall serve God and God's dominion will not be like the beast/powers which would be destroyed. Instead, God will rule the world with a peace that will not pass away. This glimpse, through Daniel, of what the world can be shows us that in the presence of God, nations and their rulers, no matter how strong they seem, are only temporal; they will pass away.

Jesus, two centuries later, used Daniel's designation of the "son of man" to identify himself as the one whom God had chosen to judge and rule humankind forever (Mark 14:62). Jesus was convinced he was standing near the end time, that from that time forward life would never be the same.

Into his message of destruction of the kingdoms of the world, Daniel imparts a message of hope for "the holy ones of the Most High" (v. 18). To the covenant community of faith Daniel's message gives the assurance and stamina to hold fast during persecution, for God's kingdom will prevail and will come with power and glory at the end of time.

Prayer: *Help me, Lord, to remember the assurances that you have given the faithful throughout all of history. And help me to live this day as a child of yours. Amen.*

Thursday, October 29   Read Luke 6:20-23.

As Jesus' ministry began, he found these among the crowds of followers: people who were just curious; some who needed medical attention and healing; people tormented by mental illness who sought peace of mind; a few who began to realize that this itinerant preacher had words of wisdom to share. Among these followers he chose twelve as his closest confidants, his disciples, his inner circle (Luke 6:12-19).

These "chosen ones" Jesus ministered to in special ways. He expected greater responsibility and accountability from them, too. Don't worry about being poor, he said; you will inherit the kingdom of God. You're hungry now, he noted, but that is only temporary. You will be satisfied.

Jesus then explained, "You are like the ancient prophets, they were persecuted, disbelieved, unheeded" (AP). Jesus urged his disciples not to give up during persecution—when that persecution was "on account of the Son of Man" (v. 22). Accept this, even rejoice in this treatment, for "your reward is great in heaven," he said.

Most of us do not experience persecution because of our faith. Or do we? Are you one of these: a teenager who refuses to use drugs, an employee who "blows the whistle," a politician who does not accept certain campaign gifts, a farmer who doesn't use harmful pesticides? Standing fast in the faith can empower us in our daily lives to take on the tasks Christ has for us. We can stand fast, refusing to do what others are doing as a matter of course and withstanding the possible shunning or jeering of the crowds. "Rejoice when that day comes and dance for joy . . . your reward will be great in heaven" (JB).

Prayer: *O Lord, help me each day as I make decisions. Help me to make the choices you would have me make. Amen.*

Friday, October 30   Read Luke 6:32-35.

Jesus continually assured his disciples that when they faced persecution they would be rewarded for their faithfulness. He also taught them that they must take a great responsibility for the welfare of others, even those who persecute them. "Treat others as you would like people to treat you," he commanded (v. 31, JB). "And you will be children of the Most High, [who] is kind to the ungrateful and the wicked" (JB).

I again saw Mother Teresa when I visited her in Calcutta in 1984 after she had been ill for some time. She looked even more frail than she had when, among other duties, I served as her chauffeur on her first visit to Washington, D.C. in 1974. I told her how sorry I was that she had been so ill for such a long time.

But with her indomitable spirit and liveliness that belied her age and ill health, she responded with the amazing power that she has accepted from God. "Don't worry," she said. "God is not done with me yet."

Mother Teresa has received worldwide acclaim and the Nobel Peace Prize because she has been a messenger of peace to all the nations of the world. She has accepted the responsibilities that Jesus told his disciples were theirs. She has truly done for others—the poor, the destitute, the depressed and the downcast of the world—as anyone of us would want done to us even in circumstances far less challenging.

She is empowered by the Holy Spirit as God has promised to each one of us who accepts and believes in God. She serves as a modern example of one who has faithfully committed her whole life in service to God.

Prayer: *Jesus, help me to be your devoted disciple in accepting the responsibilities you place on me to care for others with compassion, even those who are my enemies. Amen.*

316

Saturday, October 31   Ephesians 1:11-23.

God rejoices in those who believe in him. We have seen that in our readings throughout this week. Paul, another of God's saints, emphasizes in Ephesians in the strongest words that God delights in those of us who call ourselves Christians. "You," he says, "became God's people when you heard the true message, the Good News that brought you salvation" (TEV.) God is, has been, and always will be faithful to those who believe, and more! Paul says "how very great is [God's] power at work in us who believe" (TEV). This power is the same that raised Christ from the dead. What more could one want!

The United Methodist Council of Bishops in 1986 wrote a pastoral letter "to All United Methodists" stating their own "clear and unconditional *No* to nuclear war and to any use of nuclear weapons." The bishops called upon the people to "receive God's gracious gift of peace . . . embracing all neighbors near and far, all friends and enemies, and becoming defenders of God's good creation; and to pray without ceasing for peace in our time."*

I am convinced that the fall of the Berlin Wall in 1989, symbolizing, the end of the Cold War and diminishing the threat of nuclear war, resulted from the faithful people of God heeding the words of the bishops and others who have made similar pleas. As Paul tells us, "God chose us to be his own people . . . based on what he had decided from the very beginning" (TEV).

Prayer: *Help us to recognize your messengers, O Lord, and help us to heed the messages that you send us through them. Amen.*

---

*From "In Defense of Creation: The Nuclear Crisis and A Just Peace," a pastoral letter from the Council of Bishops of The United Methodist Church. (See *The United Methodist Reporter,* May 9, 1986, page 2).

Sunday, November 1   Read Psalm 149.

Scripture reveals a vision of shalom (peace) as God's will for all creation. Shalom is defined as well-being even in the midst of trouble. It is knowing a sense of salvation even when the world is falling around us.

The faithful have delivered to us God's messages of the path to peace. Daniel revealed that peace would come to the chosen people if they would but faithfully follow God, even if for periods of time they were under the rule of godless kings. But the faithful should have no fear because all peoples and nations and languages are expected to serve God: God's dominion is everlasting and shall not pass away (see Dan. 7:14).

Paul's message of shalom comes to those who "heard . . . the Good News that brought you salvation. You believed in Christ, and God put his stamp of ownership on you. . . . The Spirit is the guarantee that we shall receive what God as promised" (Eph. 1:13*a*, TEV).

Jesus energizes and empowers his disciples for their work after he is gone. He teaches them that "Happy are you when people hate you, reject you, insult you, and say that you are evil. . . . Be glad . . . because a great reward is kept for you in heaven" (Luke 6:22, TEV).

"The Lord takes pleasure in his people," the psalmist declares (TEV). Let us now sing God's praises as we reaffirm that we, too, are among those who will go into the future to do God's will. And that we, like those "who were the first to set [their] hope on Christ, might live for the praise of his glory" (Eph. 1:12).

Prayer: *Oh, that we might find your path to peace, O God! We know that you are ever faithful if we will but accept your commandments. Help us to follow faithfully. Amen.*

ON HONORING GOD

November 2-8, 1992   **George R. Graham†**
Monday, November 2   Read 2 Thessalonians 2:13–3:5.

In this age of self-actualization, how tempting it is to give ourselves the credit for what happens in our spiritual lives and in our churches! We want to explain our successes in terms of our actions. We would like to claim that our walk with God is going well because we have been loyal to our devotions. We want to explain growth in our churches by the number of visits made to potential members.

Paul reminds us that without God's grace, we cannot succeed. He wrote to the Thessalonians to bring reconciliation to the church there. He reminds them that their salvation does not rest on his letters or preaching. Neither will their opinions and discussions bring them salvation. God brings salvation.

This is not to say that beliefs and actions are not important. Paul urges the Thessalonians to "stand firm and hold fast to the traditions" of the faith (2:15). For us, daily devotions and visitation of prospective members are important. They are part of the tradition of which Paul speaks. A problem arises when we become so busy with our activities that we forget about God's grace. God, not our human activities, is the ultimate source of our salvation. God should be at the center of our lives.

This week's readings focus on honoring God. The texts ask: Do we honor God with all that we do?

Prayer: *Loving God, who comforts us and establishes us in every good word and work, help us remember that your grace, not our actions, is the source of salvation. Amen.*

---

†Copy editor of *The Interpreter*, published by United Methodist Communications; recent graduate of The Divinity School, Vanderbilt University; resides in Nashville, Tennessee.

Tuesday, November 3   Read Zechariah 7:1-7.

Seventy years after the destruction of the Temple, the people ask Zechariah if they should still mourn in the fifth month, the month in which the Temple was destroyed. Zechariah cuts to the core of the issue by asking them a question: Why are you fasting? Are you fasting for yourself, or are you honoring God?

What if Zechariah were to ask a similar question of us: Why do you go to worship? Do you go to worship for yourself or out of habit? Or do you go in order to honor God?

Zechariah points out that people sometimes do the right things for the wrong reasons. He challenges the people in his day to be intentional in their fasting. He challenges us to be intentional in our worship. We should recognize that the purpose of worship is to honor God.

Worship extends beyond Sunday morning services. In our work, home life, and prayer life, we can worship God by honoring God with our actions and devotion. Sunday morning worship is meant to be an expression of our everyday faith, not just an attempt to look good before God once a week.

In "Babette's Feast" by Isak Dinesan, Babette is described as a woman who "is now turning a dinner . . . into a kind of love affair . . . in which one no longer distinguishes between bodily and spiritual appetite or satiety!"* We, too, are called to turn our lives into love affairs. Our lives should be love affairs for God in which we attempt to honor God in all settings, the altar table and the dinner table. We cannot invite God into our lives in church and then refuse to take God home with us. In everything that we do, we must seek to honor God.

Prayer: *Generous God, help us to receive you at the altar table and at the dinner table. Let all aspects of our lives honor you. Amen.*

_____

*Isak Dinesen, *Babette's Feast and Other Anecdotes of Destiny* (Vintage Books, Random House, 1988), p. 38.

Wednesday, November 4   Read Zechariah 7:8-10.

Truth be told, God did not ask the people to fast to the exclusion of justice. Zechariah repeats the cry of the prophets through the ages for the people to keep their actions in line with what they professed to believe about God. Zechariah restates the core of the prophetic moral teaching, following in the tradition of Isaiah, Jeremiah, and Micah.

Perhaps Isaiah draws the clearest connection between honoring God and justice: "Is not this the fast that I choose: to loose the bonds of injustice, to undo the thongs of the yoke, to let the oppressed go free, and to break every yoke?" (Isaiah 58:6)

Indeed, this teaching of caring for the oppressed spans the life of Israel, back before the Exile and the destruction of the Temple. It reminded the people of the Law, which protected those who were most vulnerable in ancient societies (e.g., Deut. 26:12-13). It also serves as the tradition from which the Good News proclaimed by Jesus came.

Zechariah's commandment bridges ancient time to our time. It expands on the idea of honoring God at the dinner table and at the altar table. Honoring God involves whom we invite to eat with us. Do we sit down to eat with those who are most vulnerable in our society?

As the holidays approach, how might you honor God? Consider volunteering at a feeding program for the hungry or a Christmas gift program for children in need. Social agencies always need volunteers for a variety of tasks: cooking food and donating gifts, making phone calls and preparing mailings. Contact your church office for suggestions of agencies that might need your help.

Prayer: *Through all generations, O God, you have asked people to care for the oppressed. Show us ways to do this in our generation. Amen.*

Thursday, November 5   Read Psalm 9:11-20.

How often I have heard the statement "Judgment belongs to the Lord." But human beings often take judgment into their own hands. When they do, they place others in subordinate positions.

The psalmist reminds us that God does not call us to judge others. God calls us to help the oppressed. In fact, God is on the side of the oppressed. God "does not forget the cry of the afflicted."

Whose side are we on? We would like to think that we do not judge others, but all of us do. We can do it in the smallest of ways, like looking down at a co-worker or someone on the street.

God calls us to seek justice rather than to offer judgment. In contrast to judgment, justice seeks to right wrongful situations, often in which people have been judged unfairly. Human judgment maintains. Justice transforms.

God does call us through the Law, Prophets, and Gospels to lives of justice. God calls us to free the oppressed, by feeding the hungry and clothing the naked. In helping the oppressed, we must attempt to recognize and right injustice.

The best way to keep from moving from justice to judgment is to remember that we are human. "Let the nations know that they are only human," declares the psalmist (9:20). When we forget we are human, we overstep our bounds. We attempt to control others.

We must never believe we are beyond sin. We must be ready to confess our wrongdoing regularly. Our hope is in God's justice, not in our own attempts to move beyond our humanness. We honor God by confessing our sins and recognizing the ultimacy of God's justice.

Prayer: *Forgiving God, remind us that we are human. Help us confess our sins. Give us new beginnings to do your will and the assurance that we can do justice. Amen.*

Friday, November 6   Read Luke 20:27-38.

The Sadducees look like the kind of people referred to in Psalm 9. They try to snare Jesus with the work of their hands. They do not believe in resurrection and want to trap Jesus with a question. They do not succeed.

The question they raise is based on the law of Levirate marriage: if a man dies childless, his brother should marry the dead man's widow. The exaggeration of the problem in this made-up situation is designed to poke fun at the very idea of resurrection.

We need to pay attention to the way in which Jesus handles this situation. First, he does not respond to the Sadducees in the same way they treat him. He does not reply in an effort merely to spring the snare that their question sets. Nor does he attempt to set another trap with his question. Rather than take offense, Jesus views the situation as a teachable moment.

Second, Jesus speaks the Sadducees' language, they who accepted as scripture only the Pentateuch, the first five books of the Bible. Jesus refers to the book of Exodus (vv. 37-38). Jesus addresses their concerns about life and death at a deep level. The situation is transformed.

Jesus teaches us about relationships. Dealing with family, co-workers, and people at church is not always easy. If we feel that someone is trying to trap us with a question, we want to respond in kind. When these situations arise, remembering Jesus' interaction with the Sadducees is helpful. First, listen to people. Try to identify the deeper issues that are expressed in their statements. Then, speak in terms they can understand. Words can alienate, but they can also be bridges to stronger relationships.

Prayer: *Loving God, teach us to listen to other people as Jesus did. Help us to speak so that others might understand. Help us all to become closer to you. Amen.*

Saturday, November 7   Read Luke 20:27-28.

Beyond teaching us about relationships, Jesus' discussion with the Sadducees tells about new life in God.

Although we don't like to identify with the Sadducees, at times we are like them. The Sadducees accepted only the first five books of the Bible as scripture. In some ways, they did not hear what God was saying to them in their time. Many of us have no trouble accepting miracles in Jesus' time, but we fail to see God at work in our time. By saying that God was God of the living, Jesus meant that God was active in the Sadducees' world and is active in our world, too. God's actions cannot be limited to a specific time or place. We cannot control God.

The Sadducees have a hard time conceiving of an age of resurrection. We also have trouble conceiving of life after resurrection. Our society idolizes youthfulness, and if we had to imagine what heaven is like, we might think that it is full of young, beautiful people. Perhaps our image of heaven is as wrongheaded as the Sadducees. Sometimes when we wonder about heaven, we forget that God works in us in this age.

At the end of his conversation with the Sadducees, Jesus states that "all live to [God]" (v. 38, RSV). Although our culture reveres youth, God loves people of all ages equally. Because we are no longer youthful does not mean we stop living to God. God loves us all through our lives and beyond them.

Regardless of our understanding of life after death, we should attempt to live to God, listening for God's directives and honoring God with all that we do. God's works are not limited to an ancient time or restricted to a future time. God offers us new life today.

Prayer: *God of the Resurrection, help us be open to new life. Help us trust in transformation. Show us how to live to you. Amen.*

Sunday, November 8   Read 2 Thessalonians 2:13-3:5.

We end this week's meditations where we began. We see again that Paul gives God a central position in his life and the life of the church. He does not give himself credit for the Thessalonians' salvation. He gives the credit to God: "God chose you as the first fruits for salvation."

Paul shows the reciprocity of Christian relationships. Paul prays for the Thessalonians and asks that the Thessalonians pray for him. This relationship of mutual confession of God is the heart of the church.

Often the church strays from this ideal. People choose sides. They are afraid to make themselves vulnerable, and, in doing so, they forget that they are human. They lose sight of God.

Paul provides a model for us of how to live as a community of God. The relationship between Paul and the church at Thessalonica shows us that we can encourage one another to live to God. People can serve as mediators of God's grace. Paul certainly encouraged the Thessalonians in matters of faith, but he also counted on them to pray for him. Such friendships are important to cultivate in our faith journeys. These relationships support us when we are low, give us a place to celebrate when we are doing well, and remind us always of God's love for us.

Take time today to speak a word of thanks and encouragement to a friend in the faith. While passing the peace at church today, or through a visit, telephone call, or card, let this friend know you feel his or her support and that you hope you can return the support through your thoughts and prayers.

Prayer: *Loving God, direct our hearts to your love and to the steadfastness of Christ. We give thanks for friends in the faith. Help us to honor you with all of our lives. Amen.*

YEARNING FOR A JUST FUTURE

November 9-15, 1992   **Robert Brizee†**
Monday, November 9   Read Psalm 82.

Identifying with the yearning

When I first considered the four scriptures this week, I felt stymied. How could I offer something devotional based on these passages? Personally, I do not believe in a judgment day and I do not long for an end of time. Such convictions from the apocalyptic tradition violate my experience with God and my understanding of the way God relates with the world. How can I strengthen our faith from that which affronts my basic beliefs? After my initial aversion, however, images began to emerge.

In this psalm we are witnessing a scene in heaven, in which God is speaking to an assembly of "gods," or, apparently in later Hebrew history, angels. God is judging them for aiding and abetting injustice on earth. The final line of the psalm sounds forth: "Do likewise to the earth below!" (AP)

We are encircled daily with the pain of injustice. Whether from the crushing weight of corporate sin or the loss of personal unfulfilled potential, we know the pain. Sometimes we cry out in anguish and helplessness; other times we numb ourselves in denial.

So, I can wholeheartedly identify with the yearning of the psalmist! I can cry out, plead, and long for JUSTICE.

Prayer: *O Lover of Justice, as we hear the plea of our forebears, we know our deep longing for justice. May it ever be so. Amen.*

---

†Counseling psychologist, pastoral counselor; United Methodist minister; author; Wenatchee, Washington.

Tuesday, November 10   Read Malachi 4:1-3.

Appreciating our apocalyptic tradition

Things were bad, and people were despairing. In such times people have always cried out for a better future. Looking ahead is at the heart of apocalypticism: The present age is controlled by evil, but the new age will be ruled by good. God will dramatically usher in the new!

This apocalyptic tradition may be seen in the Hebrew Bible and most notably in the New Testament Book of Revelation as well as in the "Little Apocalypse" of Mark 13 with parallels in Matthew and Luke. Early Christianity folded into its sacred literature that which had been traditionally Hebrew. These visions of the future must have offered hope to a persecuted church much as they had earlier served the tiny trampled nation of Israel.

Malachi portrays the essential points: today there are the good and the wicked, but one day God will burn the evil while the good will "go forth leaping like calves from the stall." The evil are left stubble; they retain neither root nor branch. (Natural fires do not burn roots. Only Malachi's purifying fire of God does so!)

I have not personally watched the destruction of my church, been led into slavery in a foreign land, known the Holocaust, fought in combat, or lived as a powerless minority. I know that this limits my appreciation of the apocalyptic cry. However, I can feel the same longing to know that life is not meaningless chaos, and that somewhere, sometime, somehow, justice will prevail and shalom will emerge.

Prayer: *We are grateful, O God, that our forebears found hope to press on in the midst of their chaos. May it be so with us. Amen.*

Wednesday, November 11   Read Malachi 4:4.

The future influences the now

This verse summarizes the twelve minor prophets. Its conclusion to all the prophetic teaching is strangely enough, "Remember the law." The call to remember follows immediately the dramatic picture of God's coming judgment. I find an important truth within this sequence: the way in which we vision the future deeply affects the way we think, feel, and act now.

Those living in oppressive and despairing conditions could endure if they truly believed that God would have the final say and make things right. The future bounced back upon them and made a difference in their present.

But not only is hope offered, but the future vision tells what to do now. The people addressed by Malachi are to follow the Law. The other three readings for this week have similar guides about how to live in the present while anticipating the dramatic new age to be ushered in by God. Be just, do right, rescue, and deliver states Psalm 82:3-4; do not be led astray, go after false prophets, or be terrified, but bear witness and endure says Luke 21(7-8, 13, 19); while 2 Thessalonians 3:12-13 calls for working in quietness, earning a living, and not growing weary of well-doing.

The past influences the present also. The Ten Commandments begin with "I am the LORD your God, who brought you out of the land of Egypt, out of the house of bondage" (Ex. 20:2). Indeed, how we live this hour is deeply indebted to what we affirm that God has already done on our behalf and what God will do in the future. With that in mind, let us celebrate the now with gratitude for God's past action and with hope for a future that is in God's hands!

Prayer: *Grant us, O Christ, a conviction about our future with you which empowers us to live fully now. Amen.*

Thursday, November 12   Read 2 Thessalonians 3:6-11.

The idle one is within

Paul issues a command to those in the church at Thessalonica: Stay away from the idle ones! Idleness must have been a continuing problem, for Paul speaks of it in the other letter (1 Thess. 4:11-12). He uses words which we usually associate with the early pilgrims in America, "If any one will not work, let him not eat" (2 Thess. 3:10*b*).

To help my understanding, I like to try to walk in the world of the idlers. I wonder what it was like to be one of them. What would be my central concerns and goals? What might motivate me to be lazy and spend my time gossiping? Though it is difficult to enter another era and mentality, it is worth attempting.

Perhaps the people were waiting with their suitcases packed for the return of Christ, the Parousia. This expectancy permeates the New Testament. Not to work would make sense if Christ were to appear majestically on the clouds any day.

Still, they may have been immobilized by the powerful opposition and persecution from both their community and the Jewish synagogue. Perhaps they believed the criticism leveled at Paul, Timothy, and Silvanus but lacked the courage to be outspoken or to leave the new church. Instead, they would be quietly rebellious, taking a safe, apathetic middle ground.

Whoever they were in their inner selves, I find another way of understanding to be more helpful. Rather than shunning those early Christians as totally wrong, evil, or bad, which implies that I am not, I feel called to search for the idle one within me. I know that one resides there. Whenever that part of me speaks, I should listen for the message. There may, in fact, be surprising, powerful, and guiding words therein.

Prayer: *O Mysterious Voice Within, may we listen for you in the most unexpected places and be guided from idleness to action. Amen.*

Friday, November 13   Read Luke 21:5-9.

The despair of endless waiting

Jesus talks with his disciples about the end of time. The wondrous Temple they now see will be destroyed. Questions arise about when this will occur and the signs which will herald its arrival. Jesus warns of those who will proclaim the imminent end and acknowledge events before the end, then concludes, "But the end will not follow immediately."

We read about the greatest crisis of the early church—the day of the risen Christ's return. The early Christians believed that Christ was to return within their generation, but he had not. Confusion and despair resulted. A response of hope was absolutely essential.

In Luke 21, Luke's parallel of Mark's "Little Apocalypse" (Mark 13) is such a word of hope. The hope of Christ's return must now be reconciled with the dying of this particular generation. The end is surely coming, "but the end is not yet" (Mark 13:7*b*).

Other problems were mammoth: Emperor Nero's hideous persecution of the Christians in 64 A.D., the destruction of the Temple in Jerusalem in 70 A.D., and the eruption of Mount Vesuvius at Pompeii in 79 A.D. To face all this, in addition to the despair of Christ's not returning, must have been devastating.

A glance at the Book of Revelation would surely indicate that apocalypticism did not totally collapse. There was the future hope which allowed Christians to face violent death in Roman games. The Lamb of God will ultimately prevail.

Just as the early church created a revised hope for their day, so we may do with the challenges to faith in our day.

Prayer: *O Creative One, may we, too, find new hope in our world. Amen.*

Saturday, November 14   Read 2 Thessalonians 3:12-13.

Values other than immediate justice

Paul exhorts the idle "to do their work quietly and to earn their own living." This may not seem to be a particularly significant message until we hear it within the wider context, the imminent expectation of Christ's return. Paul's letters are probably the earliest written documents of the New Testament, the very time when this expectation was the most intense.

Exactly when people were eagerly anticipating the close of the age, Paul exhorts them to go about their daily routine. This sounds much like the ordinary in the midst of the climactic or cataclysmic. An analogy may be a parent telling a child to do her homework on Christmas eve. Would the child hear?

He concludes, "Brothers and sisters, do not be weary in doing what is right." I hear the call to endure, to be faithful, and to persist. Considering the opposites of *weary,* we might hear *refreshed, rejuvenated, enlivened,* or *empowered.* In the midst of expecting Christ to appear in power and glory, Paul calls the church to the ordinary and the routine.

I have become convinced that in every situation there are multiple values which we may choose. There is the value of safety and the value of adventure, of comfort and of confrontation, of conserving and of giving away. In the situation about which we read, there is the value of immediate justice, which Christ will bring, and the value of routine work. Indeed, tensions exist between such values, pulling in different directions.

I hope that while we yearn for immediate justice for the entire creation, we can continue to do our routine, ordinary tasks, those small, measured steps which move us toward justice.

Prayer: *O Wondrous Adventurer, sustain us and renew our spirits by both expectancy and the ordinary. Amen.*

Sunday, November 15   Read Luke 21:10-19.

Christ comes in each moment

After fiercely struggling through these difficult passages, with some relief I arrive at that which I can fully proclaim— even though the main thrust of the Lukan text is still apocalyptic. In describing all the travail to come, Jesus says, "I will give you a mouth and wisdom." This I wholeheartedly affirm as true!

My affirmation is that Christ comes to us in each moment. Whether or not there will be a final day of judgment, or Day of the Lord, I do not know, nor do I consider it vital to my faith. That Christ comes to me in each moment is central to my faith. In any possible future that might occur, I know that Christ will be with me whenever it unfolds, wherever it may occur, and whatever it may be like. Christ will offer me wisdom.

I affirm a "realized eschatology." That which was fervently expected has already happened. Christ has come! Christ continues to come! Into each tiny moment Christ enters!

The childlike cry of "Abba" in Jesus' prayer and the tender story of the returning prodigal move me more than all the dramatic and powerful imagery of the end. The intimacy and closeness of a Presence who enfolds me in grace while enticing me to new adventure is the reality of my faith. Nevertheless, prayer, parable, and apocalyptic are interwoven.

Cataclysms occur—Mt. Vesuvius, civil war, Hiroshima, the Holocaust, and plague. I sadly expect similar events may well occur in the future, but I do not think of them as divine judgment or signs of the end. Instead, I affirm that Christ comes, often (in Schweitzer's words) "as one unknown" and in many mysterious forms, calling us to follow.

Prayer: *O graceful Christ, may we recognize your coming in each moment of our lives. Amen.*

FAITH, JUSTICE, AND LOVE

November 16-22, 1992   **Richard L. Wood**†
Monday, November 16   Read John 12:9-19.

We reflect this week on faith and justice, temporal powers over against the Spirit's leading, the glory of God's love for us, and the suffering which the world sometimes requires of us if we are faithful to that love. Today, we first sit with the story of Jesus' triumphant entry into Jerusalem and the knowledge of his coming crucifixion.

Just after raising Lazarus from the dead, Jesus enters Jerusalem. This moment of honor contains a shadow of looming disaster. The raising of Lazarus has become a catalyst for the adulation of the people who want to make Jesus king and for the envy and venom of the authorities who want to eliminate him.

Sometimes faithfully following God's will leads persons into unpopular stances—sometimes even to death. Today marks the third anniversary of the brutal murder in El Salvador of six Jesuits, their housekeeper, and her daughter. The priests had worked tirelessly in El Salvador to love the people and to give witness to God's presence among them. They, like many Christian workers in that country in 1989 and in much of our world today, believed that love of God and neighbor means speaking of justice, and calling for true democracy and respect for human rights. Yet government troops beat down the door of their living quarters and murdered them.

Today let us remember those who have given their lives in our day because they were faithful to speaking God's word.

Prayer: *Lord, help us to seek your will, in small ways and large. If faith or justice require it, give us courage to give our very selves. Amen.*

---

†Author; Roman Catholic student at The Graduate Theological Union and the University of California at Berkeley.

Tuesday, November 17   Read 2 Samuel 5:1-5.

In this passage we learn how David, the good king David who is lauded as the central figure in much of the Hebrew scriptures, came to be king. In preceding chapters, David has positioned himself to become king through much bloodshed. But in the end, it is the people and their leaders who come to name David as their king, to anoint him. The people act together to make their own history, to choose their king.

Too often we look to great leaders to fix problems in society, for this seems easier. But it is an escape; we cannot avoid responsibility for our own future. Just as the ancient Jews do in this passage, we must trust in the presence of God enough to *act* in shaping our own lives, as individuals and as a society.

Here, too, we see hints of how the Jews, our ancestors in the faith, came to be truly a *people*. Up until the time of David, the people of Judah and Israel lived as scattered bands or in separate and divided kingdoms. Individually they were each people, but together they were not *a* people. In acting together and trusting in God, they set in motion the events which led to the unification of all Israel as one people. They built themselves up as a community, through trust in God and joint action. Only in this way could they be truly the people of God.

Prayer: *Lord God, so often our lives in this modern world*
fragment before our eyes under too many pressures.
It's all we can do just to hold our individual lives,
and maybe our families, together.
It's not life, it doesn't feel like making history;
just survival and getting by.
We offer up our lives, Lord, that you might make us a
people. Give us strength and trust to act together to
choose our future, to build up our community, to be
your people. Amen.

Wednesday, November 18   Read Colossians 1:11-14.

In this reading, Paul prays for the Colossians, and for us: that we may have strength and be prepared to endure everything. Paul's prayer assumes that Christians will need strength and will have much to endure, for that is Paul's experience: true followers of Christ will suffer. It is not that we are to glorify suffering, though often our Christian churches have mistakenly taught this. Rather, Paul simply knows the world: there is much suffering, much injustice, much loneliness and emptiness. Along with Paul, we are to acknowledge the power of these dark forces and yet trust in God's presence and goodness. Paul invites us not to run away from the power of darkness, but to face it squarely through trust in God's light.

Paul prays for our strength and endurance because he knows that in facing the sins of our world and our lives, we will suffer. He prays in confidence because he knows the power of God's light to transform the darkness—to forgive our sins and to change our world. In this context, suffering has a purpose in combining the dying pangs of our old selves with the labor pains of giving birth to a world transformed by God's love.

Prayer: *Lord, may we trust in you enough to face the darkness:*
         homelessness, poverty, greed, hard-hearted wealth.
     May we believe in your love enough to look within
         at the emptiness, fear, self-centeredness.
     Help us face these things, in search of healing,
         knowing that your light shines in the darkness.
     Touch our hearts, transform our lives
         in small ways or large
     that we might have the strength and endurance to
         act for a better world, that our
         suffering may no longer occur in isolation,
     but have meaning for the life of the world. Amen.

Thursday, November 19   Read Colossians 1:15-20.

In Jesus, the fullness of God was pleased to dwell. In him, all things were created: thrones, dominion, rulers, and powers. Herein lie two keys to the Christian experience. First, in coming to know Jesus Christ of Nazareth, we come into contact with the fullness of God. New heights and depths of life open before us, sometimes painfully slowly through long years of relationship to Jesus and the church, sometimes suddenly as God's love breaks through our fears.

Second, this relationship to God overshadows all other things, including the rulers and powers of this world, the people and influences which too often dominate our lives. We are called to be free. This is not the immature freedom of autonomous individuals unrelated to others. It is full freedom, in which we choose to relate to others as equals and to take responsibility for our world. We are free even to question those in authority over us, for their authority is not absolute. Their authority is created through Christ. Rather than absolutizing their power, this relativizes their power. It is legitimate only so long as they serve God's will. God so loved us as to make us free, not subservient; creators and lovers of life, not simply followers of orders.

Prayer: *Indeed, beloved Lord,*
this is what your Incarnation means:
somehow, the fullness of life dwelt within you,
walked with you on this earth, reached out to others who,
*   in varying ways,*
caught glimpses of your fullness and
followed that light.
May we, too, walk toward the light,
focused on your fullness—
filling up and spilling over
into our lives. Amen.

Friday, November 20   Read Psalm 95.

In recent days, we have focused on God's invitation to a life of faith and the work of justice, taking responsibility for our lives in common. Today we pause to assess our priorities.

The work of justice and service to the human community lies near the heart of the Christian faith; it is present in all of Jesus' ministry. Yet at the same time, it can become an obstacle to faith as well. All too easily, we can place ourselves and our work at the center of attention—for, indeed, this work is vital.

The psalm draws our attention back to the God who must lie at the center of our lives. When our commitment to others becomes a substitute for the encounter with God, it inevitably becomes distorted. The Christian faith experience invites us to make that commitment central in our lives as an expression of our trust in God and as a response to God's presence in the lives of those supposedly "below" us on the social ladder.

The psalm invites us to an encounter with God—the God of Jesus who calls us to work for change in this world while still keeping God as the focus of our lives. Read the psalm slowly as a prayer, stopping to invite God into your heart.

Prayer: *Lord, so often we love you so coldly,*
praise your name but forget who you are.
Warm our hearts, Lord; shake our lives
with the love that heals us,
  calls us beyond ourselves,
  speaks to us in the empty spaces of our lives
  and through those less fortunate than we.
Enter our lives anew, Lord;
Soften our hardened hearts and minds
  and fire us with passion for your justice. Amen.

Saturday, November 21   Read Psalm 95:2*a*, 6-7.

Today, you are invited to simply sit in God's presence. Simply ask God to be present with you in the joys and struggles of your life and to convert your heart and mind ever more fully to God's will.

Perhaps you will want to look back at the scriptures of the last few days. Or perhaps just review the themes of these reflections: the witness of those who have given their lives for the faith—like the Jesuits in El Salvador; like Christian martyrs through the centuries; and above all, like Jesus Christ, Son of God. The way God worked in history to lead the ancient Israelites to act together to anoint David king of Judah (2 Sam. 2:4). Think about God's call to us to trust and endure in our struggles to live faithfully. Consider the full and free life God wishes to give us, in which authority serves people rather than being served. Reflect and pray about the urgent need to place God and service to others at the center of our lives, rather than our own selfish desires.

As you review these themes, most importantly, just allow yourself to be quiet before the Lord.

Prayer: *God of life*
　　　　in the midst of the violence this world inflicts on us and
　　　　　encourages us to inflict on others,
　　　　we ask for healing and for forgiveness.
　　　　Restore us, Lord, to healthful life;
　　　　convert us more fully, that we might embrace your love.
　　　　Free us from our fears and our self-centeredness
　　　　and challenge us to go out into the world as witnesses
　　　　　to the faith and justice for which we yearn,
　　　　　and give us courage to work for your reign. Amen.

Sunday, November 22   Read John 12:9-19.

We return to where we began, to Jesus entering Jerusalem on a donkey, the crowds roaring to name him king. The authorities plot to kill both Jesus and Lazarus, as a witness to Jesus' power.

Jesus enters Jerusalem suspecting that he will be put to death as a threat to the established powers. His life and ministry are eminently political, for they call into question the priorities, values, and legitimacy of religious and political authorities who fail to serve the common good. Yet he does *not* come to take over the established religious authority or the political machinery; he does not lust for power.

This is the fine line of faithfulness which the Christian churches are called to walk: to challenge human beings and society to live up to God's standards, while allowing the political sphere its autonomy and independence. Furthermore, we are to walk this fine line in an attitude of service to the human community, without lust for power.

Two great temptations draw the churches off this path. First, we are tempted to avoid conflict by so "spiritualizing" the Christian message that it no longer challenges us here and now. Second, we are tempted to idolize power, to believe that if we could only get "our kind" of Christian into power, all would be better. This lust for power and influence leads to public scandals as the gospel is submerged to the quest for power. The good news is diluted when either temptation is allowed to triumph.

Prayer: *Lord, help us walk*
          the fine line of faithfulness.
          Our calling is to be courageous and faithful,
          trusting in your love
          to redeem our lives and our world. Amen.

LIVING INTO THE LIGHT OF GOD'S SHALOM

November 23-29, 1992   **Linda Johnson†**
Monday, November 23   Read Isaiah 2:1-5.

Just imagine: a day when all people, all nations not only believe in God but turn to God's word for instruction; a day when all people seek to know and live by God's teaching. Picture one world community in harmonious celebration of its differences, all flowing toward God's high mountain to learn how to be more faithful. Isaiah paints a vivid and compelling vision of this future reign of God. (See also Micah 4:1-4.)

With God as the active ruler in the world, there would be no more military actions, no coups or revolutions. We would study war no more. Just imagine it! Fighter planes turned into playground equipment. Navy ships docked to house homeless people. The Pentagon turned into a storehouse for food for the hungry. The military budget channeled into education. Instruments of death turned into instruments of life. Just imagine it!

We are not told when to expect this future time, but the prophet announces with certainty that the time will come when God will reign over a unified world at peace. This vision of peace, announced by prophets and echoed by angels in Bethlehem, must be kept alive. We can participate in the coming reign of God if we look for peace, work for peace, pray for peace. But first we must believe in peace. To believe in peace we have to be able to imagine it. Isaiah helps us do that.

Prayer: *Powerful God, help us to keep alive your vision of shalom. Write it on our hearts and help us to live into it. Amen.*

---

†Mother; United Methodist minister; Associate Director of Field Education, The Divinity School at Vanderbilt University, Nashville, Tennessee.

Tuesday, November 24   Read Isaiah 2:5.

When I questioned my five-and-one-half-year-old daughter, Anna, as to why she hit her four-year-old sister, she answered, "Because she wrinkled my raccoon box." She clearly felt that her actions were justified. "But," I reasoned, "sisters are more valuable than cardboard boxes. The box will be thrown away and forgotten, but Maggie will be your sister forever. Learn to express your anger with words, not hitting."

Anger is a natural part of life. When we are hurt, threatened, disappointed, violated in any way, we feel angry. I do not want to deny the very real feelings of anger in my children, but I am trying to learn ways to acknowledge their feelings while helping them find more constructive channels to express their hostilities.

Maggie says Anna hit her first; Anna says she will stop taking Maggie's toys when Maggie stops taking hers. Each one is focused on the behavior of the other rather than looking at her own deeds. They are only children, but much of the adult world models the same behavior and rationale for it.

Following his marvelous vision of God's reign of peace (Isa. 2:1-4), Isaiah adds, "O house of Jacob, come, let us walk in the light of the Lord!" Isaiah calls on Israel to begin moving into the vision, to respond to it with faithful obedience.

Waiting for God's reign is no idle waiting. Isaiah calls us to respond to the hope of a better world by first beginning our own walk toward God's light. We can work toward the day of shalom by examining our own behavior, our own motives, jealousies, and hostilities. We can seek to understand our feelings and find constructive ways of expressing them.

We can't wait for someone else to go first. In this day of nuclear stockpiles and domestic violence and abuse, the need to use words rather than force to settle conflict becomes urgent indeed.

Prayer: *O God, help us walk in the light of your great love. Amen.*

Wednesday, November 25   Read Romans 13:11-12.

There is always a tension in Paul's letters, a dual need to exhort and guide the fledgling Christian communities and to provide the deepest and most reflective observations about the mysteries of the faith. The early faith communities were profoundly affected by the death and resurrection of Jesus, already claimed by the gracious act of God in Christ. Yet, they were also expectant, hopeful of a consummation of God's faithful promise to Israel. In this passage, Paul exhibits both the "now" and the "then" of our faith. "Now" we must obey earthly rulers and pay taxes. But "then" salvation will be accomplished. "Now" the night is still with us, "then" that day will be at hand.

Time is an elusive thing. We prefer an orderly sequence of events, with one thing following naturally from another. But Paul has grasped a truth beyond our simple imaginings of a timely and ordered world. The fullness of time has brought God's act into the world and into us in the very midst of our feeble struggle to make our own order of things. With Paul, we can affirm that we know what hour it is: love has been made manifest in an instant. For that instant, the mundane "now" and the magnificent "then" are brought together, and we apprehend that majestic power of God—Creator and Redeemer.

To put on the Lord Jesus Christ is to live according to the new order of existence. Paul urges the early church in Rome to move more fully into the new order. The old order is viewed as darkness, sleeping, or a dimmer awareness of God. Wake up! Paul says. Dress in the garment of Christ and live in the light of God's magnificent day. Time is forever changed.

Prayer: *Eternal God, in this Advent season, remind us anew of your creating and redeeming power that we may see ourselves more clearly in the light of your hope for us. Amen.*

Thursday, November 26   Read Romans 13:13-14.

A few years ago a geologist predicted a great and devastating earthquake in the Mississippi Valley. Thousands of people laid in supplies of food and water; the media covered details of preparedness or of flagrant disregard for the expert's warning. Interviewed on national television, the mayor of a small town on the fault line talked about the local residents' cooperative spirit in preparing for this great and frightening event.

No earthquake happened then, or since. But, for a brief period, people's awareness of the signs of this natural event and their preparations for dealing with such a cataclysmic event were heightened. And all of the indications were that the people in the immediate area pulled together, at least to the extent that our common anxious mentality would allow.

In the face of the expected return of Jesus, Paul exhorts the Roman faithful to lead lives becoming to the faith they proclaimed. For Paul, this exhortation to an upright life is both inner- and outer-directed, focused on personal integrity and on encouraging appropriate and loving behavior among members of the community. Rather than seeking to impress with appearance and to flatter with empty words, we are encouraged to rely solely on the garment of Jesus Christ.

The common and shared anticipation of a tragedy like an earthquake prompted acts of kindness and courage; our history is full of such courageous acts and actors. How much more should a shared anticipation of joy encourage in us such acts of loving kindness and courage! How much more should the promise of God's faithfulness prompt our faithful and obedient response!

Prayer: *God of grace and mercy, help us reorder our lives after the example of Jesus. Clothe us in his righteousness that we may mature in the light of his love. Amen.*

Friday, November 27   Read Matthew 24:36-42.

There is waiting. And then there's waiting. Waiting in line is distressing if you are short and can only stare at backs or necks. Any kind of waiting is agony for certain personality types who are always in a hurry. But waiting for a birthday party or a surprise—well, the anticipation and expectation are almost as delicious as the event itself. This kind of waiting is like pregnancy; it holds life.

Today's scripture speaks of the promised return of Christ at the conclusion of human history. Earlier the disciples had asked Jesus when this would happen. "No one knows," Jesus answered, "not even the angels of heaven." (v. 36, AP). Only God knows. So, Jesus says, "Watch!" Don't get lulled into "business as usual" like the people did in the days of Noah.

Watch with anticipation. Live with the expectation that something is about to happen. Someday Jesus is going to bring history to its fulfillment and usher in the reign of God.

Watch. Not by following false prophets who announce doomsday, not by despairing over what the world is coming to, but with hopeful trusting that something grand will happen. God *will be* victorious over sin and death. All the troubles in this present time are but the birth pangs of the new age.

In the meantime we wait. We know that what we see here is not all we get. We endure suffering of every imaginable shade and degree. Even the love, joy, and peace we find are incomplete and fragile. They are but a foretaste of what is to come. And that makes a difference in how we live now. We live with an irrepressible hopefulness. Living in hope, we can see the signs of fulfillment present even now.

Prayer: *God of life, stir us from dull and lifeless living to look with expectant hope for your presence around us. Amen.*

Saturday, November 28   Matthew 24:43-44.

Those in the early church expected an imminent fulfillment of Jesus' promise to return. Initially they lived with the expectation of "any day now." When that didn't happen, they had to adjust to living more fully in the present while still living expectantly. Watchful expectation awakens awareness to be ready at all times, even if there is a delay in the expected event.

If we knew when to expect the end, we could put our lives in order and start living the way we know we should. But we do not know when, and so we are to live as a people prepared. What, exactly, does that mean? How you get ready is shaped by what you are getting ready for. Advent Christians are getting ready for Jesus. And Jesus said, "A new commandment I give to you, that you love one another. Just as I have loved you, you also should love one another" (John 13:34).

Today's scripture calls for a way of life that is always ready to receive Christ. Our lives are busy loving while our hearts are kept on alert. Advent, then, is a season for soul-searching. What about our way of life; does it operate out of love for self, God, and neighbor? How responsible are we in relationships? Are we fit stewards of the earth for the sake of our children and grand-children? Are we willing to go the extra mile for the poor?

Every year I am shocked that the scripture lessons for the first Sunday in Advent are so heavy, so foreboding. *Examine my heart and repent at the beginning of this cheery season of indulgence and revelry?* But Advent is the first Sunday in the new liturgical year. Tomorrow is the church's New Year's Day. Is it not fitting that we should reflect on our lives and acknowledge and repent of our sins in order to begin a new year with hope?

Suggestion for meditation and prayer: *Examine your life and lift up your sins to God. Accept God's forgiveness.*

Sunday, November 29   Read Psalm 122:1.

Reread the week's scripture lessons and then read Psalm 122:1.

Her timing couldn't have been worse. She knocked on the parsonage door early one Advent Sunday morning. I was hurrying to dress so that I could review my sermon. I had never seen her before, and she didn't look like the other children from the small rural church I was serving. She was alone, this seven-year-old with tangled hair and too-big dress. Someone had dropped her off for Sunday school two hours early. I gave her crayons and paper, which she eagerly accepted. Her gratitude and simple joy shamed me, for I had just wanted to keep her busy. Her happy face, framed by her poverty, haunted me. So I colored with her for a while, and we talked.

Even so, I resented the intrusion. When the worshipers began arriving, I put her in the care of an older couple. They hovered lovingly over her, aware of her ignorance of church etiquette. She was like a magnet for the congregation's eyes and hearts that Sunday. During the sermon she ate the candy cane I had given out at the children's time. I could see both the couple's futile efforts to contain the sticky messiness and her pure enjoyment of the sweetness.

She took in everything and reveled in it. Through her eyes, we saw it all fresh and new, the Advent wreath with its four candles of light-dispensing power, the rhythm of worship, the awesomeness of prayer. What a privilege to be in the house of the Lord! What joy to sing and pray! How marvelous to be treated with kindness, to be hovered over with love! She awoke us to privileges we had taken for granted.

She was Christmas for us that year, the coming of Christ so unexpected—an intrusion really—but bringing great joy.

Prayer: *Come, Lord Jesus. Come to love us that we may love others in your name. Amen.*

346

LONGING

Whether this prophecy dates from the period of the monarchy or from a later time is a matter of scholarly debate. Does the passage represent a ritualistic expression for each succeeding king or a messianic expectation? Does the "stump of Jesse" symbolize a continuing line of David or a destroyed royal house? Even if these questions were resolved, time in this passage would not be linear but a meshing of past, present, and future.

The future tense is invoked most directly. The passage promises that a leader will come. This heir of the Davidic mantle and monarchy will restore glory. This anointed one will usher in an idyllic age. The future is expected to arrive full of peaceful glory. But this poetic offering assumes a present deep yearning for wholeness and a desire for rescue. The hope described builds upon an implied searching and struggling that is of the present. The tree imagery carries the connections with the past. The leader will be rooted in the old line and shoot forth from the stump.

During Advent we experience this interwoven, non-linear enmeshing of past, present, and future. In prayer we name the pain of our present—the personal searching and public struggles. We light candles in hope of a future restoration of peace and justice. And in pageants and preparations we connect ourselves with the tradition of our story from the past.

Prayer: *God of Jesse and Jesus, you have been with us in the past. Sustaining, empowering God, you are with us in the here and now. God of hope and vision, you will be with us always. Amen.*

---

†Conference Staff, Christian Development, Manitoba and Northwestern Ontario Conference, United Church of Canada.

Tuesday, December 1   Read Isaiah 11:2.

Cleverness, wit, and street smarts are superficial substitutes for the qualities of leadership listed here. Technical and performance skills are the veneers of talent. Collecting information, facts, and figures is knowledge for knowledge's sake. True leadership is marked by intellectual discernment, deep insight, and sensitive reflection. This gift of wisdom and understanding is the first of three mentioned in this passage from Isaiah.

According to this verse, leaders must also be able to act. Putting plans into place, implementing decisions, and carrying out ideas are marks of this ability. The skills of organization and administration plus confidence to get the job done are needed.

A relationship with God is the third characteristic of leadership articulated in this verse, a relationship based on respect for and reverence and awe of God.

Leadership is often imaged as a "born-to" quality. But leadership has to be developed, nurtured, trained, and supported. And we all have the potential to be leaders. Certainly, each of us is called to Isaiah's three paths of wise reflection and faithful action and relationship with God. These are not vocations for a few elite!

Leadership is also often imaged as a power-over, hierarchical, top-down proposition. If we could respect the gifts each one brings, develop talents, and support one another, we might be able to envision a sharing of power, leadership, and ourselves.

May this Advent be a time for examining ourselves and our abilities to think, act, and pray. And may we speculate on new visions of interdependent leadership.

Prayer: *O Christ, center us in thoughtfulness.*
O Empowering Spirit, lead us into service.
O God, deepen our relationship with you. Amen.

Wednesday, December 2   Read Isaiah 11:3-4;
                                                       Psalm 72:1-8

A homeless squatter under the bridge has to stuff his oversize shoes with newspapers. A broker is dodging the traffic coming off the bridge and has to avoid a puddle so he won't get his $300 loafers wet. We tend to make assumptions about each one. To judge by appearances is a mistake. To assess a person by external features like haircuts or weight or clothing is superficial. To assume the homeless one is an irresponsible loser is shallow. To write off the broker as an arrogant materialist is too easy.

Outside, a bag lady babbles a stream of seemingly unrelated conversation to herself as she pushes her bundle buggy from garbage can to garbage can. Inside, two diners enjoy a liquid lunch in a trendy café as they wait for breaks in the conversation to make their point, to share their insight, to tell their story.

It is unfair to judge by hearsay. To depend on rumor, gossip, or innuendo can lead to conclusions that are unjust. We need to hear more, listen actively, and understand deeply. It would be unkind to dismiss the bag lady's unconnected verbiage as drunkenness. It would be unfair to label the diners as self-absorbed status-seekers.

We live our lives from the perspectives that we know. It is difficult to stand aside from those experiences and be objective. Our cultural assumptions are so entrenched, our class attitudes so ingrained, our gender bias so inbred. But the evils of wickedness, oppression, and injustice must be named. Sexism, racism, and classism must be recognized for what they are, both in ourselves and in our society.

We need our best analysis so that we may participate in "judg(ing) the poor fairly and defend(ing) the rights of the helpless" (TEV).

Prayer: *O God, judge us in our judging. Amen.*

Thursday, December 3   Read Isaiah 11:5.

This is a season when we make gift selections, and many of us give clothes. The fashion industry depends upon it. The changing fashion trends mean we purchase new wardrobes often. We don't want to get caught in yesterday's dress, suit, or pair of slacks.

But today's verse from Isaiah raises a challenge to our consumer expectations. It confronts the materialism of this season and of our society. The leader is pictured girded not with gold but with righteousness. The One who is coming will be clothed in integrity and justice. This expected One will be belted not in beauty but in authenticity of purpose and depth of caring.

The beauty of this person will be faithfulness—faithfulness which evidences trust and confidence in God with an accompanying blessing of serenity and calm; a faithfulness that is expressed in commitment to the values and ways of God; a faithfulness that results in a person's living out and putting into action God's mercy and justice.

What to buy for that male who is so difficult to shop for?
Consider making a donation to a justice-seeking agency.
If I get that sweater, do you think she'll wear it?
Consider one made at a cooperative from a developing country. The money goes back to the people who knit them. It is a gift that gives twice.
Is this my color?
It depends on whether it was made in a country where human rights are violated.

God is longing for us to wear righteousness and faithfulness inwardly. God wants us to be just and true in our relationships one-to-one, in our communities, and nation to nation.

Prayer: *Adorn our hearts with love, O God. Amen.*

Friday, December 4   Read Isaiah 11:6-8.

The words of these verses paint a picture that is unfamiliar to us. We do not know a world where enemies live together or an earth without fear. This vision of reconciliation and wholeness is beyond comprehension. This picture is unrealistic; the sound of these words utopian.

How can we take seriously this thinking? Because it is the longing of our hearts. We want to live among people who exhibit trust and companionship. We are sick of suspicion and hatred. We ache for a day when affection is the constant of human relationships.

When children can walk to school without needing to wear bulletproof vests, we will be free. When women can get into elevators with male strangers without feeling apprehensive, we will have peace. When downtown streets are safe from drug wars and crime waves, we will live in love.

Even as we long for an end to violence, we must refuse to cooperate with evil. We must stand on the side of the violated. We must not condone, hide, or neglect abuse. We must confront militarism and withhold our blessing of war. We must stop the rape of creation. We must find transforming theologies that move us out of competitive, imperialistic imagery.

During this season of Advent we acknowledge that we are waiting for a day of liberation and peace. And as we wait, we are called to commit ourselves to the work and preparation necessary to bring about this day.

Prayer: *We do not want false peace or empty harmony or simple answers, O God. We want an end to the fear, a halt to the fighting, a stop to the suffering. We want healing and wholeness and shalom. Amen.*

Saturday, December 5   Read Isaiah 11:6*d*.

And a little child shall lead them.

In context this is an image of reconciliation. Within the framework of Isaiah's idyllic vision this is further illustration of Eden-like bliss and safety. Wild animals will be tame enough to be led by infants.

My mind sees other parallels as well. I connect this phrase with a parade of faithful young people—the after-midnight calls to Samuel (1 Sam. 3), Jeremiah's protest of limited experience (Jer. 1:6–7), and Mary's magnificent song (Luke 1:46-55). During this Advent season I certainly link this phrase with an incarnational Bethlehem baby, and I am called to remember Jesus' admonition: "Whoever does not receive the kingdom as a little child will never enter it" (Mark 10:15).

I also think about the children who have ministered to and with congregations: the junior choir anthems that rose above performance expectations, the church school classes that collected contributions for significant causes, the individual young people who have delighted and touched my soul. Theirs has been a gift of vulnerability. I want to be part of a church that doesn't marginalize children. I want their names to be included on church lists. I want them to receive pastoral visits in moments of crisis. I want to experiment with intergenerational approaches. I want children to participate to whatever extent they wish. They can express their openness if there are ears to listen. If they are given opportunities, they can serve and minister to others.

In all these possibilities there is promise of growth, fresh insight, and joy if we are open to Isaiah's vision: "and a little child shall lead them."

Prayer: *Lead us, O little Child of Bethlehem, into the ways of inclusiveness. Amen.*

Sunday, December 6   Read Isaiah 11:9.

For the earth will be full of the knowledge of the LORD
as the waters that cover the sea.

Yes, we wait for that time that Isaiah foretold, and we ask:
How long, O Lord?

How long will we continue to pollute the air,
                    pump sewage into the sea,
                    and dump garbage on the land?
How long will the environment be exploited,
                the atmosphere spoiled,
                the creation destroyed?
How long will we ignore the waste,
                    act as if we're helpless,
                    be indifferent?
How long will our technological advances be encouraged
                and our consumptive excesses be allowed
                and our destructive lifestyles be affirmed?
Our resources are limited, O God.
Why do we act as if we can go on forever?

This creation is a gift and we have squandered it. Instead of
having caring dominion over the earth, we have dominated it. We
have bulldozed and paved our planet. We have cleared it and
claimed it. We have run over it and ravaged it. Forgive us, O God.

Advent is a time for waiting. We wait for the day when the holy
mountain will be green, when the land will return to wholeness.
We anticipate a restoration to right and natural order.

Prayer: *Creator of the universe,*
            we give thanks for the beauty
            and wonder of nature.
            Creator who names us co-creators,
            give us courage to turn around
            this mess we have made. Amen.

IMAGES OF ADVENT

December 7-13, 1992   **Thomas R. Hawkins†**
Monday, December 7   Read Isaiah 35:8-10.

Advent and passage through the wilderness

We must pass through an Advent wilderness to arrive at Christmas. The seers from the East followed the Star across the Arabian Desert. Mary and Joseph traveled through barren hills to arrive at Bethlehem and later crossed the desert as they fled Herod's soldiers. What are our own Advent deserts?

Busyness is one such desert. We are often so busy with baking, shopping, entertaining, and traveling that we are too tired to hear the angel voices singing in our ears.

Many of us, especially those of us who are alone, may suffer from the "holiday blues." The pressure to be cheerful, bright, and to have "the best Christmas ever" puts a strain on many of us. Some families must pass through the wilderness of excessive alcohol consumption that can lead to violence.

Isaiah, however, promises that God has prepared a highway upon which we may travel from Advent to Christmas. "A highway shall be there, and it shall be called the Holy Way." When we keep our lives centered on God during the weeks before Christmas, we can pass through the wilderness of Advent to experience Christmas joy.

What changes do we need to make in our lives in order to keep ourselves centered so we stay on the Holy Way that leads to the everlasting joy of Christ's being born in our hearts?

Prayer: *O God, help us keep our lives in balance this Advent. Guide us through the wilderness of this season so that our lives may stay centered upon your gracious presence; through Jesus Christ. Amen.*

---

†United Methodist clergy; currently Assistant Professor in Ministry at McCormick Theological Seminary, Chicago.

Tuesday, December 8   Read James 5:7-10.

Advent's patience as creative waiting

"Don't just stand there; do something!" we are often told. Our culture places a high priority on action, on keeping busy. We live in a society where we want instant action, if not instant results. We have little understanding of what it means to wait patiently.

In fact, much of our frustration with these weeks before Christmas has to do with our being made to wait: for stamps at the post office, for the store clerk to total our gift purchases, for the traffic light to change.

Advent is a time when our capacity for patience is tested. It is a time when we are reminded of the value that earlier generations of Christians placed on patience as a fruit of the Spirit. Advent represents an opportunity for us to recover a sense of patience as creative waiting. Patience is the creative waiting for the seed planted in fertile, moist soil to germinate. It is the creative waiting of parents as new life unfolds within the mother's womb. Nothing can hurry the process. We can do nothing to rush the growth, to produce instant results.

"Be patient," advises James. "Strengthen your hearts, for the coming of the Lord is near." This is the patient waiting for the Messiah's first coming as Jesus' life took shape within Mary's womb. And this is the patient waiting for Christ to come again in glory and restore all things.

During this Advent season, where in our lives do we need to rediscover the meaning of patience as creative waiting? as attention to the ways of God's power, purpose, and presence unfolding in our lives?

Suggestion for prayer: *As you go through today, pay attention to those moments when you are becoming impatient and frustrated. Ask God to reveal the deeper meaning of those situations. Turn them into occasions of prayer rather than irritation.*

Wednesday, December 9   Read Psalm 146:5-10.

Advent and the passion for justice

God's nature, God's identity, is revealed through what God does. We cannot know who God is apart from acknowledging what God continually does for us in our personal and corporate histories.

Israel's songs of praise always link knowing God as Creator with knowing God as the One who acts in history. "Happy are those . . . whose hope is in the LORD, their God who made heaven and earth . . . who executes justice for the oppressed; who gives food to the hungry."

God is the One who loves justice, who cares for the weak, the marginalized, and the forgotten. We find God not just in the beauty of nature; we discover God where the hungry are fed, the excluded are included, and the invisible are made visible.

During Advent we are painfully aware of our society's inequities. The plight of the homeless becomes more precarious as winter's cold arrives. The excluded and the invisible feel even more isolated and lonely as they stand on the fringes of our celebrations, reminding us silently of their pain. The poor are excluded from the tables spread with food and the piles of gifts that daily grow beneath Christmas trees.

"Bread for myself is a material question; bread for my neighbor is a spiritual question," observed Nikolai Berdyaev, a Russian mystic. Advent challenges us to examine our celebration of Christmas. What are we doing this Advent to include the excluded, to fill the hungry with good things?

Prayer: *O God who is our Creator as well as the One who acts in history, help us to share in your liberating purposes in human history. We pray today for those on the fringes of our society and for those who minister with them and to them; we ask this for Jesus' sake. Amen.*

Thursday, December 10   Read Isaiah 35:1-4.

Advent and our hope

The Christmas story announces the Messiah's birth. Yet our world seems little changed because the Messiah came. We proclaim the Christ Child as the Prince of Peace. Yet we know more of conflict than of peace. Sometimes our hearts are so full of turmoil that we think even inner peace is an illusion.

The author of this passage lived in a time when Israel's confidence in God's presence and purposes had been shaken. The people had been carried away into exile. The Temple lay in ruins.

Yet Isaiah invites Israel to hope for a time when they will return to their own land and God's glory will again dwell among them. Such confidence in God's ultimate victory is basic to our faith. Mary and Anna, Simeon and Joseph all hoped against hope that the Messiah would come and redeem Israel. They kept on believing even when there was little evidence to support them.

Advent challenges us to hope against hope that love can prevail. It invites us to believe that the dry, desert places of our wounded lives will blossom again and bear glad fruit. Advent asks us to embrace the foolishness of the gospel, which says justice will be done on earth.

Advent invites us to keep on doing things faithfully—guarding truth, including the marginalized, nourishing ourselves on Word and Sacrament, caring for those we love. When we act faithfully, we are living the Advent hope that our desert places will blossom with flowers.

Prayer: *Loving Creator, we offer to you those dry, wounded places within our lives that you might turn our deserts into blossoms. We offer you our inner turmoil and doubts that you might fill us with hope and trust; through Jesus Christ. Amen.*

Friday, December 11   Read Matthew 11:2-6.

Advent and our doubt

Herod had imprisoned John the Baptist in the fortress of Machaerus, on the desolate heights of Moab near the Dead Sea's eastern shore. Awaiting certain death, John began to review his life and ministry, wondering if it had been worthwhile.

He even questioned his proclamation that the Messiah was coming. He sent his disciples to ask Jesus, "Are you the one who is to come, or should we look for another?"

John asks the question all of us ask sooner or later: "Are you the one? Or should we look for another?" Some of us spend many years looking for one answer after another to our problems. We try fads, self-help movements, a variety of therapies, and numerous churches. We seem to be always looking for another answer, another way to "fix" our lives.

And some of us look for one new experience of God's salvation after another, each more profound than the last. "This must not be what we were looking for," we tell ourselves. "There must be another."

Sometimes we celebrate Christmas that way. We run from party to party, hoping for some experience that validates our worth. We eagerly unwrap each gift hoping it will prove that we are loved. When we do not experience what we hoped for, we tell ourselves, "This is not the one; there must be another."

Jesus' answer to John reminds us there is no other answer to satisfy our deepest yearnings than God's healing love made known in Jesus. The proof of our worth and value does not lie in an ideal Christmas; it lies in God's compassionate care for us.

Prayer: *O God, keep us focused and centered this Christmas season so that we do not run from experience to experience, hoping for some final proof that we are loved. Remind us that the final proof of our worth is in your love for us through Jesus Christ. Amen.*

Saturday, December 12   Read Isaiah 35:4-7.

Advent includes the excluded

Jesus quotes this passage from Isaiah when he answers the question put to him by John the Baptist's disciples, inviting John to reconsider his picture of the Messiah (Matt. 11:4-5).

The Messiah might not be one who comes in violent judgment. Instead, the Messiah might come in love, healing, and blessing. Are those not the gifts we seek in this season of gift-giving: for the blind to see, the lame to walk, the deaf to hear?

Some months ago I suffered a retinal edema. My vision was distorted. I could not read. Often I felt I could not see well enough to drive. Until that experience, I did not realize how isolating a physical handicap could be.

I was physically and emotionally distanced from others, and cut off from routine contact with them. Because I felt preoccupied with my distorted vision, I had a hard time being fully present to others.

Anyone who has had a broken bone can understand how a temporary handicap disrupts our lives. Such experiences help us understand how debilitating a permanent disability can be.

Jesus promises a time when the broken will be healed and restored to wholeness. His ministry was marked by healing and blessing. He included those whose physical limitations excluded them, made visible those whom society had made invisible.

As we approach the holidays, what can we do to include the excluded, to make visible the invisible, to offer healing and hope? Our acts of generosity are signs of the coming reign of God in which all things will be made whole.

Prayer: *Healing Spirit, give us eyes to see those around us whom society has rendered invisible and excluded; give us open hearts to include them; give us healing hands to touch their lives with love; for Jesus' sake. Amen.*

Sunday, December 13   Read Matthew 11:7-11.

Advent as a prophetic moment

What did people expect to find when they went to hear John the Baptist preaching in the wilderness, Jesus asks. A reed shaking in the wind? Someone clothed in soft raiment? A prophet?

John suffered the fate of all prophets. He paid with his life for his truth-telling. Clothed in camel hair, John was not among society's more respected members, a fact that made him even more the target of Herod's wrath and anger.

God often selects the least likely candidate to be a prophet. Like Herod and his contemporaries, we seldom honor our prophets. Modern American prophets like Martin Luther King, Jr., are more respected in their deaths than in their lives. Often, we, not unlike the scribes and Pharisees, prefer people who keep their lawns and their hair clipped short, who wash their cars and dress in the latest fashion.

If it is God's truth, then it should not matter who speaks it. But we know that it does. We want to hear God's word and to receive God's sacrament from the mouths and hands of "people like us." Yet that is seldom how God works. God selects a rough-hewn man named John, a peasant woman named Mary, an elderly woman named Anna.

Much of our energy goes into denying a voice to those people who do not fit into our categories of acceptability and respectability. Yet the John the Baptist we encounter during Advent challenges us to repent, to rethink whom God uses as God's instruments in human history. God often uses people who are very different from us.

Prayer: *O God who loves justice and truth, send your spirit upon all your people that we might support our prophets and hear your word through what they speak; through Jesus Christ. Amen.*

December 14-20, 1992   **Doug Hitt†**
Monday, December 14   Read Psalm 24:1-2.

In your mind, travel toward one of your most vivid experiences of mountains, the ocean, or another striking aspect of creation. Your recollection will likely be tinged with feeling. Let the memory of the event, feeling and all, wash over you.

It is early spring in Grand Teton National Park. In the chilly, May twilight, I see for the first time the three massive peaks jutting from the "nowhere" of Wyoming prairic. The summits, jagged and snow-covered, are blinding in brilliance. They appear unapproachable and unfathomable. Time and the endless parade of details which normally occupy my attention are swallowed up. I am moved beyond expressed thanks to wordless awe.

The psalms are so dear to us because they articulate cries of praise and desperation which arise from the very edges of our lives—those times when we can hardly find the words to express our soul's outbursts and yearnings. Like Psalm 24, a good many of the psalms are replete with images of the natural world. Contemplation of creation reminds us of the vastness and marvel of creation—and of God, the Creator. It reminds us that all creation is the Lord's: from the most minute and elusive subatomic particle in a mountain's center to a light-years-distant black hole. We stand—mute with wonder—before the Creator of such scope and variety.

Prayer: *O God, when we look at the created world and at persons as part of that world, may we be mindful of the care with which you fashioned all creation and of the grace and love by which you sustain us. Amen.*

---

†Free-lance writer; physical therapist; member of Lawrence Mennonite Fellowship, Lawrence, Kansas.

Tuesday, December 15   Read Psalm 24:3-4.

Life at the edges has a flip side. We do not long behold the wonder of creation and its Founder before we are confronted with the fact that we have been poor stewards of God's earth. The effects of greed, shortsightedness, and malignant self-interest have multiplied to the extent that parts of our planet are uninhabitable. While there are those who hoard and overconsume the earth's bounty, others perish and falter from lack of the most basic shelter and foodstuffs. Justice and mercy can hardly be found. The Creator weeps.

Corporately and individually, we all have the capacity for doing injury, whether actively or by neglect. This is sin. Weighed down with such a realization, the psalmist cries, "Who shall ascend . . . who shall stand in his holy place?" At first glance, the answer is disheartening. The words *clean* and *pure* may be mistaken for utter perfection. In meditating upon this scripture, it may be more helpful to focus on the word *falsehood* (v. 4). To lift our soul up to falsehood is to repeatedly avoid the truth about ourselves to the extent that we become compartmentalized beings. The temptation is so very subtle. Desirous of being successful and well-liked, we alter our behavior to fit a given setting. Who we are at work, in the marketplace, in our families, or in a church building has little consistency. We become impervious to God's truth-seeking Spirit.

When we dare to be honest, we find we are a hodge-podge of self-interest and charity, ugliness and beauty. The mix is uncomfortable; yet, looking the truth fully in the face, we will find ourselves at an edge where we know God's transforming love.

Prayer: *Compassionate God, help us come to grips with the hidden falsehoods which deny our gifts or disguise our faults. Amen.*

Wednesday, December 16   Read Isaiah 7:10-16.

We are pleased when things fit. Congruity feels good. It fulfills our need for order. Incongruity happens when we encounter information or events which do not fit with our experience, with our notion of what is right. When things don't fit, life seems hostile and unreliable.

Many embark upon the journey of faith with the hope that their lives will take on more order, that things will make sense at last. This is understandable. The God who creates the cosmos from out of the void is able to bring order into the chaos of our lives. Yet, as we mature, we often experience God as a *disordering* presence, One who is anything but congruous.

It may aid our understanding of today's reading if we can familiarize ourselves with the context. Assyria, an aggressive military power, seemed to have a penchant for gobbling up kingdoms. In an effort to strengthen their odds against Assyria, Israel and Syria sought to force Judah to join their alliance, usurping King Ahaz if necessary. Although hard-pressed, Ahaz rejected God's assurances of safety. Then, in the midst of amassing armies and entangling politics, Isaiah speaks a word which is startling in its incongruity, almost laughable: "Behold, a virgin shall be with child. . ." (v. 14, NASB).

Life at the edges is full of incongruity. We will often feel ill-equipped, awkward, and completely at a loss. If we run from such discomfort—if we see incongruity as a negative—we will likely miss Immanuel, God's breaking into our lives, this Advent.

Suggestion for prayer: *In your life during this season of Advent, where do you experience incongruity? Be honest with yourself. Come before God, open to the Spirit's illumination.*

Thursday, December 17   Read Matthew 1:18-19.

We should not be too quick to leave this matter of incongruity. Consider for a moment the difference between holiness and respectability. In the setting of the church, these two are regularly confused. *Holiness* describes a state of being which reflects attentiveness to God in all aspects of life and a resultant commitment to the values of the Kingdom: justice, mercy, and compassion. Respectability is context- and culture-bound. If one outwardly reflects the values of the surrounding culture, one is respected and rewarded by that culture. Much of the time, holiness is at odds with a given cultural current. Holiness may not be respectable; it may even be dangerous.

We don't know much about Joseph. He made an honest living and paid his taxes. It seems likely that he was an esteemed member of his religious community, being "a just man." Verse 19 suggests that Joseph's intentions were pure. He was motivated by compassion and concern for Mary. Sizing up the situation, he felt that a quiet divorce was the most reasonable course of action in this bizarre circumstance. Yet, God's gentle imperative directly contradicted the "respectable" course of action: "Do not be afraid to take Mary home." (v. 20*b*, NIV)

As we grow in our laboring with God toward the Kingdom vision, we will find ourselves among the poor of the world, the powerless, and the outcast. We will at times be seen as a threat to societal values with which the gospel is at odds. Encountering God at the edges, we may well be required to venture deep into the territory of irrespectability.

Prayer: *Loving God, we need the courage to turn our backs on the world's rewards for the sake of your Kingdom. May our lives exhibit a simple holiness that is at home with the lowly and the meek. Amen.*

Friday, December 18   Read Matthew 1:20-21.

The Matthew birth narrative is rather scant and to the point. Reading it, my imagination runs toward what is between the lines, toward all that is unstated. We can only wonder about the conversation between Joseph and Mary, this seemingly ordinary young couple through whom God desired to do something extraordinary. We might imagine them saying, "But this has never happened before!"

In matters of spirituality, we are especially prone to stick with what has been meaningful in the past. We memorialize the events of our lives where God has been unusually present. Certainly we should celebrate these and recite them. They are woven into our corporate and individual stories. However, if we clutch too tightly to what has been, we become a stunted people unable to live and speak the vision of the Kingdom.

Immanuel—God with us—is a terrifying prospect. It must have been doubly so for Mary and Joseph, whose religious upbringing had conveyed that God was fiery and unapproachable, that to see God's face was to die. We can imagine Joseph, repeating over and over, "How can it be? It can't be!" And Mary, how could she avoid waves of confusion and dread? Could the two have found courage in God's promise given through Isaiah: "Do not call to mind the former things. . . . Behold, I will do something new. . . . Will you not be aware of it?" (Isa. 43:18-19, NASB)

Our privilege and task is nothing less than to be bearers of God's grace and kingdom.

Suggestion for prayer: *Consider areas in your life where God may be seeking to do something new. Encouraged by the example of Joseph and Mary, come before God open and receptive to the divinely extraordinary.*

Saturday, December 19   Read Matthew 1:22-25.

Living faithfully—staying near the edge—gets tiring. We long for evidence that God is with us on this journey, that our lives make a difference, that the Kingdom is coming into fuller expression. Oftentimes, the evidence is dreadfully thin. The blind remain sightless, the captives unfreed. Come on, God! What's taking so long?

Because they are so familiar, it is easy to miss the impact of verses 22-23. Forgetting that our view of Jesus' birth has the advantage of hindsight, we fail to notice the gap between the prophecy and its fulfillment. Many years transpired between Isaiah's pronouncement of Immanuel and the birth of Jesus. As the people waited for the Messiah over the centuries, what became of the prophet's words? Were they dismissed, disregarded, totally forgotten? What about Mary and Joseph? At the time, did they fully grasp that their willingness to endure the incongruity of God's breaking in would result in the consummation of eight centuries of longing?

Undoubtedly, one of the hazards of our age is that we have lost the sense of what it means to wait. In an earlier day, the simple glory of a piece of fresh peach pie lay in the fact that it was a product of waiting: waiting for trees to bear and fruit to ripen, waiting through the washing, peeling and slicing, the artful preparation of crust.

The sum of this week's Matthew passages reminds us that all birth requires a period of gestation or of incubation. God nudges, speaks in ways nearly foolish and undiscernible. We hear—at the edge—and respond as best we know how. Then, we wait.

Prayer: *Persevering God, enable us to wait with expectation. Amen.*

Sunday, December 20   Read Romans 1:1-7.

That we will often find ourselves in the waiting gaps on this faith journey is undeniable. Still, there are rare and brief moments when we approach an edge that reveals the long view—a wide and connected panorama of God's break-ins.

Paul's letter to the Romans could be termed the "long view" epistle. It is a passionate rendition of the heart of the gospel message. Accordingly, the prologue is a sweeping, fast-forward portrayal of God's working in Israel's history. Briefly identifying his own place in the big picture, Paul goes on to trace the gospel's unfolding and fulfillment through the prophets and David's lineage, by implication, everyone from Abraham to Joseph and Mary. He then describes the divine-human Jesus, his death and resurrection. But is that the pinnacle? It doesn't appear to be. In the NIV, the section ends at verse six, which reads simply, "And you also are among those who are called . . ."

Belonging to Christ—this is where the wide view opens up into our present. If our celebration of Advent does not bring us to consider what this means, we will only be mouthing a quaint and ancient story. Advent will have no power. The world will look to a half-asleep church, then turn around and walk away.

Belonging to Christ implies a willingness to carry Christ in our personal and corporate bodies. It requires a union of our will with God's initiative. All along the way, we will be near the edge, at times astounded with wonder, at times heartsick at the brokenness we see all about us. Often, we will scream in frustration at the crazy incongruities and at waiting.

Let us find courage in Paul's long and wide view.

Prayer: *Inviting God, in the company of all the saints before us, may the "yes" of our lives contribute to the advent of your kingdom. Amen!*

EMMANUEL: GOD-WITH-US

December 21-27
Monday, December 21

Roberta Bondi†
Read: Psalm 111:1-10.

"The fear of the LORD is the beginning of wisdom." What a strange text to find in the Christmas season! Whatever could "God-with-us" have to do with fear?

For the Christian teachers who founded monasticism in fourth-century Egypt, love of God and neighbor was the whole point of the Christian life. Furthermore, for them, these two loves were so closely related that one could not love the neighbor without loving God. Conversely, one could not hate or be indifferent to the neighbor while loving God.

For these teachers who so desired to love, nothing got so much in the way of love as the desire to usurp God's role of judge. We cannot act as judges. According to the early monastics, this is because God is so infinitely more merciful to each of us than we ever are to others or to ourselves. God never judges us by some absolute scale: "She broke the law and she will pay for it." Only God sees the struggles we endure in order to be the people God wishes us to be. God is so much more ready to forgive than we.

In this context, then, for the early teachers, to fear God meant not to be afraid of God but to be careful not to usurp God's role of judge. This fear had nothing to do with the "scariness," power, and "rights" of God. It was rooted, instead, in a deep knowledge of God's gentleness with us—"God-with-us"—which we never want to lose.

Prayer: *Loving God, help us understand that you are infinitely more gentle with us and with others than we can ever imagine. Amen.*

---

†Associate Professor of Church History, Candler School of Theology, Emory University, Atlanta, Georgia.

Tuesday, December 22   Read Psalm 111:10.

"The fear of the LORD is the beginning of wisdom." These are words that have frightened many a child, and perhaps many an adult over the years, as well. They seem to reinforce in us a primitive understanding of God as an all-seeing policeman, whose main interest in us is in whether or not we break some divine law.

For many of us, actual fear of God and of God's negative judgment of us so governs the depths of our hearts that we can neither feel God's love for us nor love God in return. Who can love anyone who is only interested in judging them?

Isaac of Nineveh, a wonderful seventh-century writer on the spiritual life, was once asked what hell is. He used this analogy to explain it. "Imagine," he said, "that you have injured the person you love more than anyone in the world, and before you have any chance to apologize and relieve the suffering you have inflicted on the person you love, your beloved dies. The agony you would feel in living with the knowledge that you could no longer make things right is the pain of hell."

Seen from this angle, "fear of the Lord" means anxiety not to be careless of the love of "God-with-us," the God who loves us so tenderly. This anxiety is not rooted in a fear that God will "make us pay for it" if we do something wrong. It springs, instead, from the desire not to hurt the One who loves us, the One who never desires anything for us but life and love, "God-with-us" and God for us.

Prayer: *Loving God, help us remember that our very life is based on our mutual love: you for us and we for you. Help us never to be careless of that love. Amen.*

Wednesday, December 23   Read 1 Samuel 2:18-20, 26.

Samuel, growing up with Eli in the temple, was a special child. His mother, Hannah, had been a barren wife in an ancient culture which valued women according to their ability to become mothers. Barrenness was regarded as disgraceful, and she had been taunted intolerably over it.

One year when Hannah went up to the temple with her husband for the family's yearly sacrifice, her heart was in anguish. In her bitterness and pain, she wept and prayed so distraughtly that Eli the priest thought her drunk. In this prayer she begged God for a son, and she vowed that if God were to give her this child, she would dedicate him to God for the whole of his life.

Would God hear the prayer of one who was not necessarily righteous or saintly? Of course! The baffling and wonderful God we meet in scripture is especially concerned not with the righteous or the successful but with the least in society, with the one who cries out in pain, "Help me." Hannah's prayer was answered, and she gave birth to a child.

Jesus' birth is not parallel to Samuel's in many ways. Mary certainly did not ask for the child she bore. Nevertheless, in God's choosing of Mary as Jesus' mother, God showed the same paradoxical lack of interest in her "suitability" by human standards that God had shown in responding to Hannah. The wonder of Christmas is this: that God has chosen human beings among whom to live ever since without any regard to human standards of "suitability."

Prayer: *Thank you, loving God, that I am always "somebody" in your eyes and that you will always hear me. Help me to see other people as you see them. Amen.*

Thursday, December 24   Read Luke 1:26-38.

How amazing God is! Throughout the Bible we hear God described as a God of power and might. Surely, it would not be unreasonable to expect God to rule the world simply by "laying down the law" and demanding unquestioning obedience to it.

But "God-with-us" does not relate to us this way. Those whom God chooses must choose God freely in return. God promised Abraham that he would become the father of a whole nation, but Abraham had to choose in return to go to a new land he did not know at all. God called Moses to lead the people out of Egypt, and God promised to help him, but Moses himself had to decide to accept what God offered. In the same way, Mary had to choose to accept the task God wished to give her, to become a mother under very ambiguous circumstances.

Could Mary have said no to God? Yes, of course. Irenaeus, a great second-century Christian, taught that God created human beings not to be God's slaves but to be God's companions. God is infinitely respectful of us human beings. God does not override our choices, even when those choices hurt both God and us.

Because God loves us, God works with us; God does not *do* things to us. God is like this for us at Christmas too. God comes to us in the birth of Jesus, "God-with-us"—to claim us, to heal us, to bring us peace, to turn our world upside down. But God will not overpower us. We must choose to be claimed to be healed, to be granted peace, to have our world overturned. We must learn to say for ourselves, "Behold, the servant of the Lord; may it be, according to your will" (AP).

Prayer: *Loving God, help us like Mary to choose what you hold out to us. Amen.*

Friday, December 25 (Christmas)
Read Luke 2:1-7.

When the angel Gabriel told Mary about the wonderful son she would bear, how awed she must have been! Her baby would be no ordinary child. He would be "the Son of the Most High" (1:37), the inheritor of the throne of David, whose reign would never have an end.

We imagine Mary and Joseph with very mixed emotions as they leave Nazareth for Bethlehem. We picture Mary as close to delivery and the couple aware of the hardship of the trip. Did they give in to the temptation to tell each other that God would spare them a difficult childbirth because this was to be such a special baby?

The birth must have been hard. Perhaps they were in complete darkness. Probably there was no hot water, no blankets, no help other than the two of them. I imagine that they felt great fear and anxiety. Whatever the birth scene was, it was not the peaceful, idyllic family scene the church has made it.

We place so many expectations on ourselves at Christmas. Instead of remembering what that first Christmas must really have been like and drawing comfort from it, we substitute in our minds an image of family harmony and coziness that leaves no room for the brokenness we all experience at some time in ourselves and in our families. With our false picture of that first Christmas, we exclude ourselves from the real comfort and hope of "God-with-us," who came to us not to congratulate the whole but to heal the brokenhearted.

Prayer: *Loving God, help us know you on Christmas Day as "God-with-us," the God who is with us as we actually are and not as we think we should be. Amen.*

Saturday, December 26
Read: Luke 2:8-20;
Luke 2:41-52.

What was Jesus really like? Popular pictures of Jesus as an infant, as a boy, and as an adult seem to portray him not only as innocent of any kind of real-life experience but also as having a kind of passive obedience. One trouble with these pictures is that they preach to us that Jesus was this kind of person and imply that this is the kind of person God wants each of us to be: simple, obedient, without any messy life experiences.

The picture of "simple Jesus, meek and mild" prevents us from being able to see Jesus as the Gospels actually present him: as the one who repeatedly tells those around him (as he seems to do in the Temple passage), "Things are not as they appear. God does not judge as human beings judge. Do not make the mistake of confusing family, social, or even religious harmony for God's will."

Mary and Joseph, frantic with worry about Jesus' whereabouts, discover him still in the Temple. But rather than apologizing to his parents, Jesus says to them, "Did you not know that I must be in my Father's house?"

I imagine Jesus must have been a hard child to rear. I know he can be a hard person for us to live with. He never seems to allow us simply to let things be. He makes us ask: Is the way things are—in our families, in our churches, in our society, in our world—the way God really wants them to be?

Prayer: *Loving God, we ask you for courage and strength to hear Jesus when he pushes us not to accept things as they are. Amen.*

Sunday, December 27
Read Galatians 4:4-7;
Colossians 3:12-17.

"God-is-with-us" means that God loves us as children and heirs, that God frees us from slavery to our sins, and that God wishes for peace to reign in our hearts.

Yet, we know we do not experience this love, forgiveness, and peace all by ourselves or for ourselves alone. If we are loved, then we must try to exercise the characteristics of God's love for us toward the rest of "God's holy people" with whom we share a common life: compassion, generosity, humility, gentleness, and patience. If we know ourselves to be forgiven by God, then we must forgive each other. If we have been given a measure of internal peace, we must remember that we have also been called to unity in the Body of Christ as adopted children of God and, thereby, as joint heirs.

How good all this sounds in the abstract, but how very hard it can be to try to live out in our local churches as we struggle with the budget, the mission of the church, maintaining the building, worship, Sunday school, and all the other things that make up the everyday realities of our life together! The passage from Colossians asks that we really be *for* each other and *with* each other as God is with us—and God is with us as we really are.

Being together in the church like this is not easy. For this we need the courage to try, together and individually, to live out the promises of Christmas.

Prayer: *Loving God, help us claim the courage to live out your promises for us in our churches. Amen.*

JOY TO THE WORLD

December 28-31, 1992   **Myron F. Wicke†**
Monday, December 28   Jeremiah 31:7-11.

Our reading comes from Jeremiah, often called the "weeping prophet." So it may seem strange to begin a series of meditations with Jeremiah under the topic "Joy to the World." To be sure, Jeremiah had reason to sorrow over what he saw happening in Israel. Yet he stood steadfast in his faith that in the end God's way would prevail. He knew this was still God's world; his faith was strong enough to cause sheer rejoicing.

Even as we rejoice in God's promise: "I have loved you with an everlasting love" (31:3), we too find ourselves almost overcome with sorrow when we look at the modern world, including our own nation. Everywhere we are troubled by signs that our nation is the product of greed, selfishness, and faithlessness, resulting in hopelessness for so many. Consider the problems of AIDS, scandals in business and government, countless lost children, and thousands of homeless on our streets.

Jeremiah wept because the Jewish nation had been sent into exile, its own people blown into captivity. Jeremiah believed that the disaster had occurred because Israel had forgotten promises to God. But always to Jeremiah, whatever the catastrophe, there was God "keeping watch above his own." So Jeremiah breaks into poetry of joy: "I will lead them back, I will make them walk by brooks of water." Joy to the world!

Prayer: *Dear Lord and Father of mankind, forgive our foolish ways. Reclothe us in our rightful mind, in purer lives thy service find, in deeper reverence praise.*Amen.*

*From "Dear Lord and Father of Mankind" by John Greenleaf Whittier.
†General Secretary, Board of Higher Education and Ministry, UMC, retired; Nashville, Tennessee.

Tuesday, December 29   Read Jeremiah 31:11-14.

Yesterday we had a hint of Jeremiah's poetic imagery. In today's scripture there are more pictures written with high emotion, seemingly just flowing out, and expressing a faith experience of absolute trust. It is a faith at its most profound, radiant even in disaster, in the goodness of the Lord.

The images are beautiful and direct—the grain which sustains us, the watered garden, the wine, the oil—all gifts without which life would be much poorer. Who can explain these gifts? The question is what amazed Alfred Lord Tennyson in his lovely poem "Flower in the Crannied Wall." How, the poet wondered, could a flower under such stress become so beautiful? One look at a beautiful apple, an orange, or a banana makes one wonder what manufacturing skill could match even the beauty of the packaging of these marvelous fruits.

From Jeremiah there is more: "Then shall the young women rejoice in the dance, and the young men and the old shall be merry," for, says the Lord, "I will turn their mourning into joy, I will comfort them, and give them gladness for sorrow." The words make us think of the Afro-American spiritual, "Go, tell it on the mountain, over the hills and everywhere." Clearly to Jeremiah, however, the joyous homecoming was altogether dependent upon a true recommitment between God and Israel. It was a promise with a condition. We too must take notice. Time to remember the promise: "I have loved you with an everlasting love." Joy to the world!

Prayer: *O love that wilt not let me go, I rest my weary soul in thee; I give thee back the life I owe, that in thine ocean depths its flow may richer, fuller be.*Amen.*

---

*From "O Love That Wilt Not Let Me Go" by George Matheson.

Wednesday, December 30   Read Psalm 147:12-20.

Recently, the Public Broadcasting System presented Bill
Moyers's ninety-minute program on John Newton's hymn
"Amazing Grace." Before he became a Christian, John Newton
was a slave trader. Again and again those who took part in the
program—many of whom were black, the grandchildren of
slaves—confessed that the hymn had been instrumental in
changing their lives. The psalms had the same effect upon the
Hebrews.

Psalm 147 must have greatly affected the ancient Israelites,
returning again from the exile which Jeremiah had so deplored.
Here is a deeply felt song of faith picturing a joy that only poetry
and song could satisfy. It was an expression which welded the
congregation together.

Hymns and psalms are more than ideas; they are experiences.
The psalmist celebrates God's wonderful goodness—"the finest
of the wheat," "snow like wool," "frost like ashes."

Stop long enough to look thoughtfully at a tree or a rose, to
experience a storm or to see a mountain in the fall, and begin to
comprehend the psalmist's wonder. As an astronomer once put
it: The world looks more and more like a great thought rather
than a machine. Indeed, says the psalmist, a thought in the mind
of God. Joy to the world!

Prayer: *This is my Father's world, and to my listening ears all nature
sings, and round me rings, the music of the spheres. This is my Father's
world: I rest me in the thought of rocks and trees, of skies and seas; his
hand the wonders wrought.* * *Amen.*

---

*From "This Is My Father's World" by Maltbie D. Babcock.

Thursday, December 31   Read Ephesians 1:1-6.

The reading for today expresses again the joy to be found in the miracle of faith in Jesus the Christ. It comes from the man who dramatically encountered the one he had been persecuting. The man was, of course, Saul of Tarsus, who became Paul.

Was there ever a life turned more upside down than Paul's? An active Jewish zealot, he was determined to wipe out the sect called Christian. According to Acts 7:58, Paul guarded the coats of those who stoned Stephen, the first Christian martyr. Then as Saul traveled to Damascus to continue his war on the Christians, he had an encounter with the living Christ. From one point of view the experience was a disaster, for a lifetime of suffering was to follow. To Paul, however, it was anything but a disaster; rather, it was the saving of his spirit. He saw himself as truly a child of God through Christ. He agreed with John, who, in his old age, proclaimed to his fellow Christians: "We are God's children now" (1 John 3:2). The "now" was what Paul had learned.

In this letter to the young church at Ephesus, Paul begins with a prayer for the saints, the followers of Christ. He was pleading that their hearts might be "enlightened" to serve God in a dying world. It is a prayer for all of us. A group of visitors to an African hospital was being conducted through horrifying evidence of disease. They saw a Catholic sister carefully washing a patient with leprosy. One woman in the group approached the nurse and said, "I wouldn't do that for a million dollars." The sister continued her work as she responded, "Neither would I." Love "toward all the saints." Joy to the world!

Prayer: *God of glory, give us the spirit of wisdom and revelation, that our hearts may be enlightened and our lives changed. Amen.*

The Common Lectionary 1992
(*Disciplines* Edition)

January 1-5
Epiphany

Isaiah 60:1-6
Psalm 72:1-14
Ephesians 3:1-12
Matthew 2:1-12

January 6-12

Isaiah 61:1-4
Psalm 29
Acts 8:14-17
Luke 3:15-17, 21-22

January 13-19

Isaiah 62:1-5
Psalm 36:5-10
1 Corinthians 12:1-11
John 2:1-11

January 20-26

Nehemiah 8:1-4a, 5-6, 8-10
Psalm 19:7-14
1 Corinthians 12:12-30
Luke 4:14-21

January 27–February 2

Jeremiah 1:4-10
Psalm 71:1-6
1 Corinthians 13:1-13
Luke 4:21-30

February 3-9

Isaiah 6:1-8 (or 13)
Psalm 138
1 Corinthians 15:1-11
Luke 5:1-11

February 10-16

Jeremiah 17:5-10
Psalm 1
1 Corinthians 15:12-20
Luke 6:17-26

February 17-23

Genesis 45:3-11, 15
Psalm 37:1-11
1 Corinthians 15:35-38, 42-50
Luke 6:27-38

February 24–March 1

Exodus 34:29-35
Psalm 99
2 Corinthians 3:12–4:2
Luke 9:28-36

March 2-8
First Sunday in Lent

Deuteronomy 26:1-11
Psalm 91:9-16
Romans 10:8b-13
Luke 4:1-13
**(Includes these lections
for Ash Wednesday)**
Joel 2:1-2, 12-17a
Psalm 51:1-12
2 Corinthians 5:20b–6:2
    Matthew 6:1-6, 16-21

March 9-15

Genesis 15:1-12, 17-18
Psalm 127
Philippians 3:17–4:1
Luke 13:31-35

March 16 - 22
Exodus 3:1-15
Psalm 103:1-13
1 Corinthians 10:1-13
Luke 13:1-9

March 23 - 29
Joshua 5:9-12
Psalm 34:1-8
2 Corinthians 5:16-21
Luke 15:1-3, 11-32

March 30 – April 5
Isaiah 43:16-21
Psalm 126
Philippians 3:8-14
John 12:1-8

April 6 – 12
  Passion / Palm
Isaiah 50:4-9a
Psalm 31:9-16
Psalm 118:19-29
Philippians 2:5-11
Luke 22:14–23:56
  or Luke 23:1-49

April 13 - 19
  Holy Week
  Easter
Isaiah 42:1-9
John 13:21-30
John 19:17-30
John 20:1-18
Luke 22:7-20
Hebrews 4:14-16; 5:7-9
Acts 10:34-43
1 Corinthians 15:19-26
Luke 24:1-12

April 20 - 26
Acts 5:27-32
Psalm 2
Revelation 1:4-8
John 20:19-31

April 27 – May 3
Acts 9:1-20
Psalm 30:4-12
Revelation 5:11-14
John 21:1 (or 15-19)

May 4 - 10
Acts 13:15-16, 26-33
Psalm 23
Revelation 7:9-17
John 10:22-30

May 11 - 17
Acts 14:8-18
Psalm 145:13b-21
Revelation 21:1-6
John 13:31-35

May 18 - 24
Acts 15:1-2, 22-29
Psalm 67
Revelation 21:10, 22-27
John 14:23-29

May 25 - 31
Acts 16:16-34
Psalm 97
Revelation 22:12-14, 16-17, 20
John 17:20-26

June 1 – 7
  Pentecost
Acts 2:1-21 or Genesis 11:1-9
Psalm 104:24-34
Romans 8:14-17
John 14:8-17, 25-27

June 8 - 14
  Trinity
Proverbs 8:22-31
Psalm 8
Romans 5:1-5
John 16:12-15

June 15-21
1 Kings 19:9-14
Psalm 43
Galatians 3:23-29
Luke 9:18-24

June 22-28
1 Kings 19:15-21
Psalm 44:1-8
Galatians 5:1, 13-25
Luke 9:51-62

June 29–July 5
1 Kings 21:1-3, 17-21
Psalm 5:1-8
Galatians 6:7-18
Luke 10:1-12, 17-20

July 6-12
2 Kings 2:1, 6-14
Psalm 139:1-12
Colossians 1:1-14
Luke 10:25-37

July 13-19
2 Kings 4:8-17
Psalm 139:13-18
Colossians 1:21-29
Luke 10:38-42

July 20-26
2 Kings 5:1-15*ab*
Psalm 21:1-7
Colossians 2:6-15
Luke 11:1-13

July 27–August 2
2 Kings 13:14-20*a*
Psalm 28
Colossians 3:1-11
Luke 12:13-21

August 3-9
Jeremiah 18:1-11
Psalm 14
Hebrews 11:1-3, 8-19
Luke 12:32-40

August 10-16
Jeremiah 20:7-13
Psalm 10:12-18
Hebrews 12:1-2, 12-17
Luke 12:49-56

August 17-23
Jeremiah 28:1-9
Psalm 84
Hebrews 12:18-29
Luke 13:22-30

August 24-30
Ezekiel 18:1-9, 25-29
Psalm 15
Hebrews 13:1-8
Luke 14:1, 7-14

August 31–September 6
Ezekiel 33:1-11
Psalm 94:12-22
Philemon 1-20
Luke 14:25-33

September 7-13
Hosea 4:1-3; 5:15–6:6
Psalm 77:11-20
1 Timothy 1:12-17
Luke 15:1-10

September 14-20
Hosea 11:1-11
Psalm 107:1-9
1 Timothy 2:1-7
Luke 16:1-13

September 21-27
Joel 2:23-30
Psalm 107:1, 33-43
1 Timothy 6:6-19
Luke 16:19-31

September 28–October 4
Amos 5:6-7, 10-15
Psalm 101
2 Timothy 1:1-14
Luke 17:5-10

October 5-11

Micah 1:2; 2:1-10
Psalm 26
2 Timothy 2:8-15
Luke 17:11-19

October 12-18

Habakkuk 1:1-3; 2:1-4
Psalm 119:137-144
2 Timothy 3:14−4:5
Luke 18:1-8

October 19-25

Zephaniah 3:1-9
Psalm 3
2 Timothy 4:6-8, 16-18
Luke 18:9-14

October 26−November 1

Daniel 7:1-3, 15-18
Psalm 149
Ephesians 1:11-23
Luke 6:20-36

November 2-8

Zechariah 7:1-10
Psalm 9:11-20
2 Thessalonians 2:13−3:5
Luke 20:27-38

November 9-15

Malachi 4:1-6
Psalm 82
2 Thessalonians 3:6-13
Luke 21:5-19

November 16-22

2 Samuel 5:1-5
Psalm 95
Colossians 1:11-20
John 12:9-19

November 23-29
First Sunday in Advent

Isaiah 2:1-5
Psalm 122
Romans 13:11-14
Matthew 24:36-44

November 30−December 6

Isaiah 11:1-10
Psalm 72:1-8
Romans 15:4-13
Matthew 3:1-12

December 7-13

Isaiah 35:1-10
Psalm 146:5-10
James 5:7-10
Matthew 11:2-11

December 14-20

Isaiah 7:10-16
Psalm 24
Romans 1:1-7
Matthew 1:18-25

December 21-27
Christmas

Isaiah 9:2-7
Psalm 96
Luke 2:1-20
Isaiah 63:7-9
Psalm 111
Hebrews 2:10-18
Matthew 2:13-15, 19-23
Galatians 4:4-7

December 28−January 3

Jeremiah 31:7-14
Psalm 147:12-20
Ephesians 1:3-6, 15-18
John 1:1-18